DICTIONARY
THEME-BASED

ENGLISH-UKRAINIAN

The most useful words
To expand your lexicon and sharpen
your language skills

7000 words

Theme-based dictionary British English-Ukrainian - 7000 words

By Andrey Taranov

T&P Books vocabularies are intended for helping you learn, memorize and review foreign words. The dictionary is divided into themes, covering all major spheres of everyday activities, business, science, culture, etc.

The process of learning words using T&P Books' theme-based dictionaries gives you the following advantages:

- Correctly grouped source information predetermines success at subsequent stages of word memorization
- Availability of words derived from the same root allowing memorization of word units (rather than separate words)
- Small units of words facilitate the process of establishing associative links needed for consolidation of vocabulary
- Level of language knowledge can be estimated by the number of learned words

T&P Books Publishing
www.tpbooks.com

This book is also available in E-book formats.
Please visit www.tpbooks.com or the major online bookstores.

UKRAINIAN THEME-BASED DICTIONARY
British English collection

T&P Books vocabularies are intended to help you learn, memorize, and review foreign words. The vocabulary contains over 7000 commonly used words arranged thematically.

- Vocabulary contains the most commonly used words
- Recommended as an addition to any language course
- Meets the needs of beginners and advanced learners of foreign languages
- Convenient for daily use, revision sessions, and self-testing activities
- Allows you to assess your vocabulary

Special features of the vocabulary

- Words are organized according to their meaning, not alphabetically
- Words are presented in three columns to facilitate the reviewing and self-testing processes
- Words in groups are divided into small blocks to facilitate the learning process
- The vocabulary offers a convenient and simple transcription of each foreign word

The vocabulary has 198 topics including:

Basic Concepts, Numbers, Colors, Months, Seasons, Units of Measurement, Clothing & Accessories, Food & Nutrition, Restaurant, Family Members, Relatives, Character, Feelings, Emotions, Diseases, City, Town, Sightseeing, Shopping, Money, House, Home, Office, Working in the Office, Import & Export, Marketing, Job Search, Sports, Education, Computer, Internet, Tools, Nature, Countries, Nationalities and more …

TABLE OF CONTENTS

PRONUNCIATION GUIDE

Letter	Ukrainian example	T&P phonetic alphabet	English example

Vowels

Letter	Ukrainian example	T&P phonetic alphabet	English example
А а	акт	[a]	shorter than in 'ask'
Е е	берет	[e], [ɛ]	absent, pet
Є є	модельєр	[ɛ]	man, bad
И и	ритм	[k]	clock, kiss
I і	компанія	[i]	shorter than in 'feet'
Ï ï	поїзд	[ji]	playing, spying
О о	око	[ɔ]	bottle, doctor
У у	буря	[u]	book
Ю ю	костюм	[ʲu]	cued, cute
Я я	маяк	[ja], [ʲa]	royal

Consonants

Letter	Ukrainian example	T&P phonetic alphabet	English example
Б б	бездна	[b]	baby, book
В в	вікно	[w]	vase, winter
Г г	готель	[ɦ]	between [g] and [h]
Ґ ґ	ґудзик	[g]	game, gold
Д д	дефіс	[d]	day, doctor
Ж ж	жанр	[ʒ]	forge, pleasure
З з	зброя	[z]	zebra, please
Й й	йти	[j]	yes, New York
К к	крок	[k]	clock, kiss
Л л	лев	[l]	lace, people
М м	мати	[m]	magic, milk
Н н	назва	[n]	name, normal
П п	приз	[p]	pencil, private
Р р	радість	[r]	rice, radio
С с	сон	[s]	city, boss
Т т	тир	[t]	tourist, trip
Ф ф	фарба	[f]	face, food
Х х	холод	[h]	home, have
Ц ц	церква	[ts]	cats, tsetse fly
Ч ч	час	[tʃ]	church, French
Ш ш	шуба	[ʃ]	machine, shark
Щ щ	щука	[ɕ]	sheep, shop
ь	камінь	[ʲ]	soft sign - no sound
ъ	ім'я	[ʼ]	hard sign, no sound

ABBREVIATIONS
used in the dictionary

English abbreviations

ab.	-	about
adj	-	adjective
adv	-	adverb
anim.	-	animate
as adj	-	attributive noun used as adjective
e.g.	-	for example
etc.	-	et cetera
fam.	-	familiar
fem.	-	feminine
form.	-	formal
inanim.	-	inanimate
masc.	-	masculine
math	-	mathematics
mil.	-	military
n	-	noun
pl	-	plural
pron.	-	pronoun
sb	-	somebody
sing.	-	singular
sth	-	something
v aux	-	auxiliary verb
vi	-	intransitive verb
vi, vt	-	intransitive, transitive verb
vt	-	transitive verb

Ukrainian abbreviations

ж	-	feminine noun
мн	-	plural
с	-	neuter
ч	-	masculine noun

BASIC CONCEPTS

Basic concepts. Part 1

I, me	я	[ja]
you	ти	[tɨ]
he	він	[win]
she	вона	[wo'na]
we	ми	[mɨ]
you (to a group)	ви	[wɨ]
they	вони	[wo'nɨ]

Hello! (fam.)	Здрастуй!	['zdrastuj]
Hello! (form.)	Здрастуйте!	['zdrastujtɛ]
Good morning!	Доброго ранку!	['dɔbrofio 'ranku]
Good afternoon!	Добрий день!	['dɔbrij dɛnʲ]
Good evening!	Добрий вечір!	['dɔbrij 'wɛʧir]
to say hello	вітатися	[wi'tatisʲa]
Hi! (hello)	Привіт!	[pri'wit]
greeting (n)	вітання (с)	[wi'tanʲa]
to greet (vt)	вітати	[wi'tati]
How are you?	Як справи?	[jak 'sprawɨ]
What's new?	Що нового?	[ɕo no'wɔfio]
Bye-Bye! Goodbye!	До побачення!	[do po'baʧɛnʲa]
See you soon!	До швидкої зустрічі!	[do ʃwid'kɔjɨ 'zustriʧi]
Farewell! (to a friend)	Прощавай!	[proɕa'waj]
Farewell! (form.)	Прощавайте!	[proɕa'wajtɛ]
to say goodbye	прощатися	[pro'ɕatisʲa]
Cheers!	Бувай!	[bu'waj]
Thank you! Cheers!	Дякую!	['dʲakuʲu]
Thank you very much!	Щиро дякую!	['ɕiro 'dʲakuʲu]
My pleasure!	Будь ласка.	[budʲ 'laska]
Don't mention it!	Не варто подяки	[nɛ 'warto po'dʲaki]
It was nothing	Нема за що.	[nɛ'ma za ɕo]
Excuse me! (fam.)	Вибач!	['wɨbaʧ]
Excuse me! (form.)	Вибачте!	['wɨbaʧtɛ]
to excuse (forgive)	вибачати	[wɨba'ʧati]

to apologize (vi)	вибачатися	[wɨbaˈʧatisʲa]
My apologies	Моє вибачення.	[moˈɛ ˈwɨbaʧɛnʲa]
I'm sorry!	Вибачте!	[ˈwɨbaʧtɛ]
to forgive (vt)	пробачати	[probaˈʧati]
please (adv)	будь ласка	[budʲ ˈlaska]

Don't forget!	Не забудьте!	[nɛ zaˈbudʲtɛ]
Certainly!	Звичайно!	[zwɨˈʧajno]
Of course not!	Звичайно ні!	[zwɨˈʧajno ni]
Okay! (I agree)	Згоден!	[ˈzɦodɛn]
That's enough!	Досить!	[ˈdɔsitʲ]

3. Cardinal numbers. Part 1

0 zero	нуль	[nulʲ]
1 one	один	[oˈdɨn]
2 two	два	[dwa]
3 three	три	[tri]
4 four	чотири	[ʧoˈtiri]

5 five	п'ять	[pʲatʲ]
6 six	шість	[ʃistʲ]
7 seven	сім	[sim]
8 eight	вісім	[ˈwisim]
9 nine	дев'ять	[ˈdɛwʲatʲ]

10 ten	десять	[ˈdɛsʲatʲ]
11 eleven	одинадцять	[odɨˈnadʦʲatʲ]
12 twelve	дванадцять	[dwaˈnadʦʲatʲ]
13 thirteen	тринадцять	[triˈnadʦʲatʲ]
14 fourteen	чотирнадцять	[ʧotirˈnadʦʲatʲ]

15 fifteen	п'ятнадцять	[pʲatˈnadʦʲatʲ]
16 sixteen	шістнадцять	[ʃistˈnadʦʲatʲ]
17 seventeen	сімнадцять	[simˈnadʦʲatʲ]
18 eighteen	вісімнадцять	[wisimˈnadʦʲatʲ]
19 nineteen	дев'ятнадцять	[dɛwʲatˈnadʦʲatʲ]

20 twenty	двадцять	[ˈdwadʦʲatʲ]
21 twenty-one	двадцять один	[ˈdwadʦʲatʲ oˈdɨn]
22 twenty-two	двадцять два	[ˈdwadʦʲatʲ dwa]
23 twenty-three	двадцять три	[ˈdwadʦʲatʲ tri]

30 thirty	тридцять	[ˈtridʦʲatʲ]
31 thirty-one	тридцять один	[ˈtridʦʲatʲ oˈdɨn]
32 thirty-two	тридцять два	[ˈtridʦʲatʲ dwa]
33 thirty-three	тридцять три	[ˈtridʦʲatʲ tri]

40 forty	сорок	[ˈsɔrok]
41 forty-one	сорок один	[ˈsɔrok oˈdɨn]
42 forty-two	сорок два	[ˈsɔrok dwa]
43 forty-three	сорок три	[ˈsɔrok tri]
50 fifty	п'ятдесят	[pʲatdɛˈsʲat]
51 fifty-one	п'ятдесят один	[pʲatdɛˈsʲat oˈdɨn]

52 fifty-two	п'ятдесят два	[pʲatdɛˈsʲat dwa]
53 fifty-three	п'ятдесят три	[pʲatdɛˈsʲat trɨ]
60 sixty	шістдесят	[ʃizdɛˈsʲat]
61 sixty-one	шістдесят один	[ʃizdɛˈsʲat oˈdin]
62 sixty-two	шістдесят два	[ʃizdɛˈsʲat dwa]
63 sixty-three	шістдесят три	[ʃizdɛˈsʲat trɨ]
70 seventy	сімдесят	[simdɛˈsʲat]
71 seventy-one	сімдесят один	[simdɛˈsʲat odin]
72 seventy-two	сімдесят два	[simdɛˈsʲat dwa]
73 seventy-three	сімдесят три	[simdɛˈsʲat trɨ]
80 eighty	вісімдесят	[wisimdɛˈsʲat]
81 eighty-one	вісімдесят один	[wisimdɛˈsʲat oˈdin]
82 eighty-two	вісімдесят два	[wisimdɛˈsʲat dwa]
83 eighty-three	вісімдесят три	[wisimdɛˈsʲat trɨ]
90 ninety	дев'яносто	[dɛwʲaˈnɔsto]
91 ninety-one	дев'яносто один	[dɛwʲaˈnɔsto oˈdin]
92 ninety-two	дев'яносто два	[dɛwʲaˈnɔsto dwa]
93 ninety-three	дев'яносто три	[dɛwʲaˈnɔsto trɨ]

4. Cardinal numbers. Part 2

100 one hundred	сто	[sto]
200 two hundred	двісті	[ˈdwisti]
300 three hundred	триста	[ˈtrista]
400 four hundred	чотириста	[t͡ʃoˈtɨrista]
500 five hundred	п'ятсот	[pʲaˈt͡sɔt]
600 six hundred	шістсот	[ʃistˈsɔt]
700 seven hundred	сімсот	[simˈsɔt]
800 eight hundred	вісімсот	[wisimˈsɔt]
900 nine hundred	дев'ятсот	[dɛwʲaˈt͡sɔt]
1000 one thousand	тисяча	[ˈtɨsʲat͡ʃa]
2000 two thousand	дві тисячі	[dwi ˈtɨsʲat͡ʃi]
3000 three thousand	три тисячі	[tri ˈtɨsʲat͡ʃi]
10000 ten thousand	десять тисяч	[ˈdɛsʲatʲ ˈtɨsʲat͡ʃ]
one hundred thousand	сто тисяч	[sto ˈtɨsʲat͡ʃ]
million	мільйон (ч)	[milʲˈjɔn]
billion	мільярд (ч)	[miˈlʲjard]

5. Numbers. Fractions

fraction	дріб (ч)	[drib]
one half	одна друга	[odˈna ˈdruɦa]
one third	одна третя	[odˈna ˈtrɛtʲa]
one quarter	одна четверта	[odˈna t͡ʃɛtˈwɛrta]
one eighth	одна восьма	[odˈna ˈwɔsʲma]
one tenth	одна десята	[odˈna dɛˈsʲata]

| two thirds | дві третіх | [dwi 'trɛtih] |
| three quarters | три четвертих | [tri ʧɛt'wɛrtih] |

6. Numbers. Basic operations

subtraction	віднімання (c)	[widni'manʲa]
to subtract (vi, vt)	відняти	[wid'nʲatɨ]
division	ділення (c)	['dilɛnʲa]
to divide (vt)	ділити	[di'litɨ]
addition	додавання (c)	[doda'wanʲa]
to add up (vt)	додати	[do'datɨ]
to add (vi)	додавати	[doda'watɨ]
multiplication	множення (c)	['mnɔʒɛnʲa]
to multiply (vt)	множити	['mnɔʒɨtɨ]

7. Numbers. Miscellaneous

digit, figure	цифра (ж)	['ʦifra]
number	число (c)	[ʧis'lɔ]
numeral	числівник (ч)	[ʧis'liwnik]
minus sign	мінус (ч)	['minus]
plus sign	плюс (ч)	[plʲus]
formula	формула (ж)	['fɔrmula]
calculation	розрахунок (ч)	[rozra'hunok]
to count (vi, vt)	рахувати	[rahu'watɨ]
to count up	підраховувати	[pidra'howuwatɨ]
to compare (vt)	зрівнювати	['zriwnʲuwatɨ]
How much?	Скільки?	['skilʲki]
sum, total	сума (ж)	['suma]
result	результат (ч)	[rɛzulʲ'tat]
remainder	залишок (ч)	['zaliʃok]
a few (e.g., ~ years ago)	декілька	['dɛkilʲka]
little (I had ~ time)	небагато ...	[nɛba'hato]
the rest	решта (ж)	['rɛʃta]
one and a half	півтора	[piwto'ra]
dozen	дюжина (ж)	['dʲuʒɨna]
in half (adv)	навпіл	['nawpil]
equally (evenly)	порівну	['pɔriwnu]
half	половина (ж)	[polo'wina]
time (three ~s)	раз (ч)	[raz]

8. The most important verbs. Part 1

| to advise (vt) | радити | ['radɨtɨ] |
| to agree (say yes) | погоджуватися | [po'hɔʤuwatɨsʲa] |

to answer (vi, vt)	відповідати	[widpowi'dati]
to apologize (vi)	вибачатися	[wiba'tʃatisʲa]
to arrive (vi)	приїжджати	[prijiʲ'ʐati]

to ask (~ oneself)	запитувати	[za'pituwati]
to ask (~ sb to do sth)	просити	[pro'siti]
to be (vi)	бути	['buti]

to be afraid	боятися	[boʲ'atisʲa]
to be hungry	хотіти їсти	[ho'titi 'jisti]
to be interested in …	цікавитися	[tsi'kawitisʲa]
to be needed	бути потрібним	['buti po'tribnim]
to be surprised	дивуватись	[diwu'watisʲ]

to be thirsty	хотіти пити	[ho'titi 'piti]
to begin (vt)	починати	[potʃi'nati]
to belong to …	належати	[na'lɛʐati]
to boast (vi)	хвастатися	['hwastatisʲa]
to break (split into pieces)	ламати	[la'mati]
to call (~ for help)	кликати	['klikati]

can (v aux)	могти	[moh'ti]
to catch (vt)	ловити	[lo'witi]
to change (vt)	поміняти	[pomi'nʲati]
to choose (select)	вибирати	[wibiʲ'rati]
to come down (the stairs)	спускатися	[spus'katisʲa]

to compare (vt)	зрівнювати	['zriwnʲuwati]
to complain (vi, vt)	скаржитися	['skarʒitisʲa]
to confuse (mix up)	помилятися	[pomiʲ'lʲatisʲa]
to continue (vt)	продовжувати	[pro'dowʒuwati]
to control (vt)	контролювати	[kontrolʲu'wati]
to cook (dinner)	готувати	[ɦotu'wati]

to cost (vt)	коштувати	['koʃtuwati]
to count (add up)	лічити	[li'tʃiti]
to count on …	розраховувати на …	[rozra'howuwati na]
to create (vt)	створити	[stwo'riti]
to cry (weep)	плакати	['plakati]

9. The most important verbs. Part 2

to deceive (vi, vt)	обманювати	[ob'manʲuwati]
to decorate (tree, street)	прикрашати	[prikra'ʃati]
to defend (a country, etc.)	захищати	[zahiʲ'ɕati]
to demand (request firmly)	вимагати	[wima'ɦati]
to dig (vt)	рити	['riti]

to discuss (vt)	обговорювати	[obɦo'worʲuwati]
to do (vt)	робити	[ro'biti]
to doubt (have doubts)	сумніватися	[sumni'watisʲa]
to drop (let fall)	упускати	[upus'kati]
to enter (room, house, etc.)	входити	['whoditi]
to exist (vi)	існувати	[isnu'wati]

to expect (foresee)	передбачити	[pɛrɛd'batʃiti]
to explain (vt)	пояснювати	[po'ⁱasnⁱuwati]
to fall (vi)	падати	['padati]
to fancy (vt)	подобатися	[po'dobatisⁱa]
to find (vt)	знаходити	[zna'hoditi]
to finish (vt)	закінчувати	[za'kintʃuwati]
to fly (vi)	летіти	[lɛ'titi]
to follow ... (come after)	іти слідом	[i'tɨ 'slidom]
to forget (vi, vt)	забувати	[zabu'wati]
to forgive (vt)	прощати	[pro'ɕati]
to give (vt)	давати	[da'wati]
to give a hint	натякати	[natⁱa'kati]
to go (on foot)	йти	[jtɨ]
to go for a swim	купатися	[ku'patisⁱa]
to go out (for dinner, etc.)	виходити	[wɨ'hoditi]
to guess (the answer)	відгадати	[widɦa'dati]
to have (vt)	мати	['mati]
to have breakfast	снідати	['snidati]
to have dinner	вечеряти	[wɛ'tʃɛrⁱati]
to have lunch	обідати	[o'bidati]
to hear (vt)	чути	['tʃuti]
to help (vt)	допомагати	[dopoma'ɦati]
to hide (vt)	ховати	[ho'wati]
to hope (vi, vt)	сподіватися	[spodi'watisⁱa]
to hunt (vi, vt)	полювати	[polⁱu'wati]
to hurry (vi)	поспішати	[pospi'ʃati]

10. The most important verbs. Part 3

to inform (vt)	інформувати	[informu'wati]
to insist (vi, vt)	наполягати	[napolⁱa'ɦati]
to insult (vt)	ображати	[obra'ʒati]
to invite (vt)	запрошувати	[za'proʃuwati]
to joke (vi)	жартувати	[ʒartu'wati]
to keep (vt)	зберігати	[zbɛri'ɦati]
to keep silent, to hush	мовчати	[mow'tʃati]
to kill (vt)	убивати	[ubɨ'wati]
to know (sb)	знати	['znati]
to know (sth)	знати	['znati]
to laugh (vi)	сміятися	[smi'ⁱatisⁱa]
to liberate (city, etc.)	звільняти	[zwilⁱ'nⁱati]
to look for ... (search)	шукати	[ʃu'kati]
to love (sb)	кохати	[ko'hati]
to make a mistake	помилятися	[pomⁱ'lⁱatisⁱa]
to manage, to run	керувати	[kɛru'wati]
to mean (signify)	означати	[ozna'tʃati]
to mention (talk about)	згадувати	['zɦaduwati]

to miss (school, etc.)	пропускати	[propus'kati]
to notice (see)	помічати	[pomi'tʃati]
to object (vi, vt)	заперечувати	[zapɛ'rɛtʃuwati]

to observe (see)	спостерігати	[spostɛri'hati]
to open (vt)	відчинити	[widtʃi'niti]
to order (meal, etc.)	замовляти	[zamow'lʲati]
to order (mil.)	наказувати	[na'kazuwati]
to own (possess)	володіти	[wolo'diti]

to participate (vi)	брати участь	['brati 'utʃastʲ]
to pay (vi, vt)	платити	[pla'titi]
to permit (vt)	дозволяти	[dozwo'lʲati]
to plan (vt)	планувати	[planu'wati]
to play (children)	грати	['hrati]

to pray (vi, vt)	молитися	[mo'litisʲa]
to prefer (vt)	воліти	[wo'liti]
to promise (vt)	обіцяти	[obi'tsʲati]
to pronounce (vt)	вимовляти	[wimow'lʲati]
to propose (vt)	пропонувати	[proponu'wati]
to punish (vt)	покарати	[poka'rati]

11. The most important verbs. Part 4

to read (vi, vt)	читати	[tʃi'tati]
to recommend (vt)	рекомендувати	[rɛkomɛndu'wati]
to refuse (vi, vt)	відмовлятися	[widmow'lʲatisʲa]
to regret (be sorry)	жалкувати	[ʒalku'wati]
to rent (sth from sb)	наймати	[naj'mati]

to repeat (say again)	повторювати	[pow'torʲuwati]
to reserve, to book	резервувати	[rɛzɛrwu'wati]
to run (vi)	бігти	['bihti]
to save (rescue)	рятувати	[rʲatu'wati]

to say (~ thank you)	сказати	[ska'zati]
to scold (vt)	лаяти	['laʲati]
to see (vt)	бачити	['batʃiti]
to sell (vt)	продавати	[proda'wati]

to send (vt)	відправляти	[widpraw'lʲati]
to shoot (vi)	стріляти	[stri'lʲati]
to shout (vi)	кричати	[kri'tʃati]
to show (vt)	показувати	[po'kazuwati]
to sign (document)	підписувати	[pid'pisuwati]

to sit down (vi)	сідати	[si'dati]
to smile (vi)	посміхатися	[posmi'hatisʲa]
to speak (vi, vt)	розмовляти	[rozmow'lʲati]
to steal (money, etc.)	красти	['krasti]
to stop (for pause, etc.)	зупинятися	[zupi'nʲatisʲa]
to stop (please ~ calling me)	припиняти	[pripi'nʲati]
to study (vt)	вивчати	[wiw'tʃati]

to swim (vi)	плавати	['plawati]
to take (vt)	брати	['brati]
to think (vi, vt)	думати	['dumati]

to threaten (vt)	погрожувати	[poɦ'rɔʒuwati]
to touch (with hands)	торкати	[tor'kati]
to translate (vt)	перекладати	[pɛrɛkla'dati]
to trust (vt)	довіряти	[dowi'rʲati]
to try (attempt)	пробувати	['prɔbuwati]

to turn (e.g., ~ left)	повертати	[powɛr'tati]
to underestimate (vt)	недооцінювати	[nɛdoo'tsinʲuwati]
to understand (vt)	розуміти	[rozu'miti]
to unite (vt)	об'єднувати	[o'bʲɛdnuwati]
to wait (vt)	чекати	[tʃɛ'kati]

to want (wish, desire)	хотіти	[ho'titi]
to warn (vt)	попереджувати	[popɛ'rɛdʒuwati]
to work (vi)	працювати	[pratsʲu'wati]
to write (vt)	писати	[pi'sati]
to write down	записувати	[za'pisuwati]

12. Colours

colour	колір (ч)	['kɔlir]
shade (tint)	відтінок (ч)	[wid'tinok]
hue	тон (ч)	[ton]
rainbow	веселка (ж)	[wɛ'sɛlka]

white (adj)	білий	['bilij]
black (adj)	чорний	['tʃɔrnij]
grey (adj)	сірий	['sirij]

green (adj)	зелений	[zɛ'lɛnij]
yellow (adj)	жовтий	['ʒɔwtij]
red (adj)	червоний	[tʃɛr'wɔnij]

blue (adj)	синій	['sinij]
light blue (adj)	блакитний	[bla'kitnij]
pink (adj)	рожевий	[ro'ʒɛwij]
orange (adj)	помаранчевий	[poma'rantʃɛwij]
violet (adj)	фіолетовий	[fio'lɛtowij]
brown (adj)	коричневий	[ko'ritʃnɛwij]

| golden (adj) | золотий | [zolo'tij] |
| silvery (adj) | сріблястий | [srib'lʲastij] |

beige (adj)	бежевий	['bɛʒɛwij]
cream (adj)	кремовий	['krɛmowij]
turquoise (adj)	бірюзовий	[birʲu'zɔwij]
cherry red (adj)	вишневий	[wiʃ'nɛwij]
lilac (adj)	бузковий	[buz'kɔwij]
crimson (adj)	малиновий	[ma'linowij]
light (adj)	світлий	['switlij]

dark (adj)	темний	['tɛmnij]
bright, vivid (adj)	яскравий	[jas'krawij]
coloured (pencils)	кольоровий	[kolʲo'rɔwij]
colour (e.g. ~ film)	кольоровий	[kolʲo'rɔwij]
black-and-white (adj)	чорно-білий	['ʧɔrno 'bilij]
plain (one-coloured)	однобарвний	[odno'barwnij]
multicoloured (adj)	різнобарвний	[rizno'barwnij]

13. Questions

Who?	Хто?	[hto]
What?	Що?	[ɕo]
Where? (at, in)	Де?	[dɛ]
Where (to)?	Куди?	[ku'dɨ]
From where?	Звідки?	['zwidkɨ]
When?	Коли?	[ko'lɨ]
Why? (What for?)	Навіщо?	[na'wiɕo]
Why? (~ are you crying?)	Чому?	[ʧo'mu]
What for?	Для чого?	[dlʲa 'ʧɔho]
How? (in what way)	Як?	[jak]
What? (What kind of …?)	Який?	[ja'kij]
Which?	Котрий?	[kot'rij]
To whom?	Кому?	[ko'mu]
About whom?	Про кого?	[pro 'kɔho]
About what?	Про що?	[pro ɕo]
With whom?	З ким?	[z kɨm]
How many? How much?	Скільки?	['skilʲkɨ]
Whose?	Чий?	[ʧij]

14. Function words. Adverbs. Part 1

Where? (at, in)	Де?	[dɛ]
here (adv)	тут	[tut]
there (adv)	там	[tam]
somewhere (to be)	десь	[dɛsʲ]
nowhere (not in any place)	ніде	[ni'dɛ]
by (near, beside)	біля	['bilʲa]
by the window	біля вікна	['bilʲa wik'na]
Where (to)?	Куди?	[ku'dɨ]
here (e.g. come ~!)	сюди	[sʲu'dɨ]
there (e.g. to go ~)	туди	[tu'dɨ]
from here (adv)	звідси	['zwidsɨ]
from there (adv)	звідти	['zwidtɨ]
close (adv)	близько	['blizʲko]
far (adv)	далеко	[da'lɛko]

near (e.g. ~ Paris)	біля	['bilʲa]
nearby (adv)	поряд	['porʲad]
not far (adv)	недалеко	[nɛda'lɛko]
left (adj)	лівий	['liwɨj]
on the left	зліва	['zliwa]
to the left	ліворуч	[li'worutʃ]
right (adj)	правий	['prawɨj]
on the right	справа	['sprawa]
to the right	праворуч	[pra'worutʃ]
in front (adv)	спереду	['spɛrɛdu]
front (as adj)	передній	[pɛ'rɛdnij]
ahead (the kids ran ~)	уперед	[upɛ'rɛd]
behind (adv)	позаду	[po'zadu]
from behind	ззаду	['zzadu]
back (towards the rear)	назад	[na'zad]
middle	середина (ж)	[sɛ'rɛdɨna]
in the middle	посередині	[posɛ'rɛdɨni]
at the side	збоку	['zbɔku]
everywhere (adv)	скрізь	[skrizʲ]
around (in all directions)	навколо	[naw'kɔlo]
from inside	зсередини	[zsɛ'rɛdɨni]
somewhere (to go)	кудись	[ku'disʲ]
straight (directly)	напрямки	[naprʲam'kɨ]
back (e.g. come ~)	назад	[na'zad]
from anywhere	звідки-небудь	['zwidkɨ 'nɛbudʲ]
from somewhere	звідкись	['zwidkɨsʲ]
firstly (adv)	по-перше	[po 'pɛrʃɛ]
secondly (adv)	по-друге	[po 'druɦɛ]
thirdly (adv)	по-третє	[po t'rɛtɛ]
suddenly (adv)	раптом	['raptom]
at first (in the beginning)	спочатку	[spo'tʃatku]
for the first time	уперше	[u'pɛrʃɛ]
long before …	задовго до …	[za'dɔwɦo do]
anew (over again)	заново	['zanowo]
for good (adv)	назовсім	[na'zɔwsim]
never (adv)	ніколи	[ni'kɔlɨ]
again (adv)	знову	['znɔwu]
now (at present)	тепер	[tɛ'pɛr]
often (adv)	часто	['tʃasto]
then (adv)	тоді	[to'di]
urgently (quickly)	терміново	[tɛrmi'nɔwo]
usually (adv)	звичайно	[zwɨ'tʃajno]
by the way, …	до речі	[do 'rɛtʃi]
possibly	можливо	[moʒ'lɨwo]

probably (adv)	мабуть	[ma'butʲ]
maybe (adv)	може бути	['mɔʒɛ 'buti]
besides ...	крім того, ...	[krim 'tɔɦo]
that's why ...	тому	[to'mu]
in spite of ...	незважаючи на ...	[nɛzwa'ʒaʲuʧi na]
thanks to ...	завдяки ...	[zawdʲa'kɨ]

what (pron.)	що	[ɕo]
that (conj.)	що	[ɕo]
something	щось	[ɕosʲ]
anything (something)	що-небудь	[ɕo 'nɛbudʲ]
nothing	нічого	[ni'ʧɔɦo]

who (pron.)	хто	[hto]
someone	хтось	[htosʲ]
somebody	хто-небудь	[hto 'nɛbudʲ]

nobody	ніхто	[nih'tɔ]
nowhere (a voyage to ~)	нікуди	['nikudɨ]
nobody's	нічий	[ni'ʧij]
somebody's	чий-небудь	[ʧij 'nɛbudʲ]

so (I'm ~ glad)	так	[tak]
also (as well)	також	[ta'kɔʒ]
too (as well)	також	[ta'kɔʒ]

15. Function words. Adverbs. Part 2

Why?	Чому?	[ʧo'mu]
for some reason	чомусь	[ʧo'musʲ]
because ...	тому, що ...	[to'mu, ɕo ...]
for some purpose	навіщось	[na'wiɕosʲ]

and	і	[i]
or	або	[a'bɔ]
but	але	[a'lɛ]
for (e.g. ~ me)	для	[dlʲa]

too (excessively)	занадто	[za'nadto]
only (exclusively)	тільки	['tilʲkɨ]
exactly (adv)	точно	['tɔʧno]
about (more or less)	приблизно	[prib'lizno]

approximately (adv)	приблизно	[prib'lizno]
approximate (adj)	приблизний	[prib'liznij]
almost (adv)	майже	['majʒɛ]
the rest	решта (ж)	['rɛʃta]

each (adj)	кожен	['kɔʒɛn]
any (no matter which)	будь-який	[budʲ ja'kij]
many, much (a lot of)	багато	[ba'ɦato]
many people	багато хто	[ba'ɦato hto]
all (everyone)	всі	[wsi]
in return for ...	в обмін на ...	[w 'ɔbmin na]

in exchange (adv)	натомість	[na'tɔmistʲ]
by hand (made)	вручну	[wrutʃʲnu]
hardly (negative opinion)	навряд чи	[naw'rʲad tʃi]

probably (adv)	мабуть	[ma'butʲ]
on purpose (intentionally)	навмисно	[naw'misno]
by accident (adv)	випадково	[wipad'kɔwo]

very (adv)	дуже	['duʒɛ]
for example (adv)	наприклад	[na'priklad]
between	між	[miʒ]
among	серед	['sɛrɛd]
so much (such a lot)	стільки	['stilʲki]
especially (adv)	особливо	[osob'liwo]

Basic concepts. Part 2

rich (adj)	багатий	[ba'ɦatij]
poor (adj)	бідний	['bidnij]
ill, sick (adj)	хворий	['hwɔrij]
well (not sick)	здоровий	[zdo'rɔwij]
big (adj)	великий	[wɛ'likij]
small (adj)	маленький	[ma'lɛnʲkij]
quickly (adv)	швидко	['ʃwidko]
slowly (adv)	повільно	[po'wilʲno]
fast (adj)	швидкий	[ʃwid'kij]
slow (adj)	повільний	[po'wilʲnij]
glad (adj)	веселий	[wɛ'sɛlij]
sad (adj)	сумний	[sum'nij]
together (adv)	разом	['razom]
separately (adv)	окремо	[ok'rɛmo]
aloud (to read)	вголос	['wɦɔlos]
silently (to oneself)	про себе	[pro 'sɛbɛ]
tall (adj)	високий	[wi'sɔkij]
low (adj)	низький	[nizʲ'kij]
deep (adj)	глибокий	[ɦli'bɔkij]
shallow (adj)	мілкий	[mil'kij]
yes	так	[tak]
no	ні	[ni]
distant (in space)	далекий	[da'lɛkij]
nearby (adj)	близький	[blizʲ'kij]
far (adv)	далеко	[da'lɛko]
nearby (adv)	поруч	['pɔruʧ]
long (adj)	довгий	['dɔwɦij]
short (adj)	короткий	[ko'rɔtkij]
good (kindhearted)	добрий	['dɔbrij]
evil (adj)	злий	['zlij]

married (adj)	одружений	[od'ruʒɛnij]
single (adj)	холостий	[holos'tij]
to forbid (vt)	заборонити	[zaboro'niti]
to permit (vt)	дозволити	[doz'woliti]
end	кінець (ч)	[ki'nɛts]
beginning	початок (ч)	[po'tʃatok]
left (adj)	лівий	['liwij]
right (adj)	правий	['prawij]
first (adj)	перший	['pɛrʃij]
last (adj)	останній	[os'tanij]
crime	злочин (ч)	['zlotʃin]
punishment	кара (ж)	['kara]
to order (vt)	наказати	[naka'zati]
to obey (vi, vt)	підкоритися	[pidko'ritisˈa]
straight (adj)	прямий	[prˈa'mij]
curved (adj)	кривий	[kriˈwij]
paradise	рай (ч)	[raj]
hell	пекло (с)	['pɛklo]
to be born	народитися	[naro'ditisˈa]
to die (vi)	померти	[po'mɛrti]
strong (adj)	сильний	['silˈnij]
weak (adj)	слабкий	[slab'kij]
old (adj)	старий	[sta'rij]
young (adj)	молодий	[molo'dij]
old (adj)	старий	[sta'rij]
new (adj)	новий	[no'wij]
hard (adj)	твердий	[twɛr'dij]
soft (adj)	м'який	[mˈʲa'kij]
warm (tepid)	теплий	['tɛplij]
cold (adj)	холодний	[ho'lɔdnij]
fat (adj)	товстий	[tows'tij]
thin (adj)	худий	[hu'dij]
narrow (adj)	вузький	[wuziˈ'kij]
wide (adj)	широкий	[ʃi'rɔkij]
good (adj)	добрий	['dɔbrij]
bad (adj)	поганий	[po'ɦanij]
brave (adj)	хоробрий	[ho'rɔbrij]
cowardly (adj)	боягузливий	[boja'ɦuzliwij]

17. Weekdays

Monday	понеділок (ч)	[pɔnɛ'dilok]
Tuesday	вівторок (ч)	[wiw'tɔrok]
Wednesday	середа (ж)	[sɛrɛ'da]
Thursday	четвер (ч)	[ʧɛt'wɛr]
Friday	п'ятниця (ж)	['pʲatnitsʲa]
Saturday	субота (ж)	[su'bɔta]
Sunday	неділя (ж)	[nɛ'dilʲa]
today (adv)	сьогодні	[sʲo'ɦɔdni]
tomorrow (adv)	завтра	['zawtra]
the day after tomorrow	післязавтра	[pislʲa'zawtra]
yesterday (adv)	вчора	['wʧora]
the day before yesterday	позавчора	[pozaw'ʧɔra]
day	день (ч)	[dɛnʲ]
working day	робочий день (ч)	[ro'bɔʧij dɛnʲ]
public holiday	святковий день (ч)	[swʲat'kɔwij dɛnʲ]
day off	вихідний день (ч)	[wiɦid'nij dɛnʲ]
weekend	вихідні (мн)	[wiɦid'ni]
all day long	весь день	[wɛsʲ dɛnʲ]
the next day (adv)	на наступний день	[na na'stupnij dɛnʲ]
two days ago	2 дні тому	[dwa dni 'tomu]
the day before	напередодні	[napɛrɛ'dɔdni]
daily (adj)	щоденний	[ɕo'dɛnij]
every day (adv)	щодня	[ɕod'nʲa]
week	тиждень (ч)	['tiʒdɛnʲ]
last week (adv)	на минулому тижні	[na mi'nulomu 'tiʒni]
next week (adv)	на наступному тижні	[na na'stupnomu 'tiʒni]
weekly (adj)	щотижневий	[ɕotiʒ'nɛwij]
every week (adv)	щотижня	[ɕo'tiʒnʲa]
twice a week	два рази на тиждень	[dwa 'razi na 'tiʒdɛnʲ]
every Tuesday	кожен вівторок	['kɔʒɛn wiw'tɔrok]

18. Hours. Day and night

morning	ранок (ч)	['ranok]
in the morning	вранці	['wrantsi]
noon, midday	полудень (ч)	['pɔludɛnʲ]
in the afternoon	після обіду	['pislʲa o'bidu]
evening	вечір (ч)	['wɛʧir]
in the evening	увечері	[u'wɛʧeri]
night	ніч (ж)	[niʧ]
at night	уночі	[uno'ʧi]
midnight	північ (ж)	['piwniʧ]
second	секунда (ж)	[sɛ'kunda]
minute	хвилина (ж)	[hwi'lina]
hour	година (ж)	[ɦo'dina]

half an hour	півгодини (мн)	[piwɦo'dɨnɨ]
a quarter-hour	чверть (ж) години	[ʧwɛrtʲ ɦo'dɨnɨ]
fifteen minutes	15 хвилин	[pʲat'nadʦʲatʲ hwɨ'lɨn]
24 hours	доба (ж)	[do'ba]

sunrise	схід (ч) сонця	[shid 'sɔnʦʲa]
dawn	світанок (ч)	[swi'tanok]
early morning	ранній ранок (ч)	['ranij 'ranok]
sunset	захід (ч)	['zahid]

early in the morning	рано вранці	['rano 'wranʦi]
this morning	сьогодні вранці	[sʲo'ɦodni 'wranʦi]
tomorrow morning	завтра вранці	['zawtra 'wranʦi]

this afternoon	сьогодні вдень	[sʲo'ɦodni wdɛnʲ]
in the afternoon	після обіду	['pislʲa o'bidu]
tomorrow afternoon	завтра після обіду (ч)	['zawtra 'pislʲa o'bidu]

| tonight (this evening) | сьогодні увечері | [sʲo'ɦodni u'wɛʧɛri] |
| tomorrow night | завтра увечері | ['zawtra u'wɛʧɛri] |

at 3 o'clock sharp	рівно о третій годині	['riwno o t'retij ɦo'dɨni]
about 4 o'clock	біля четвертої години	['bilʲa ʧɛt'wɛrtoji ɦo'dɨni]
by 12 o'clock	до дванадцятої години	[do dwa'nadʦʲatoji ɦo'dɨni]

in 20 minutes	за двадцять хвилин	[za 'dwadʦʲatʲ hwɨ'lɨn]
in an hour	за годину	[za ɦo'dɨnu]
on time (adv)	вчасно	['wʧasno]

a quarter to …	без чверті	[bɛz 'ʧwɛrti]
within an hour	на протязі години	[na 'protʲazi ɦo'dɨni]
every 15 minutes	що п'ятнадцять хвилин	[ɕo pʲat'nadʦʲatʲ hwɨ'lɨn]
round the clock	цілодобово	[ʦilodo'bɔwo]

19. Months. Seasons

January	січень (ч)	['siʧɛnʲ]
February	лютий (ч)	['lʲutɨj]
March	березень (ч)	['bɛrɛzɛnʲ]
April	квітень (ч)	['kwitɛnʲ]
May	травень (ч)	['trawɛnʲ]
June	червень (ч)	['ʧɛrwɛnʲ]

July	липень (ч)	['lɨpɛnʲ]
August	серпень (ч)	['sɛrpɛnʲ]
September	вересень (ч)	['wɛrɛsɛnʲ]
October	жовтень (ч)	['ʒɔwtɛnʲ]
November	листопад (ч)	[lɨsto'pad]
December	грудень (ч)	['ɦrudɛnʲ]

spring	весна (ж)	[wɛs'na]
in spring	навесні	[nawɛs'ni]
spring (as adj)	весняний	[wɛs'nʲanɨj]
summer	літо (с)	['lito]

in summer	влітку	['wlitku]
summer (as adj)	літній	['litnij]
autumn	осінь (ж)	['ɔsinʲ]
in autumn	восени	[wosɛ'nɨ]
autumn (as adj)	осінній	[o'sinij]
winter	зима (ж)	[zɨ'ma]
in winter	взимку	['wzɨmku]
winter (as adj)	зимовий	[zɨ'mɔwɨj]
month	місяць (ч)	['misʲaʦ]
this month	в цьому місяці (ч)	[w ʦʲomu 'misʲaʦi]
next month	в наступному місяці (ч)	[w na'stupnomu 'misʲaʦi]
last month	в минулому місяці (ч)	[w mɨ'nulomu 'misʲaʦi]
a month ago	місяць (ч) тому	['misʲaʦ to'mu]
in a month (a month later)	через місяць	['ʧɛrɛz 'misʲaʦ]
in 2 months (2 months later)	через 2 місяці	['ʧɛrɛz dwa 'misʲaʦi]
the whole month	весь місяць (ч)	[wɛsʲ 'misʲaʦ]
all month long	цілий місяць	['ʦilɨj 'misʲaʦ]
monthly (~ magazine)	щомісячний	[ɕo'misʲaʧnɨj]
monthly (adv)	щомісяця	[ɕo'misʲaʦʲa]
every month	кожний місяць (ч)	['kɔʒnɨj 'misʲaʦ]
twice a month	два рази на місяць	[dwa 'razɨ na 'misʲaʦ]
year	рік (ч)	[rik]
this year	в цьому році	[w ʦʲomu 'rɔʦi]
next year	в наступному році	[w na'stupnomu 'rɔʦi]
last year	в минулому році	[w mɨ'nulomu 'rɔʦi]
a year ago	рік тому	[rik 'tɔmu]
in a year	через рік	['ʧɛrɛz rik]
in two years	через два роки	['ʧɛrɛz dwa 'rɔkɨ]
the whole year	увесь рік	[u'wɛsʲ rik]
all year long	цілий рік	['ʦilɨj rik]
every year	кожен рік	['kɔʒɛn 'rik]
annual (adj)	щорічний	[ɕo'riʧnɨj]
annually (adv)	щороку	[ɕo'rɔku]
4 times a year	чотири рази на рік	[ʧo'tɨrɨ 'razɨ na rik]
date (e.g. today's ~)	число (с)	[ʧɨs'lɔ]
date (e.g. ~ of birth)	дата (ж)	['data]
calendar	календар (ч)	[kalɛn'dar]
half a year	півроку	[piw'rɔku]
six months	півріччя (с)	[piw'riʧʲa]
season (summer, etc.)	сезон (ч)	[sɛ'zɔn]
century	вік (ч)	[wik]

20. Time. Miscellaneous

time	час (с)	[ʧas]
moment	мить (ж)	[mɨtʲ]

instant (n)	момент (ч)	[mo'mɛnt]
instant (adj)	миттєвий	[mit'tɛwij]
lapse (of time)	відрізок (ч)	[wid'rizok]
life	життя (с)	[ʒit'tʲa]
eternity	вічність (ж)	['witʃnistʲ]

epoch	епоха (ж)	[ɛ'pɔha]
era	ера (ж)	['ɛra]
cycle	цикл (ч)	['tsikl]
period	період (ч)	[pɛ'riod]
term (short-~)	термін (ч)	['tɛrmin]

the future	майбутнє (с)	[maj'butnɛ]
future (as adj)	майбутній	[maj'butnij]
next time	наступного разу (ч)	[na'stupnoɦo 'razu]
the past	минуле (с)	[mi'nulɛ]
past (recent)	минулий	[mi'nulij]
last time	минулого разу	[mi'nuloɦo 'razu]

later (adv)	пізніше	[piz'niʃɛ]
after (prep.)	після	['pislʲa]
nowadays (adv)	сьогодення	[sʲoɦo'dɛnʲa]
now (at this moment)	зараз	['zaraz]
immediately (adv)	негайно	[nɛ'ɦajno]
soon (adv)	незабаром	[nɛza'barom]
in advance (beforehand)	завчасно	[zaw'tʃasno]

a long time ago	давно	[daw'nɔ]
recently (adv)	нещодавно	[nɛɕo'dawno]
destiny	доля (ж)	['dɔlʲa]
recollections	пам'ять (ж)	['pamʲʲatʲ]
archives	архів (ч)	[ar'ɦiw]
during …	під час	[pid 'tʃas]
long, a long time (adv)	довго	['dɔwɦo]
not long (adv)	недовго	[nɛ'dɔwɦo]
early (in the morning)	рано	['rano]
late (not early)	пізно	['pizno]

forever (for good)	назавжди	[na'zawʒdi]
to start (begin)	починати	[potʃi'nati]
to postpone (vt)	перенести	[pɛrɛ'nɛsti]

at the same time	одночасно	[odno'tʃasno]
permanently (adv)	постійно	[pos'tijno]
constant (noise, pain)	постійний	[pos'tijnij]
temporary (adj)	тимчасовий	[timtʃa'sɔwij]
sometimes (adv)	інколи	['inkoli]
rarely (adv)	рідко	['ridko]
often (adv)	часто	['tʃasto]

21. Lines and shapes

| square | квадрат (ч) | [kwad'rat] |
| square (as adj) | квадратний | [kwad'ratnij] |

circle	коло (с)	['kɔlo]
round (adj)	круглий	['kruɦlij]
triangle	трикутник (ч)	[tri'kutnik]
triangular (adj)	трикутний	[tri'kutnij]
oval	овал (ч)	[o'wal]
oval (as adj)	овальний	[o'walʲnij]
rectangle	прямокутник (ч)	[prʲamo'kutnik]
rectangular (adj)	прямокутний	[prʲamo'kutnij]
pyramid	піраміда (ж)	[pira'mida]
rhombus	ромб (ч)	[romb]
trapezium	трапеція (ж)	[tra'pɛtsiʲa]
cube	куб (ч)	[kub]
prism	призма (ж)	['prizma]
circumference	коло (с)	['kɔlo]
sphere	сфера (ж)	['sfɛra]
ball (solid sphere)	куля (ж)	['kulʲa]
diameter	діаметр (ч)	[di'amɛtr]
radius	радіус (ч)	['radius]
perimeter (circle's ~)	периметр (ч)	[pɛ'rimɛtr]
centre	центр (ч)	[tsɛntr]
horizontal (adj)	горизонтальний	[ɦorizon'talʲnij]
vertical (adj)	вертикальний	[wɛrti'kalʲnij]
parallel (n)	паралель (ж)	[para'lɛlʲ]
parallel (as adj)	паралельний	[para'lɛlʲnij]
line	лінія (ж)	['liniʲa]
stroke	риса (ж)	['risa]
straight line	пряма (ж)	[prʲa'ma]
curve (curved line)	крива (ж)	[kri'wa]
thin (line, etc.)	тонкий	[ton'kij]
contour (outline)	контур (ч)	['kɔntur]
intersection	перетин (ч)	[pɛ'rɛtin]
right angle	прямий кут (ч)	[prʲa'mij kut]
segment	сегмент (ч)	[sɛɦ'mɛnt]
sector (circular ~)	сектор (ч)	['sɛktor]
side (of a triangle)	бік (ч)	[bik]
angle	кут (ч)	[kut]

22. Units of measurement

weight	вага (ж)	[wa'ɦa]
length	довжина (ж)	[dowʒi'na]
width	ширина (ж)	[ʃiri'na]
height	висота (ж)	[wiso'ta]
depth	глибина (ж)	[ɦlibi'na]
volume	об'єм (ч)	[o'b'ɛm]
area	площа (ж)	['plɔɕa]
gram	грам (ч)	[ɦram]
milligram	міліграм (ч)	[mili'ɦram]

kilogram	кілограм (ч)	[kilo'ɦram]
ton	тонна (ж)	['tɔna]
pound	фунт (ч)	['funt]
ounce	унція (ж)	['unt͡sʲiˌa]

metre	метр (ч)	[mɛtr]
millimetre	міліметр (ч)	[mili'mɛtr]
centimetre	сантиметр (ч)	[santi'mɛtr]
kilometre	кілометр (ч)	[kilo'mɛtr]
mile	миля (ж)	['miɫʲʲa]

inch	дюйм (ч)	[dʲujm]
foot	фут (ч)	[fut]
yard	ярд (ч)	[jard]

| square metre | квадратний метр (ч) | [kwad'ratnij mɛtr] |
| hectare | гектар (ч) | [ɦɛk'tar] |

litre	літр (ч)	[litr]
degree	градус (ч)	['ɦradus]
volt	вольт (ч)	[wolʲt]
ampere	ампер (ч)	[am'pɛr]
horsepower	кінська сила (ж)	['kinsʲka 'siɫa]

quantity	кількість (ж)	['kilʲkistʲ]
a little bit of …	небагато …	[nɛba'ɦato]
half	половина (ж)	[polo'wina]
dozen	дюжина (ж)	['dʲuʒina]
piece (item)	штука (ж)	['ʃtuka]

| size | розмір (ч) | ['rɔzmir] |
| scale (map ~) | масштаб (ч) | [masʃ'tab] |

minimal (adj)	мінімальний	[mini'malʲnij]
the smallest (adj)	найменший	[naj'mɛnʃij]
medium (adj)	середній	[sɛ'rɛdnij]
maximal (adj)	максимальний	[maksi'malʲnij]
the largest (adj)	найбільший	[naj'bilʲʃij]

23. Containers

canning jar (glass ~)	банка (ж)	['banka]
tin, can	банка (ж)	['banka]
bucket	відро (с)	[wid'rɔ]
barrel	бочка (ж)	['bɔt͡ʃka]

wash basin (e.g., plastic ~)	таз (ч)	[taz]
tank (100L water ~)	бак (ч)	[bak]
hip flask	фляжка (ж)	['flʲaʒka]
jerrycan	каністра (ж)	[ka'nistra]
tank (e.g., tank car)	цистерна (ж)	[t͡sis'tɛrna]

| mug | кухоль (ч) | ['kuholʲ] |
| cup (of coffee, etc.) | чашка (ж) | ['t͡ʃaʃka] |

saucer	блюдце (с)	['blʲudtsɛ]
glass (tumbler)	склянка (ж)	['sklʲanka]
wine glass	келих (ч)	['kɛlɨh]
stock pot (soup pot)	каструля (ж)	[kas'trulʲa]
bottle (~ of wine)	пляшка (ж)	['plʲaʃka]
neck (of the bottle, etc.)	шийка (ж)	['ʃɨjka]
carafe (decanter)	карафа (ж)	[ka'rafa]
pitcher	глечик (ч)	['hlɛtʃɨk]
vessel (container)	посудина (ж)	[po'sudɨna]
pot (crock, stoneware ~)	горщик (ч)	['horɕik]
vase	ваза (ж)	['waza]
flacon, bottle (perfume ~)	флакон (ч)	[fla'kɔn]
vial, small bottle	пляшечка (ж)	['plʲaʃɛtʃka]
tube (of toothpaste)	тюбик (ч)	['tʲubɨk]
sack (bag)	мішок (ч)	[mi'ʃɔk]
bag (paper ~, plastic ~)	пакет (ч)	[pa'kɛt]
packet (of cigarettes, etc.)	пачка (ж)	['patʃka]
box (e.g. shoebox)	коробка (ж)	[ko'rɔbka]
crate	ящик (ч)	['ʲaɕik]
basket	кошик (ч)	['kɔʃik]

24. Materials

material	матеріал (ч)	[matɛri'al]
wood (n)	дерево (с)	['dɛrɛwo]
wood-, wooden (adj)	дерев'яний	[dɛrɛ'wʲanij]
glass (n)	скло (с)	['sklo]
glass (as adj)	скляний	[sklʲa'nij]
stone (n)	камінь (ч)	['kaminʲ]
stone (as adj)	кам'яний	[kam'ʲa'nij]
plastic (n)	пластмаса (ж)	[plast'masa]
plastic (as adj)	пластмасовий	[plast'masowij]
rubber (n)	гума (ж)	['huma]
rubber (as adj)	гумовий	['humowij]
cloth, fabric (n)	тканина (ж)	[tka'nɨna]
fabric (as adj)	з тканини	[z tka'nɨnɨ]
paper (n)	папір (ч)	[pa'pir]
paper (as adj)	паперовий	[papɛ'rɔwij]
cardboard (n)	картон (ч)	[kar'tɔn]
cardboard (as adj)	картоновий	[kar'tɔnowij]
polyethylene	поліетилен (ч)	[poliɛti'lɛn]
cellophane	целофан (ч)	[tsɛlo'fan]

plywood	фанера (ж)	[fa'nɛra]
porcelain (n)	фарфор (ч)	['farfor]
porcelain (as adj)	порцеляновий	[portsɛ'lʲanowij]
clay (n)	глина (ж)	['ɦlina]
clay (as adj)	глиняний	['ɦlinʲanij]
ceramic (n)	кераміка (ж)	[kɛ'ramika]
ceramic (as adj)	керамічний	[kɛra'mitʃnij]

25. Metals

metal (n)	метал (ч)	[mɛ'tal]
metal (as adj)	металевий	[mɛta'lɛwij]
alloy (n)	сплав (ч)	[splaw]

gold (n)	золото (с)	['zɔloto]
gold, golden (adj)	золотий	[zolo'tij]
silver (n)	срібло (с)	['sriblo]
silver (as adj)	срібний	['sribnij]

iron (n)	залізо (с)	[za'lizo]
iron-, made of iron (adj)	залізний	[za'liznij]
steel (n)	сталь (ж)	[stalʲ]
steel (as adj)	сталевий	[sta'lɛwij]
copper (n)	мідь (ж)	[midʲ]
copper (as adj)	мідний	['midnij]

aluminium (n)	алюміній (ч)	[alʲu'minij]
aluminium (as adj)	алюмінієвий	[alʲu'miniɛwij]
bronze (n)	бронза (ж)	['brɔnza]
bronze (as adj)	бронзовий	['brɔnzowij]

brass	латунь (ж)	[la'tunʲ]
nickel	нікель (ч)	['nikɛlʲ]
platinum	платина (ж)	['platina]
mercury	ртуть (ж)	[rtutʲ]
tin	олово (с)	['ɔlowo]
lead	свинець (ч)	[swi'nɛts]
zinc	цинк (ч)	['tsink]

HUMAN BEING

Human being. The body

human being	людина (ж)	[lʲu'dɨna]
man (adult male)	чоловік (ч)	[ʧolo'wik]
woman	жінка (ж)	['ʒinka]
child	дитина (ж)	[dɨ'tɨna]
girl	дівчинка (ж)	['diwʧɨnka]
boy	хлопчик (ч)	['hlopʧik]
teenager	підліток (ч)	['pidlitok]
old man	старий (ч)	[sta'rij]
old woman	стара (ж)	[sta'ra]

organism (body)	організм (ч)	[orɦa'nizm]
heart	серце (с)	['sɛrʦɛ]
blood	кров (ж)	[krow]
artery	артерія (ж)	[ar'tɛriʲa]
vein	вена (ж)	['wɛna]
brain	мозок (ч)	['mɔzok]
nerve	нерв (ч)	[nɛrw]
nerves	нерви (мн)	['nɛrwɨ]
vertebra	хребець (ч)	[hrɛ'bɛʦ]
spine (backbone)	хребет (ч)	[hrɛ'bɛt]
stomach (organ)	шлунок (ч)	['ʃlunok]
intestines, bowels	кишечник (ч)	[ki'ʃɛʧnik]
intestine (e.g. large ~)	кишка (ж)	['kiʃka]
liver	печінка (ж)	[pɛ'ʧinka]
kidney	нирка (ж)	['nɨrka]
bone	кістка (ж)	['kistka]
skeleton	скелет (ч)	[skɛ'lɛt]
rib	ребро (с)	[rɛb'rɔ]
skull	череп (ч)	['ʧɛrɛp]
muscle	м'яз (ч)	['mʲʲaz]
biceps	біцепс (ч)	['biʦɛps]
triceps	трицепс (ч)	['triʦɛps]
tendon	сухожилля (с)	[suho'ʒilʲa]
joint	суглоб (ч)	[suɦ'lɔb]

lungs	легені (мн)	[lɛ'ɦɛni]
genitals	статеві органи (мн)	[sta'tɛwi 'ɔrɦani]
skin	шкіра (ж)	['ʃkira]

28. Head

head	голова (ж)	[ɦolo'wa]
face	обличчя (с)	[ob'litʃa]
nose	ніс (ч)	[nis]
mouth	рот (ч)	[rot]

eye	око (с)	['ɔko]
eyes	очі (мн)	['ɔtʃi]
pupil	зіниця (ч)	[zi'nitsia]
eyebrow	брова (ж)	[bro'wa]
eyelash	вія (ж)	['wiia]
eyelid	повіка (ж)	[po'wika]

tongue	язик (ч)	[ja'zɨk]
tooth	зуб (ч)	[zub]
lips	губи (мн)	['ɦubɨ]
cheekbones	вилиці (мн)	['wɨlɨtsi]
gum	ясна (мн)	['iasna]
palate	піднебіння (с)	[pidnɛ'binia]

nostrils	ніздрі (мн)	['nizdri]
chin	підборіддя (с)	[pidbo'riddia]
jaw	щелепа (ж)	[ɕɛ'lɛpa]
cheek	щока (ж)	[ɕo'ka]

forehead	чоло (с)	[tʃo'lɔ]
temple	скроня (ж)	['skronia]
ear	вухо (с)	['wuho]
back of the head	потилиця (ж)	[po'tɨlɨtsia]
neck	шия (ж)	['ʃiia]
throat	горло (с)	['ɦɔrlo]

hair	волосся (с)	[wo'lɔssia]
hairstyle	зачіска (ж)	['zatʃiska]
haircut	стрижка (ж)	['striʒka]
wig	парик (ч)	[pa'rɨk]

moustache	вуса (мн)	['wusa]
beard	борода (ж)	[boro'da]
to have (a beard, etc.)	носити	[no'sɨtɨ]
plait	коса (ж)	[ko'sa]
sideboards	бакенбарди (мн)	[bakɛn'bardɨ]

red-haired (adj)	рудий	[ru'dɨj]
grey (hair)	сивий	['sɨwɨj]
bald (adj)	лисий	['lɨsɨj]
bald patch	лисина (ж)	['lɨsɨna]
ponytail	хвіст (ч)	[hwist]
fringe	чубчик (ч)	['tʃubtʃɨk]

29. Human body

hand	кисть (ж)	[kistʲ]
arm	рука (ж)	[ru'ka]
finger	палець (ч)	['palɛts]
thumb	великий палець (ч)	[wɛ'likij 'palɛts]
little finger	мізинець (ч)	[mi'zinɛts]
nail	ніготь (ч)	['niɦotʲ]
fist	кулак (ч)	[ku'lak]
palm	долоня (ж)	[do'lɔnʲa]
wrist	зап'ясток (ч)	[za'pʲastok]
forearm	передпліччя (с)	[pɛrɛdp'litʃʲa]
elbow	лікоть (ч)	['likotʲ]
shoulder	плече (с)	[plɛ'tʃɛ]
leg	гомілка (ж)	[ɦo'milka]
foot	ступня (ж)	[stup'nʲa]
knee	коліно (с)	[ko'lino]
calf	литка (ж)	['litka]
hip	стегно (с)	[stɛɦ'nɔ]
heel	п'ятка (ж)	['pʲatka]
body	тіло (с)	['tilo]
stomach	живіт (ч)	[ʒiˈwit]
chest	груди (мн)	['ɦrudi]
breast	груди (мн)	['ɦrudi]
flank	бік (ч)	[bik]
back	спина (ж)	['spina]
lower back	поперек (ч)	[popɛ'rɛk]
waist	талія (ж)	['taliʲa]
navel (belly button)	пупок (ч)	[pu'pɔk]
buttocks	сідниці (мн)	[sid'nitsi]
bottom	зад (ч)	[zad]
beauty spot	родимка (ж)	['rɔdimka]
birthmark (café au lait spot)	родима пляма (ж)	[ro'dima 'plʲama]
tattoo	татуювання (с)	[tatuʲu'wanʲa]
scar	рубець (ч)	[ru'bɛts]

Clothing & Accessories

30. Outerwear. Coats

clothes	одяг (ч)	['ɔdʲaɦ]
outerwear	верхній одяг (ч)	['wɛrhnij 'ɔdʲaɦ]
winter clothing	зимовий одяг (ч)	[ziˈmɔwij 'ɔdʲaɦ]
coat (overcoat)	пальто (с)	[palʲˈtɔ]
fur coat	шуба (ж)	['ʃuba]
fur jacket	кожушок (ч)	[koʒuˈʃɔk]
down coat	пуховик (ч)	[puhoˈwɨk]
jacket (e.g. leather ~)	куртка (ж)	['kurtka]
raincoat (trenchcoat, etc.)	плащ (ч)	[plaɕ]
waterproof (adj)	непромокальний	[nɛpromoˈkalʲnij]

31. Men's & women's clothing

shirt (button shirt)	сорочка (ж)	[soˈrɔtʃka]
trousers	штани (мн)	[ʃtaˈnɨ]
jeans	джинси (мн)	['dʒɨnsɨ]
suit jacket	піджак (ч)	[piˈdʒak]
suit	костюм (ч)	[kosˈtʲum]
dress (frock)	сукня (ж)	['suknʲa]
skirt	спідниця (ж)	[spidˈnɨtsʲa]
blouse	блузка (ж)	['bluzka]
knitted jacket (cardigan, etc.)	кофта (ж)	['kɔfta]
jacket (of a woman's suit)	жакет (ч)	[ʒaˈkɛt]
T-shirt	футболка (ж)	[futˈbɔlka]
shorts (short trousers)	шорти (мн)	['ʃɔrtɨ]
tracksuit	спортивний костюм (ч)	[sporˈtɨwnij kosˈtʲum]
bathrobe	халат (ч)	[haˈlat]
pyjamas	піжама (ж)	[piˈʒama]
jumper (sweater)	светр (ч)	[swɛtr]
pullover	пуловер (ч)	[puloˈwɛr]
waistcoat	жилет (ч)	[ʒiˈlɛt]
tailcoat	фрак (ч)	[frak]
dinner suit	смокінг (ч)	['smɔkinɦ]
uniform	форма (ж)	['fɔrma]
workwear	робочий одяг (ж)	[roˈbɔtʃij 'ɔdʲaɦ]
boiler suit	комбінезон (ч)	[kombinɛˈzɔn]
coat (e.g. doctor's smock)	халат (ч)	[haˈlat]

32. Clothing. Underwear

underwear	білизна (ж)	[bi'lizna]
vest (singlet)	майка (ж)	['majka]
socks	шкарпетки (мн)	[ʃkar'pɛtki]
nightdress	нічна сорочка (ж)	[nitʃ'na so'rotʃka]
bra	бюстгальтер (ч)	[bʲust'halʲtɛr]
knee highs (knee-high socks)	гольфи (мн)	['holʲfi]
tights	колготки (мн)	[kol'hotki]
stockings (hold ups)	панчохи (мн)	[pan'tʃohi]
swimsuit, bikini	купальник (ч)	[ku'palʲnik]

33. Headwear

hat	шапка (ж)	['ʃapka]
trilby hat	капелюх (ч)	[kapɛ'lʲuh]
baseball cap	бейсболка (ж)	[bɛjs'bolka]
flatcap	кашкет (ч)	[kaʃ'kɛt]
beret	берет (ч)	[bɛ'rɛt]
hood	каптур (ч)	[kap'tur]
panama hat	панамка (ж)	[pa'namka]
knit cap (knitted hat)	в'язана шапочка (ж)	['wʲazana 'ʃapotʃka]
headscarf	хустка (ж)	['hustka]
women's hat	капелюшок (ч)	[kapɛ'lʲuʃok]
hard hat	каска (ж)	['kaska]
forage cap	пілотка (ж)	[pi'lotka]
helmet	шолом (ч)	[ʃo'lom]
bowler	котелок (ч)	[kotɛ'lok]
top hat	циліндр (ч)	[tsi'lindr]

34. Footwear

footwear	взуття (с)	[wzut'tʲa]
shoes (men's shoes)	черевики (мн)	[tʃɛrɛ'wiki]
shoes (women's shoes)	туфлі (мн)	['tufli]
boots (e.g., cowboy ~)	чоботи (мн)	['tʃoboti]
carpet slippers	капці (мн)	['kaptsi]
trainers	кросівки (мн)	[kro'siwki]
trainers	кеди (мн)	['kɛdi]
sandals	сандалі (мн)	[san'dali]
cobbler (shoe repairer)	чоботар (ч)	[tʃobo'tar]
heel	каблук (ч)	[kab'luk]
pair (of shoes)	пара (ж)	['para]
lace (shoelace)	шнурок (ч)	[ʃnu'rok]

to lace up (vt)	шнурувати	[ʃnuru'watɨ]
shoehorn	ложка (ж)	['lɔʒka]
shoe polish	крем (ч) для взуття	[krɛm dlʲa wzut'tʲa]

35. Textile. Fabrics

cotton (n)	бавовна (ж)	[ba'wɔwna]
cotton (as adj)	з бавовни	[z ba'wɔwnɨ]
flax (n)	льон (ч)	[lʲon]
flax (as adj)	з льону	[z lʲonu]

silk (n)	шовк (ч)	['ʃɔwk]
silk (as adj)	шовковий	[ʃow'kɔwɨj]
wool (n)	вовна (ж)	['wɔwna]
wool (as adj)	вовняний	['wɔwnʲanɨj]

velvet	оксамит (ч)	[oksa'mɨt]
suede	замша (ж)	['zamʃa]
corduroy	вельвет (ч)	[wɛlʲ'wɛt]

nylon (n)	нейлон (ч)	[nɛj'lɔn]
nylon (as adj)	з нейлону	[z nɛj'lɔnu]
polyester (n)	поліестр (ч)	[poli'ɛstr]
polyester (as adj)	поліестровий	[poli'ɛstrowɨj]

leather (n)	шкіра (ж)	['ʃkira]
leather (as adj)	зі шкіри	[zi 'ʃkirɨ]
fur (n)	хутро (с)	['hutro]
fur (e.g. ~ coat)	хутряний	[hu'trʲanɨj]

36. Personal accessories

gloves	рукавички (мн)	[ruka'wɨtʃkɨ]
mittens	рукавиці (мн)	[ruka'wɨtsi]
scarf (muffler)	шарф (ч)	[ʃarf]

glasses	окуляри (мн)	[oku'lʲarɨ]
frame (eyeglass ~)	оправа (ж)	[op'rawa]
umbrella	парасолька (ж)	[para'sɔlʲka]
walking stick	ціпок (ч)	[tsi'pɔk]
hairbrush	щітка (ж) для волосся	['ɕitka dlʲa wo'lɔssʲa]
fan	віяло (с)	['wiʲalo]

tie (necktie)	краватка (ж)	[kra'watka]
bow tie	краватка-метелик (ж)	[kra'watka mɛ'tɛlɨk]
braces	шлейки (мн)	['ʃlɛjkɨ]
handkerchief	носовичок (ч)	[nosowɨ'tʃɔk]

comb	гребінець (ч)	[hrɛbi'nɛts]
hair slide	заколка (ж)	[za'kɔlka]
hairpin	шпилька (ж)	['ʃpɨlʲka]
buckle	пряжка (ж)	['prʲaʒka]

belt	пасок (ч)	['pasok]
shoulder strap	ремінь (ч)	['rɛminʲ]
bag (handbag)	сумка (ж)	['sumka]
handbag	сумочка (ж)	['sumotʃka]
rucksack	рюкзак (ч)	[rʲuk'zak]

37. Clothing. Miscellaneous

fashion	мода (ж)	['mɔda]
in vogue (adj)	модний	['mɔdnij]
fashion designer	модельєр (ч)	[modɛ'ljɛr]
collar	комір (ч)	['kɔmir]
pocket	кишеня (ж)	[ki'ʃɛnʲa]
pocket (as adj)	кишеньковий	[kiʃɛnʲ'kɔwij]
sleeve	рукав (ч)	[ru'kaw]
hanging loop	петелька (ж)	[pɛ'tɛlʲka]
flies (on trousers)	ширінка (ж)	[ʃiʲ'rinka]
zip (fastener)	змійка (ж)	['zmijka]
fastener	застібка (ж)	['zastibka]
button	ґудзик (ч)	['gudzik]
buttonhole	петля (ж)	[pɛt'lʲa]
to come off (ab. button)	відірватися	[widir'watisʲa]
to sew (vi, vt)	шити	['ʃiti]
to embroider (vi, vt)	вишивати	[wiʃiʲ'wati]
embroidery	вишивка (ж)	['wiʃiwka]
sewing needle	голка (ж)	['hɔlka]
thread	нитка (ж)	['nitka]
seam	шов (ч)	[ʃow]
to get dirty (vi)	забруднитися	[zabrud'nitisʲa]
stain (mark, spot)	пляма (ж)	['plʲama]
to crease, to crumple	пом'ятися	[po'm'ʲatisʲa]
to tear, to rip (vt)	порвати	[por'wati]
clothes moth	міль (ж)	[milʲ]

38. Personal care. Cosmetics

toothpaste	зубна паста (ж)	[zub'na 'pasta]
toothbrush	зубна щітка (ж)	[zub'na 'ɕitka]
to clean one's teeth	чистити зуби	['tʃistiti 'zubi]
razor	бритва (ж)	['britwa]
shaving cream	крем (ч) для гоління	[krɛm dlʲa ɦo'linʲa]
to shave (vi)	голитися	[ɦo'litisʲa]
soap	мило (с)	['miɬo]
shampoo	шампунь (ч)	[ʃam'punʲ]
scissors	ножиці (мн)	['nɔʒitsi]

nail file	пилочка (ж) для нігтів	['pɪlotʃka dlʲa 'niɦtiw]
nail clippers	щипчики (мн)	['ɕiptʃiki]
tweezers	пінцет (ч)	[pin'tsɛt]
cosmetics	косметика (ж)	[kos'mɛtika]
face mask	маска (ж)	['maska]
manicure	манікюр (ч)	[mani'kʲur]
to have a manicure	робити манікюр	[ro'biti mani'kʲur]
pedicure	педикюр (ч)	[pɛdi'kʲur]
make-up bag	косметичка (ж)	[kosmɛ'titʃka]
face powder	пудра (ж)	['pudra]
powder compact	пудрениця (ж)	['pudrɛnitsʲa]
blusher	рум'яна (мн)	[ru'mʲʲana]
perfume (bottled)	парфуми (мн)	[par'fumi]
toilet water (lotion)	туалетна вода (ж)	[tua'lɛtna wo'da]
lotion	лосьйон (ч)	[lo'sjon]
cologne	одеколон (ч)	[odɛko'lɔn]
eyeshadow	тіні (мн) для повік	['tini dlʲa po'wik]
eyeliner	олівець (ч) для очей	[oli'wɛts dlʲa o'tʃɛj]
mascara	туш (ж)	[tuʃ]
lipstick	губна помада (ж)	[ɦub'na po'mada]
nail polish	лак (ч) для нігтів	[lak dlʲa 'niɦtiw]
hair spray	лак (ч) для волосся	[lak dlʲa wo'lɔssʲa]
deodorant	дезодорант (ч)	[dɛzodo'rant]
cream	крем (ч)	[krɛm]
face cream	крем (ч) для обличчя	[krɛm dlʲa ob'litʃʲa]
hand cream	крем (ч) для рук	[krɛm dlʲa ruk]
anti-wrinkle cream	крем (ч) проти зморшок	[krɛm 'prɔti 'zmɔrʃok]
day (as adj)	денний	['dɛnij]
night (as adj)	нічний	[nitʃ'nij]
tampon	тампон (ч)	[tam'pɔn]
toilet paper (toilet roll)	туалетний папір (ч)	[tua'lɛtnij pa'pir]
hair dryer	фен (ч)	[fɛn]

39. Jewellery

jewellery, jewels	коштовність (ж)	[koʃ'townistʲ]
precious (e.g. ~ stone)	коштовний	[koʃ'townij]
hallmark stamp	проба (ж)	['prɔba]
ring	каблучка (ж)	[kab'lutʃka]
wedding ring	обручка (ж)	[ob'rutʃka]
bracelet	браслет (ч)	[bras'lɛt]
earrings	сережки (мн)	[sɛ'rɛʒki]
necklace (~ of pearls)	намисто (с)	[na'misto]
crown	корона (ж)	[ko'rɔna]
bead necklace	буси (мн)	['busi]

diamond	діамант (ч)	[diaˈmant]
emerald	смарагд (ч)	[smaˈraɦd]
ruby	рубін (ч)	[ruˈbin]
sapphire	сапфір (ч)	[sapˈfir]
pearl	перли (мн)	[ˈpɛrlɨ]
amber	бурштин (ч)	[burʃˈtɨn]

40. Watches. Clocks

watch (wristwatch)	годинник (ч)	[ɦoˈdɨnɨk]
dial	циферблат (ч)	[ʦɨfɛrbˈlat]
hand (clock, watch)	стрілка (ж)	[ˈstrilka]
metal bracelet	браслет (ч)	[brasˈlɛt]
watch strap	ремінець (ч)	[rɛmiˈnɛʦ]

battery	батарейка (ж)	[bataˈrɛjka]
to be flat (battery)	сісти	[ˈsistɨ]
to change a battery	поміняти батарейку	[pomiˈnʲatɨ bataˈrɛjku]
to run fast	поспішати	[pospiˈʃatɨ]
to run slow	відставати	[widstaˈwatɨ]

wall clock	годинник (ч)	[ɦoˈdɨnɨk]
hourglass	годинник (ч) пісковий	[ɦoˈdɨnɨk pisˈkowɨj]
sundial	годинник (ч) сонячний	[ɦoˈdɨnɨk ˈsonʲaʧnɨj]
alarm clock	будильник (ч)	[buˈdɨlʲnɨk]
watchmaker	годинникар (ч)	[ɦodɨnɨˈkar]
to repair (vt)	ремонтувати	[rɛmontuˈwatɨ]

Food. Nutricion

41. Food

meat	м'ясо (с)	['m⁷jaso]
chicken	курка (ж)	['kurka]
poussin	курча (с)	[kur'ʧa]
duck	качка (ж)	['katʃka]
goose	гусак (ч)	[ɦu'sak]
game	дичина (ж)	[diʧi'na]
turkey	індичка (ж)	[in'diʧka]
pork	свинина (ж)	[swi'nina]
veal	телятина (ж)	[tɛ'lʲatina]
lamb	баранина (ж)	[ba'ranina]
beef	яловичина (ж)	['ʲalowiʧina]
rabbit	кріль (ч)	[krilʲ]
sausage (bologna, etc.)	ковбаса (ж)	[kowba'sa]
vienna sausage (frankfurter)	сосиска (ж)	[so'siska]
bacon	бекон (ч)	[bɛ'kɔn]
ham	шинка (ж)	['ʃinka]
gammon	окіст (ч)	['ɔkist]
pâté	паштет (ч)	[paʃ'tɛt]
liver	печінка (ж)	[pɛ'ʧinka]
mince (minced meat)	фарш (ч)	[farʃ]
tongue	язик (ч)	[ja'zik]
egg	яйце (с)	[jaj'tsɛ]
eggs	яйця (мн)	['ʲajtsʲa]
egg white	білок (ч)	[bi'lɔk]
egg yolk	жовток (ч)	[ʒow'tɔk]
fish	риба (ж)	['riba]
seafood	морепродукти (мн)	[morɛpro'dukti]
caviar	ікра (ж)	[ik'ra]
crab	краб (ч)	[krab]
prawn	креветка (ж)	[krɛ'wɛtka]
oyster	устриця (ж)	['ustritsʲa]
spiny lobster	лангуст (ч)	[lan'ɦust]
octopus	восьминіг (ч)	[wosʲmi'niɦ]
squid	кальмар (ч)	[kalʲ'mar]
sturgeon	осетрина (ж)	[osɛt'rina]
salmon	лосось (ч)	[lo'sɔsʲ]
halibut	палтус (ч)	['paltus]
cod	тріска (ж)	[tris'ka]
mackerel	скумбрія (ж)	['skumbriʲa]

| tuna | тунець (ч) | [tu'nɛts] |
| eel | вугор (ч) | [wu'ɦɔr] |

trout	форель (ж)	[fo'rɛlʲ]
sardine	сардина (ж)	[sar'dina]
pike	щука (ж)	['ɕuka]
herring	оселедець (ч)	[osɛ'lɛdɛts]

bread	хліб (ч)	[hlib]
cheese	сир (ч)	[sir]
sugar	цукор (ч)	['tsukor]
salt	сіль (ж)	[silʲ]

rice	рис (ч)	[ris]
pasta (macaroni)	макарони (мн)	[maka'rɔni]
noodles	локшина (ж)	[lokʃi'na]

butter	вершкове масло (с)	[wɛrʃ'kɔwɛ 'maslo]
vegetable oil	олія (ж) рослинна	[o'liʲa ros'lina]
sunflower oil	соняшникова олія (ж)	['sonʲaʃnikowa o'liʲa]
margarine	маргарин (ч)	[marɦa'rin]

| olives | оливки (мн) | [o'liwki] |
| olive oil | олія (ж) оливкова | [o'liʲa o'liwkowa] |

milk	молоко (с)	[molo'kɔ]
condensed milk	згущене молоко (с)	['zɦuɕɛnɛ molo'kɔ]
yogurt	йогурт (ч)	['jɔɦurt]
soured cream	сметана (ж)	[smɛ'tana]
cream (of milk)	вершки (мн)	[wɛrʃ'ki]

| mayonnaise | майонез (ч) | [maʲo'nɛz] |
| buttercream | крем (ч) | [krɛm] |

groats (barley ~, etc.)	крупа (ж)	[kru'pa]
flour	борошно (с)	['bɔrɔʃno]
tinned food	консерви (мн)	[kon'sɛrwi]

cornflakes	кукурудзяні пластівці (мн)	[kuku'rudzʲani plastiw'tsi]
honey	мед (ч)	[mɛd]
jam	джем (ч)	[ʤɛm]
chewing gum	жувальна гумка (ж)	[ʒu'walʲna 'ɦumka]

42. Drinks

water	вода (ж)	[wo'da]
drinking water	питна вода (ж)	[pit'na wo'da]
mineral water	мінеральна вода (ж)	[minɛ'ralʲna wo'da]

still (adj)	без газу	[bɛz 'ɦazu]
carbonated (adj)	газований	[ɦa'zɔwanij]
sparkling (adj)	з газом	[z 'ɦazom]
ice	лід (ч)	[lid]
with ice	з льодом	[z lʲodom]

non-alcoholic (adj)	безалкогольний	[bɛzalko'hɔlʲnɨj]
soft drink	безалкогольний напій (ч)	[bɛzalko'hɔlʲnɨj na'pij]
refreshing drink	прохолодній напій (ч)	[proho'lɔdnij na'pij]
lemonade	лимонад (ч)	[lɨmo'nad]

spirits	алкогольні напої (мн)	[alko'hɔlʲni na'pɔjɨ]
wine	вино (с)	[wɨ'nɔ]
white wine	біле вино (с)	['bilɛ wɨ'nɔ]
red wine	червоне вино (с)	[tʃɛr'wɔnɛ wɨ'nɔ]

liqueur	лікер (ч)	[li'kɛr]
champagne	шампанське (с)	[ʃam'pansʲkɛ]
vermouth	вермут (ч)	['wɛrmut]

whisky	віскі (с)	['wiski]
vodka	горілка (ж)	[ɦo'rilka]
gin	джин (ч)	[dʒin]
cognac	коньяк (ч)	[ko'nʲak]
rum	ром (ч)	[rom]

coffee	кава (ж)	['kawa]
black coffee	чорна кава (ж)	['tʃɔrna 'kawa]
white coffee	кава (ж) з молоком	['kawa z molo'kɔm]
cappuccino	кава (ж) з вершками	['kawa z wɛrʃ'kamɨ]
instant coffee	розчинна кава (ж)	[roz'tʃɨna 'kawa]

milk	молоко (с)	[molo'kɔ]
cocktail	коктейль (ч)	[kok'tɛjlʲ]
milkshake	молочний коктейль (ч)	[mo'lɔtʃnɨj kok'tɛjlʲ]

juice	сік (ч)	[sik]
tomato juice	томатний сік (ч)	[to'matnɨj 'sik]
orange juice	апельсиновий сік (ч)	[apɛlʲ'sinowɨj sik]
freshly squeezed juice	свіжовижатий сік (ч)	[swiʒo'wɨʒatɨj sik]

beer	пиво (с)	['pɨwo]
lager	світле пиво (с)	['switlɛ 'pɨwo]
bitter	темне пиво (с)	['tɛmnɛ 'pɨwo]

tea	чай (ч)	[tʃaj]
black tea	чорний чай (ч)	['tʃɔrnɨj tʃaj]
green tea	зелений чай (ч)	[zɛ'lɛnɨj tʃaj]

43. Vegetables

| vegetables | овочі (мн) | ['ɔwotʃi] |
| greens | зелень (ж) | ['zɛlɛnʲ] |

tomato	помідор (ч)	[pomi'dɔr]
cucumber	огірок (ч)	[ofhi'rɔk]
carrot	морква (ж)	['mɔrkwa]
potato	картопля (ж)	[kar'tɔplʲa]
onion	цибуля (ж)	[tsɨ'bulʲa]
garlic	часник (ч)	[tʃas'nɨk]

cabbage	капуста (ж)	[ka'pusta]
cauliflower	кольорова капуста (ж)	[kolʲo'rɔwa ka'pusta]
Brussels sprouts	брюссельська капуста (ж)	[brʲu'sɛlʲsʲka ka'pusta]
broccoli	капуста броколі (ж)	[ka'pusta 'brɔkoli]

beetroot	буряк (ч)	[bu'rʲak]
aubergine	баклажан (ч)	[bakla'ʒan]
courgette	кабачок (ч)	[kaba'ʧɔk]
pumpkin	гарбуз (ч)	[ɦar'buz]
turnip	ріпа (ж)	['ripa]

parsley	петрушка (ж)	[pɛt'ruʃka]
dill	кріп (ч)	[krip]
lettuce	салат (ч)	[sa'lat]
celery	селера (ж)	[sɛ'lɛra]
asparagus	спаржа (ж)	['sparʒa]
spinach	шпинат (ч)	[ʃpɨ'nat]

pea	горох (ч)	[ɦo'rɔh]
beans	боби (мн)	[bo'bɨ]
maize	кукурудза (ж)	[kuku'ruʣa]
kidney bean	квасоля (ж)	[kwa'sɔlʲa]

sweet paper	перець (ч)	['pɛrɛʦ]
radish	редька (ж)	['rɛdʲka]
artichoke	артишок (ч)	[artɨ'ʃɔk]

44. Fruits. Nuts

fruit	фрукт (ч)	[frukt]
apple	яблуко (с)	['ʲabluko]
pear	груша (ж)	['ɦruʃa]
lemon	лимон (ч)	[lɨ'mɔn]
orange	апельсин (ч)	[apɛlʲ'sɨn]
strawberry (garden ~)	полуниця (ж)	[polu'nɨʦʲa]

tangerine	мандарин (ч)	[manda'rɨn]
plum	слива (ж)	['slɨwa]
peach	персик (ч)	['pɛrsɨk]
apricot	абрикос (ч)	[abrɨ'kɔs]
raspberry	малина (ж)	[ma'lɨna]
pineapple	ананас (ч)	[ana'nas]

banana	банан (ч)	[ba'nan]
watermelon	кавун (ч)	[ka'wun]
grape	виноград (ч)	[wɨno'ɦrad]
sour cherry	вишня (ж)	['wɨʃnʲa]
sweet cherry	черешня (ж)	[ʧɛ'rɛʃnʲa]
melon	диня (ж)	['dɨnʲa]

grapefruit	грейпфрут (ч)	[ɦrɛjp'frut]
avocado	авокадо (с)	[awo'kado]
papaya	папайя (ж)	[pa'paʲa]
mango	манго (с)	['manɦo]

pomegranate	гранат (ч)	[ɦra'nat]
redcurrant	порічки (мн)	[po'ritʃkɨ]
blackcurrant	чорна смородина (ж)	['tʃorna smo'rodɨna]
gooseberry	аґрус (ч)	['agrus]
bilberry	чорниця (ж)	[tʃor'nɨtsʲa]
blackberry	ожина (ж)	[o'ʒɨna]

raisin	родзинки (мн)	[ro'dzɨnkɨ]
fig	інжир (ч)	[in'ʒɨr]
date	фінік (ч)	['finik]

peanut	арахіс (ч)	[a'rahis]
almond	мигдаль (ч)	[mɨɦ'dalʲ]
walnut	горіх (ч) волоський	[ɦo'rih wo'losʲkɨj]
hazelnut	ліщина (ж)	[li'ɕina]
coconut	горіх (ч) кокосовий	[ɦo'rih ko'kosowɨj]
pistachios	фісташки (мн)	[fis'taʃkɨ]

45. Bread. Sweets

bakers' confectionery (pastry)	кондитерські вироби (мн)	[kon'dɨtɛrsʲki 'wɨrobɨ]
bread	хліб (ч)	[hlib]
biscuits	печиво (с)	['pɛtʃɨwo]

chocolate (n)	шоколад (ч)	[ʃoko'lad]
chocolate (as adj)	шоколадний	[ʃoko'ladnɨj]
candy (wrapped)	цукерка (ж)	[tsu'kɛrka]
cake (e.g. cupcake)	тістечко (с)	['tistɛtʃko]
cake (e.g. birthday ~)	торт (ч)	[tort]

| pie (e.g. apple ~) | пиріг (ч) | [pɨ'riɦ] |
| filling (for cake, pie) | начинка (ж) | [na'tʃɨnka] |

jam (whole fruit jam)	варення (с)	[wa'rɛnʲa]
marmalade	мармелад (ч)	[marmɛ'lad]
wafers	вафлі (мн)	['wafli]
ice-cream	морозиво (с)	[mo'rozɨwo]

46. Cooked dishes

course, dish	страва (ж)	['strawa]
cuisine	кухня (ж)	['kuhnʲa]
recipe	рецепт (ч)	[rɛ'tsɛpt]
portion	порція (ж)	['portsiʲa]

| salad | салат (ч) | [sa'lat] |
| soup | юшка (ж) | ['ʲuʃka] |

clear soup (broth)	бульйон (ч)	[bulʲon]
sandwich (bread)	канапка (ж)	[ka'napka]
fried eggs	яєчня (ж)	[ja'ɛʃnʲa]
hamburger (beefburger)	гамбургер (ч)	['ɦamburɦɛr]

beefsteak	біфштекс (ч)	[bif'ʃtɛks]
side dish	гарнір (ч)	[ɦar'nir]
spaghetti	спагеті (мн)	[spa'ɦɛti]
mash	картопляне пюре (с)	[kartop'lʲanɛ pʲu'rɛ]
pizza	піца (ж)	['pitsa]
porridge (oatmeal, etc.)	каша (ж)	['kaʃa]
omelette	омлет (ч)	[om'lɛt]

boiled (e.g. ~ beef)	варений	[wa'rɛnij]
smoked (adj)	копчений	[kop'ʧɛnij]
fried (adj)	смажений	['smaʒɛnij]
dried (adj)	сушений	['suʃɛnij]
frozen (adj)	заморожений	[zamo'rɔʒɛnij]
pickled (adj)	маринований	[mari'nɔwanij]

sweet (sugary)	солодкий	[so'lɔdkij]
salty (adj)	солоний	[so'lɔnij]
cold (adj)	холодний	[ho'lɔdnij]
hot (adj)	гарячий	[ɦa'rʲaʧij]
bitter (adj)	гіркий	[ɦir'kij]
tasty (adj)	смачний	[smaʧ'nij]

to cook in boiling water	варити	[wa'riti]
to cook (dinner)	готувати	[ɦotu'wati]
to fry (vt)	смажити	['smaʒiti]
to heat up (food)	розігрівати	[roziɦri'wati]

to salt (vt)	солити	[so'liti]
to pepper (vt)	перчити	[pɛr'ʧiti]
to grate (vt)	терти	['tɛrti]
peel (n)	шкірка (ж)	['ʃkirka]
to peel (vt)	чистити	['ʧistiti]

47. Spices

salt	сіль (ж)	[silʲ]
salty (adj)	солоний	[so'lɔnij]
to salt (vt)	солити	[so'liti]

black pepper	чорний перець (ч)	['ʧornij 'pɛrɛts]
red pepper (milled ~)	червоний перець (ч)	[ʧɛr'wonij 'pɛrɛts]
mustard	гірчиця (ж)	[ɦir'ʧitsʲa]
horseradish	хрін (ч)	[hrin]

condiment	приправа (ж)	[prip'rawa]
spice	прянощі (мн)	[prʲa'nɔɕi]
sauce	соус (ч)	['sɔus]
vinegar	оцет (ч)	['ɔtsɛt]

anise	аніс (ч)	['anis]
basil	базилік (ч)	[bazi'lik]
cloves	гвоздика (ж)	[ɦwoz'dika]
ginger	імбир (ч)	[im'bir]
coriander	коріандр (ч)	[kori'andr]

cinnamon	кориця (ж)	[ko'ritsʲa]
sesame	кунжут (ч)	[kun'ʒut]
bay leaf	лавровий лист (ч)	[law'rɔwij list]
paprika	паприка (ж)	['paprika]
caraway	кмин (ч)	[kmin]
saffron	шафран (ч)	[ʃaf'ran]

48. Meals

food	їжа (ж)	['jiʒa]
to eat (vi, vt)	їсти	['jisti]
breakfast	сніданок (ч)	[sni'danok]
to have breakfast	снідати	['snidati]
lunch	обід (ч)	[o'bid]
to have lunch	обідати	[o'bidati]
dinner	вечеря (ж)	[wɛ'tʃɛrʲa]
to have dinner	вечеряти	[wɛ'tʃɛrʲati]
appetite	апетит (ч)	[apɛ'tit]
Enjoy your meal!	Смачного!	[smatʃ'nɔho]
to open (~ a bottle)	відкривати	[widkri'wati]
to spill (liquid)	пролити	[prɔ'liti]
to spill out (vi)	пролитись	[prɔ'litisʲ]
to boil (vi)	кипіти	[ki'piti]
to boil (vt)	кип'ятити	[kipʲa'titi]
boiled (~ water)	кип'ячений	[kipʲa'tʃɛnij]
to chill, cool down (vt)	охолодити	[oholo'diti]
to chill (vi)	охолоджуватись	[oho'lɔdʒuwatisʲ]
taste, flavour	смак (ч)	[smak]
aftertaste	присмак (ч)	['prismak]
to slim down (lose weight)	худнути	['hudnuti]
diet	дієта (ж)	[di'ɛta]
vitamin	вітамін (ч)	[wita'min]
calorie	калорія (ж)	[ka'lɔrʲa]
vegetarian (n)	вегетаріанець (ч)	[wɛɦɛtari'anɛts]
vegetarian (adj)	вегетаріанський	[wɛɦɛtari'ansʲkij]
fats (nutrient)	жири (мн)	[ʒi'ri]
proteins	білки (мн)	[bil'ki]
carbohydrates	вуглеводи (ч)	[wuɦlɛ'wɔdi]
slice (of lemon, ham)	скибка (ж)	['skibka]
piece (of cake, pie)	шматок (ч)	[ʃma'tɔk]
crumb (of bread, cake, etc.)	крихта (ж)	['krihta]

49. Table setting

spoon	ложка (ж)	['lɔʒka]
knife	ніж (ч)	[niʒ]

fork	виделка (ж)	[wi'dɛlka]
cup (e.g., coffee ~)	чашка (ж)	['ʧaʃka]
plate (dinner ~)	тарілка (ж)	[ta'rilka]
saucer	блюдце (с)	['blʲudtsɛ]
serviette	серветка (ж)	[sɛr'wɛtka]
toothpick	зубочистка (ж)	[zubo'ʧistka]

50. Restaurant

restaurant	ресторан (ч)	[rɛsto'ran]
coffee bar	кав'ярня (ж)	[ka'wʲarnʲa]
pub, bar	бар (ч)	[bar]
tearoom	чайна (ж)	['ʧajna]

waiter	офіціант (ч)	[ofitsi'ant]
waitress	офіціантка (ж)	[ofitsi'antka]
barman	бармен (ч)	[bar'mɛn]

menu	меню (с)	[mɛ'nʲu]
wine list	карта (ж) вин	['karta win]
to book a table	забронювати столик	[zabronʲu'wati 'stɔlik]

course, dish	страва (ж)	['strawa]
to order (meal)	замовити	[za'mɔwiti]
to make an order	зробити замовлення	[zro'biti za'mɔwlɛnʲa]

aperitif	аперитив (ч)	[apɛri'tiw]
starter	закуска (ж)	[za'kuska]
dessert, pudding	десерт (ч)	[dɛ'sɛrt]

bill	рахунок (ч)	[ra'hunok]
to pay the bill	оплатити рахунок	[opla'titi ra'hunok]
to give change	дати решту	['dati 'rɛʃtu]
tip	чайові (мн)	[ʧajo'wi]

Family, relatives and friends

51. Personal information. Forms

name (first name)	ім'я (с)	[i'm²ia]
surname (last name)	прізвище (с)	['prizwiɕɛ]
date of birth	дата (ж) народження	['data na'rɔdʒɛnia]
place of birth	місце (с) народження	['mistsɛ na'rɔdʒɛnia]
nationality	національність (ж)	[natsio'nalinisti]
place of residence	місце (с) проживання	['mistsɛ prɔʒi'wania]
country	країна (ж)	[kra'jina]
profession (occupation)	професія (ж)	[pro'fɛsiia]
gender, sex	стать (ж)	[stati]
height	зріст (ч)	[zrist]
weight	вага (ж)	[wa'ɦa]

52. Family members. Relatives

mother	мати (ж)	['mati]
father	батько (ч)	['batiko]
son	син (ч)	[sin]
daughter	дочка (ж)	[dotʃ'ka]
younger daughter	молодша дочка (ж)	[mo'lɔdʃa dotʃ'ka]
younger son	молодший син (ч)	[mo'lɔdʃij sin]
eldest daughter	старша дочка (ж)	['starʃa dotʃ'ka]
eldest son	старший син (ч)	['starʃij sin]
brother	брат (ч)	[brat]
sister	сестра (ж)	[sɛst'ra]
cousin (masc.)	двоюрідний брат (ч)	[dwoiu'ridnij brat]
cousin (fem.)	двоюрідна сестра (ж)	[dwoiu'ridna sɛst'ra]
mummy	мати (ж)	['mati]
dad, daddy	тато (ч)	['tato]
parents	батьки (мн)	[bati'ki]
child	дитина (ж)	[di'tina]
children	діти (мн)	['diti]
grandmother	бабуся (ж)	[ba'busia]
grandfather	дід (ч)	['did]
grandson	онук (ч)	[o'nuk]
granddaughter	онука (ж)	[o'nuka]
grandchildren	онуки (мн)	[o'nuki]
uncle	дядько (ч)	['diadiko]
aunt	тітка (ж)	['titka]

nephew	племінник (ч)	[plɛ'minɨk]
niece	племінниця (ж)	[plɛ'minɨtsʲa]
mother-in-law (wife's mother)	теща (ж)	['tɛɕa]
father-in-law (husband's father)	свекор (ч)	['swɛkor]
son-in-law (daughter's husband)	зять (ч)	[zʲatʲ]
stepmother	мачуха (ж)	['matʃuha]
stepfather	вітчим (ч)	['witʃim]
infant	немовля (с)	[nɛmow'lʲa]
baby (infant)	немовля (с)	[nɛmow'lʲa]
little boy, kid	малюк (ч)	[ma'lʲuk]
wife	дружина (ж)	[dru'ʒina]
husband	чоловік (ч)	[tʃolo'wik]
spouse (husband)	чоловік (ч)	[tʃolo'wik]
spouse (wife)	дружина (ж)	[dru'ʒina]
married (masc.)	одружений	[od'ruʒɛnɨj]
married (fem.)	заміжня	[za'miʒnʲa]
single (unmarried)	холостий	[holos'tɨj]
bachelor	холостяк (ч)	[holos'tʲak]
divorced (masc.)	розведений	[roz'wɛdɛnɨj]
widow	вдова (ж)	[wdo'wa]
widower	вдівець (ч)	[wdi'wɛts]
relative	родич (ч)	['rɔditʃ]
close relative	близький родич (ч)	[blizʲ'kij 'rɔditʃ]
distant relative	далекий родич (ч)	[da'lɛkij 'rɔditʃ]
relatives	рідні (мн)	['ridni]
orphan (boy or girl)	сирота (ч)	[sɨro'ta]
guardian (of a minor)	опікун (ч)	[opi'kun]
to adopt (a boy)	усиновити	[usino'wɨti]
to adopt (a girl)	удочерити	[udotʃɛ'riti]

53. Friends. Colleagues

friend (masc.)	товариш (ч)	[to'wariʃ]
friend (fem.)	подруга (ж)	['pɔdruha]
friendship	дружба (ж)	['druʒba]
to be friends	дружити	[dru'ʒɨti]
pal (masc.)	приятель (ч)	['prijatɛlʲ]
pal (fem.)	приятелька (ж)	['prijatɛlʲka]
partner	партнер (ч)	[part'nɛr]
chief (boss)	шеф (ч)	[ʃɛf]
superior (n)	начальник (ч)	[na'tʃalʲnɨk]
subordinate (n)	підлеглий (ч)	[pid'lɛhlɨj]
colleague	колега (ч)	[ko'lɛha]

acquaintance (person)	знайомий (ч)	[zna'jɔmij]
fellow traveller	попутник (ч)	[po'putnɨk]
classmate	однокласник (ч)	[odno'klasnɨk]

neighbour (masc.)	сусід (ч)	[su'sid]
neighbour (fem.)	сусідка (ж)	[su'sidka]
neighbours	сусіди (мн)	[su'sidɨ]

54. Man. Woman

woman	жінка (ж)	['ʒinka]
girl (young woman)	дівчина (ж)	['diwtʃina]
bride	наречена (ж)	[narɛ'tʃɛna]

beautiful (adj)	гарна	['ɦarna]
tall (adj)	висока	[wɨ'sɔka]
slender (adj)	струнка	[stru'nka]
short (adj)	невисокого зросту	[nɛwɨ'sɔkoɦo 'zrɔstu]

| blonde (n) | блондинка (ж) | [blon'dɨnka] |
| brunette (n) | брюнетка (ж) | [brʲu'nɛtka] |

ladies' (adj)	дамський	['damsʲkij]
virgin (girl)	незаймана дівчина (ж)	[nɛ'zajmana 'diwtʃina]
pregnant (adj)	вагітна	[wa'ɦitna]

man (adult male)	чоловік (ч)	[tʃolo'wik]
blonde haired man	блондин (ч)	[blon'dɨn]
dark haired man	брюнет (ч)	[brʲu'nɛt]
tall (adj)	високий	[wɨ'sɔkij]
short (adj)	невисокого зросту	[nɛwɨ'sɔkoɦo 'zrɔstu]

rude (rough)	брутальний	[bru'talʲnij]
stocky (adj)	кремезний	[krɛ'mɛznɨj]
robust (adj)	міцний	[mits'nij]
strong (adj)	сильний	['sɨlʲnij]
strength	сила (ж)	['sɨla]

plump, fat (adj)	повний	['pɔwnɨj]
swarthy (dark-skinned)	смаглявий	[smaɦ'lʲawɨj]
slender (well-built)	стрункий	[stru'nkij]
elegant (adj)	елегантний	[ɛlɛ'ɦantnɨj]

55. Age

age	вік (ч)	[wik]
youth (young age)	юність (ж)	['ʲunistʲ]
young (adj)	молодий	[molo'dɨj]

younger (adj)	молодший	[mo'lɔdʃij]
older (adj)	старший	['starʃij]
young man	юнак (ч)	[ʲu'nak]

| teenager | підліток (ч) | ['pidlitok] |
| guy, fellow | хлопець (ч) | ['hlɔpɛʦ] |

| old man | старий (ч) | [sta'rij] |
| old woman | стара (ж) | [sta'ra] |

| adult (adj) | дорослий | [do'rɔslij] |
| middle-aged (adj) | середніх років | [sɛ'rɛdnih ro'kiw] |

| elderly (adj) | похилий | [po'hiłij] |
| old (adj) | старий | [sta'rij] |

retirement	пенсія (ж)	['pɛnsiˡa]
to retire (from job)	вийти на пенсію	['wijtɨ na 'pɛnsiˡu]
retiree, pensioner	пенсіонер (ч)	[pɛnsio'nɛr]

56. Children

child	дитина (ж)	[dɨ'tɨna]
children	діти (мн)	['ditɨ]
twins	близнюки (мн)	[blɨznˡu'kɨ]

cradle	колиска (ж)	[ko'lɨska]
rattle	брязкальце (с)	['brˡazkalˡʦɛ]
nappy	підгузок (ч)	[pid'ɦuzok]

| dummy, comforter | соска (ж) | ['sɔska] |
| pram | коляска (ж) | [ko'lˡaska] |

| nursery | дитячий садок (ч) | [dɨ'tˡatʃij sa'dɔk] |
| babysitter | няня (ж) | ['nˡanˡa] |

| childhood | дитинство (с) | [dɨ'tɨnstwo] |
| doll | лялька (ж) | ['lˡalˡka] |

| toy | іграшка (ж) | ['iɦraʃka] |
| construction set (toy) | конструктор (ч) | [kon'struktor] |

well-bred (adj)	вихований	['wɨhowanɨj]
ill-bred (adj)	невихований	[nɛ'wɨhowanɨj]
spoilt (adj)	розбещений	[roz'bɛɕɛnɨj]

| to be naughty | бешкетувати | [bɛʃkɛtu'watɨ] |
| mischievous (adj) | пустотливий | [pustot'lɨwɨj] |

| mischievousness | витівка (ж) | ['wɨtiwka] |
| mischievous child | пустун (ч) | [pus'tun] |

| obedient (adj) | слухняний | [sluh'nˡanɨj] |
| disobedient (adj) | неслухняний | [nɛsluh'nˡanɨj] |

docile (adj)	розумний	[ro'zumnɨj]
clever (intelligent)	розумний	[ro'zumnɨj]
child prodigy	вундеркінд (ч)	[wundɛr'kind]

57. Married couples. Family life

to kiss (vt)	цілувати	[ʦilu'wati]
to kiss (vi)	цілуватися	[ʦilu'watisʲa]
family (n)	сім'я (ж)	[si'mʲʲa]
family (as adj)	сімейний	[si'mɛjnij]
couple	пара (ж)	['para]
marriage (state)	шлюб (ч)	[ʃlʲub]
hearth (home)	домашнє вогнище (с)	[do'maʃnɛ 'woɦniɕɛ]
dynasty	династія (ж)	[diʲnastiʲa]
date	побачення (с)	[po'baʧɛnʲa]
kiss	поцілунок (ч)	[poʦi'lunok]
love (for sb)	кохання (с)	[ko'hanʲa]
to love (sb)	кохати	[ko'hati]
beloved	кохана людина (ж)	[ko'hana lʲu'dina]
tenderness	ніжність (ж)	['niʒnistʲ]
tender (affectionate)	ніжний	['niʒnij]
faithfulness	незрадливість (ж)	[nɛzrad'liwistʲ]
faithful (adj)	незрадливий	[nɛzrad'liwij]
care (attention)	турбота (ж)	[tur'bota]
caring (~ father)	турботливий	[tur'botliwij]
newlyweds	молодята (мн)	[molo'dʲata]
honeymoon	медовий місяць (ч)	[mɛ'dowij 'misʲaʦ]
to get married (ab. woman)	вийти заміж	['wijti 'zamiʒ]
to get married (ab. man)	одружуватися	[od'ruʒuwatisʲa]
wedding	весілля (с)	[wɛ'silʲa]
golden wedding	золоте весілля (с)	[zolo'tɛ wɛ'silʲa]
anniversary	річниця (ж)	[riʧ'niʦʲa]
lover (masc.)	коханець (ч)	[ko'hanɛʦs]
mistress (lover)	коханка (ж)	[ko'hanka]
adultery	зрада (ж)	['zrada]
to cheat on ... (commit adultery)	зрадити	['zraditi]
jealous (adj)	ревнивий	[rɛw'niwij]
to be jealous	ревнувати	[rɛwnu'wati]
divorce	розлучення (с)	[roz'luʧɛnʲa]
to divorce (vi)	розлучитися	[rozlu'ʧitisʲa]
to quarrel (vi)	сваритися	[swa'ritisʲa]
to be reconciled (after an argument)	миритися	[mi'ritisʲa]
together (adv)	разом	['razom]
sex	секс (ч)	[sɛks]
happiness	щастя (с)	['ɕastʲa]
happy (adj)	щасливий	[ɕas'liwij]
misfortune (accident)	нещастя (с)	[nɛ'ɕastʲa]
unhappy (adj)	нещасний	[nɛ'ɕasnij]

Character. Feelings. Emotions

58. Feelings. Emotions

feeling (emotion)	почуття (с)	[potʃut'tʲa]
feelings	почуття (мн)	[potʃut'tʲa]
hunger	голод (ч)	['ɦɔlod]
to be hungry	хотіти їсти	[ho'titɨ 'jisti]
thirst	спрага (ж)	['spraɦa]
to be thirsty	хотіти пити	[ho'titɨ 'pɨtɨ]
sleepiness	сонливість (ж)	[son'lɨwistʲ]
to feel sleepy	хотіти спати	[ho'titɨ 'spatɨ]
tiredness	втома (ж)	['wtɔma]
tired (adj)	втомлений	['wtɔmlɛnɨj]
to get tired	втомитися	[wto'mɨtɨsʲa]
mood (humour)	настрій (ч)	['nastrij]
boredom	нудьга (ж)	[nudʲ'ɦa]
to be bored	нудьгувати	[nudʲɦu'wati]
seclusion	самота (ж)	[samo'ta]
to seclude oneself	усамітнюватися	[usa'mitnʲuwatɨsʲa]
to worry (make anxious)	хвилювати	[hwɨlʲu'wati]
to be worried	хвилюватися	[hwɨlʲu'watɨsʲa]
worrying (n)	хвилювання (с)	[hwɨlʲu'wanʲa]
anxiety	занепокоєння (с)	[zanɛpo'kɔɛnʲa]
preoccupied (adj)	занепокоєний	[zanɛpo'kɔɛnɨj]
to be nervous	нервуватися	[nɛrwu'watɨsʲa]
to panic (vi)	панікувати	[paniku'wati]
hope	надія (ж)	[na'diʲa]
to hope (vi, vt)	сподіватися	[spodi'watɨsʲa]
certainty	упевненість (ж)	[u'pɛwnɛnistʲ]
certain, sure (adj)	упевнений	[u'pɛwnɛnɨj]
uncertainty	непевність (ж)	[nɛ'pɛwnistʲ]
uncertain (adj)	невпевнений	[nɛw'pɛwnɛnɨj]
drunk (adj)	п'яний	['pʲʲanɨj]
sober (adj)	тверезий	[twɛ'rɛzɨj]
weak (adj)	слабкий	[slab'kij]
happy (adj)	щасливий	[ɕas'lɨwɨj]
to scare (vt)	налякати	[nalʲa'kati]
fury (madness)	шаленство (с)	[ʃa'lɛnstwo]
rage (fury)	лють (ж)	[lʲutʲ]
depression	депресія (ж)	[dɛ'prɛsiʲa]
discomfort (unease)	дискомфорт (ч)	[dɨskom'fɔrt]

comfort	комфорт (ч)	[kɔmˈfɔrt]
to regret (be sorry)	жалкувати	[ʒalkuˈwatɨ]
regret	жаль (ч)	[ʒalʲ]
bad luck	невезіння (с)	[nɛwɛˈzinʲa]
sadness	прикрість (ж)	[ˈprikristʲ]

shame (remorse)	сором (ч)	[ˈsɔrom]
gladness	веселість (ж)	[wɛˈsɛlistʲ]
enthusiasm, zeal	ентузіазм (ч)	[ɛntuziˈazm]
enthusiast	ентузіаст (ч)	[ɛntuziˈast]
to show enthusiasm	проявити ентузіазм	[projaˈwitɨ ɛntuziˈazm]

59. Character. Personality

character	характер (ч)	[haˈraktɛr]
character flaw	вада (ж)	[ˈwada]
mind	ум (ч)	[um]
reason	розум (ч)	[ˈrɔzum]

conscience	совість (ж)	[ˈsɔwistʲ]
habit (custom)	звичка (ж)	[ˈzwitʃka]
ability (talent)	здібність (ж)	[ˈzdibnistʲ]
can (e.g. ~ swim)	уміти	[uˈmitɨ]

patient (adj)	терплячий	[tɛrpˈlʲatʃij]
impatient (adj)	нетерплячий	[nɛtɛrˈplʲatʃij]
curious (inquisitive)	допитливий	[doˈpɨtlɨwɨj]
curiosity	цікавість (ж)	[tsiˈkawistʲ]

modesty	скромність (ж)	[ˈskrɔmnistʲ]
modest (adj)	скромний	[ˈskrɔmnɨj]
immodest (adj)	нескромний	[nɛˈskrɔmnɨj]

laziness	лінь (ж)	[linʲ]
lazy (adj)	ледачий	[lɛˈdatʃij]
lazy person (masc.)	ледар (ч)	[ˈlɛdar]

cunning (n)	хитрість (ж)	[ˈhitristʲ]
cunning (as adj)	хитрий	[ˈhitrɨj]
distrust	недовіра (ж)	[nɛdoˈwira]
distrustful (adj)	недовірливий	[nɛdoˈwirlɨwɨj]

generosity	щедрість (ж)	[ˈɕɛdristʲ]
generous (adj)	щедрий	[ˈɕɛdrɨj]
talented (adj)	талановитий	[talanoˈwitɨj]
talent	талант (ч)	[taˈlant]

courageous (adj)	сміливий	[smiˈliwɨj]
courage	сміливість (ж)	[smiˈliwistʲ]
honest (adj)	чесний	[ˈtʃɛsnɨj]
honesty	чесність (ж)	[ˈtʃɛsnistʲ]

| careful (cautious) | обережний | [obɛˈrɛʒnɨj] |
| brave (courageous) | відважний | [widˈwaʒnɨj] |

| serious (adj) | серйозний | [sɛrˈoznij] |
| strict (severe, stern) | суворий | [suˈwɔrij] |

decisive (adj)	рішучий	[riˈʃutʃij]
indecisive (adj)	нерішучий	[nɛriˈʃutʃij]
shy, timid (adj)	сором'язливий	[soroˈmʲazlɨwij]
shyness, timidity	сором'язливість (ж)	[soroˈmʲazlɨwistʲ]

confidence (trust)	довіра (ж)	[doˈwira]
to believe (trust)	вірити	[ˈwirɨtɨ]
trusting (credulous)	довірливий	[doˈwirlɨwij]

sincerely (adv)	щиро	[ˈɕiro]
sincere (adj)	щирий	[ˈɕirij]
sincerity	щирість (ж)	[ˈɕiristʲ]
open (person)	відкритий	[widˈkritij]

calm (adj)	тихий	[ˈtihij]
frank (sincere)	відвертий	[widˈwɛrtij]
naïve (adj)	наївний	[naˈjiwnij]
absent-minded (adj)	неуважний	[nɛuˈwaʒnij]
funny (odd)	кумедний	[kuˈmɛdnij]

greed, stinginess	жадібність (ж)	[ˈʒadibnistʲ]
greedy, stingy (adj)	жадібний	[ˈʒadibnij]
stingy (adj)	скупий	[skuˈpij]
evil (adj)	злий	[ˈzlij]
stubborn (adj)	впертий	[ˈwpɛrtij]
unpleasant (adj)	неприємний	[nɛpriˈɛmnij]

selfish person (masc.)	егоїст (ч)	[ɛhoˈjist]
selfish (adj)	егоїстичний	[ɛhojisˈtitʃnij]
coward	боягуз (ч)	[bojaˈɦuz]
cowardly (adj)	боягузливий	[bojaˈɦuzlɨwij]

60. Sleep. Dreams

to sleep (vi)	спати	[ˈspatɨ]
sleep, sleeping	сон (ч)	[son]
dream	сон (ч)	[son]
to dream (in sleep)	бачити сни	[ˈbatʃitɨ snɨ]
sleepy (adj)	сонний	[ˈsɔnij]

bed	ліжко (с)	[ˈliʒko]
mattress	матрац (ч)	[matˈrats]
blanket (eiderdown)	ковдра (ж)	[ˈkɔwdra]
pillow	подушка (ж)	[poˈduʃka]
sheet	простирадло (с)	[prostiˈradlo]

insomnia	безсоння (с)	[bɛzˈsɔnʲa]
sleepless (adj)	безсонний	[bɛzˈsɔnij]
sleeping pill	снодійне (с)	[snoˈdijnɛ]
to take a sleeping pill	прийняти снодійне	[prijˈnʲatɨ snoˈdijnɛ]
to feel sleepy	хотіти спати	[hoˈtitɨ ˈspatɨ]

to yawn (vi)	позіхати	[pozi'hati]
to go to bed	йти спати	[jtɨ 'spati]
to make up the bed	стелити ліжко	[stɛ'litɨ 'liʒko]
to fall asleep	заснути	[zas'nuti]

nightmare	страхіття (c)	[stra'hittʲa]
snore, snoring	хропіння (c)	[hro'pinʲa]
to snore (vi)	хропіти	[hro'piti]

alarm clock	будильник (ч)	[bu'dɨlʲnɨk]
to wake (vt)	розбудити	[rozbu'diti]
to wake up	прокидатися	[prokɨ'datisʲa]
to get up (vi)	вставати	[wsta'wati]
to have a wash	умитися	[u'mitisʲa]

61. Humour. Laughter. Gladness

humour (wit, fun)	гумор (ч)	['ɦumor]
sense of humour	почуття (c)	[potʃut'tʲa]
to enjoy oneself	веселитися	[wɛsɛ'litisʲa]
cheerful (merry)	веселий	[wɛ'sɛlɨj]
merriment (gaiety)	веселощі (мн)	[wɛ'sɛloɕi]

smile	посмішка (ж)	['pɔsmiʃka]
to smile (vi)	посміхатися	[posmi'hatisʲa]
to start laughing	засміятися	[zasmi'ʲatisʲa]
to laugh (vi)	сміятися	[smi'ʲatisʲa]
laugh, laughter	сміх (ч)	[smih]

anecdote	анекдот (ч)	[anɛk'dɔt]
funny (anecdote, etc.)	смішний	[smiʃ'nɨj]
funny (odd)	кумедний	[ku'mɛdnɨj]

to joke (vi)	жартувати	[ʒartu'wati]
joke (verbal)	жарт (ч)	[ʒart]
joy (emotion)	радість (ж)	['radistʲ]
to rejoice (vi)	радіти	[ra'diti]
joyful (adj)	радісний	['radisnɨj]

62. Discussion, conversation. Part 1

| communication | спілкування (c) | [spilku'wanʲa] |
| to communicate | спілкуватися | [spilku'watisʲa] |

conversation	розмова (ж)	[roz'mɔwa]
dialogue	діалог (ч)	[dia'lɔɦ]
discussion (discourse)	дискусія (ж)	[dis'kusiʲa]
dispute (debate)	суперечка (ч)	[supɛ'rɛtʃka]
to dispute, to debate	сперечатися	[spɛrɛ'tʃatisʲa]

| interlocutor | співрозмовник (ч) | [spiwroz'mɔwnɨk] |
| topic (theme) | тема (ж) | ['tɛma] |

point of view	точка (ж) зору	['tɔtʃka 'zɔru]
opinion (point of view)	погляд (ч)	['pɔɦlʲad]
speech (talk)	промова (ж)	[pro'mɔwa]

discussion (of a report, etc.)	обговорення (с)	[obɦo'wɔrɛnʲa]
to discuss (vt)	обговорювати	[obɦo'wɔrʲuwatɨ]
talk (conversation)	бесіда (ж)	['bɛsida]
to talk (to chat)	розмовляти	[rozmow'lʲatɨ]
meeting (encounter)	зустріч (ж)	['zustritʃ]
to meet (vi, vt)	зустрічатися	[zustri'tʃatɨsʲa]

proverb	прислів'я (с)	[pris'liwʲʲa]
saying	приказка (ж)	['prɨkazka]
riddle (poser)	загадка (ж)	['zaɦadka]
to pose a riddle	загадувати загадку	[za'ɦaduwatɨ 'zaɦadku]
password	пароль (ч)	[pa'rɔlʲ]
secret	секрет (ч)	[sɛk'rɛt]

oath (vow)	клятва (ж)	['klʲatwa]
to swear (an oath)	клястися	['klʲastɨsʲa]
promise	обіцянка (ж)	[obi'tsʲanka]
to promise (vt)	обіцяти	[obi'tsʲatɨ]

advice (counsel)	порада (ж)	[po'rada]
to advise (vt)	радити	['radɨtɨ]
to listen to … (obey)	слухатись	['sluhatɨsʲ]

news	новина (ж)	[nowɨ'na]
sensation (news)	сенсація (ж)	[sɛn'satsʲia]
information (report)	відомості (мн)	[wi'dɔmosti]
conclusion (decision)	висновок (ч)	['wɨsnowok]
voice	голос (ч)	['ɦɔlos]
compliment	комплімент (ч)	[kompli'mɛnt]
kind (nice)	люб'язний	[lʲu'bʲʲaznɨj]

word	слово (с)	['slɔwo]
phrase	фраза (ж)	['fraza]
answer	відповідь (ж)	['widpowidʲ]

| truth | правда (ж) | ['prawda] |
| lie | брехня (ж) | [brɛh'nʲa] |

thought	думка (ж)	['dumka]
idea (inspiration)	думка (ж)	['dumka]
fantasy	вигадка (ж)	['wɨɦadka]

63. Discussion, conversation. Part 2

respected (adj)	шановний	[ʃa'nownɨj]
to respect (vt)	поважати	[powa'ʒatɨ]
respect	повага (ж)	[po'waɦa]
Dear … (letter)	Шановний …	[ʃa'nownɨj]
to introduce (sb to sb)	познайомити	[pozna'jɔmitɨ]
intention	намір (ч)	['namir]

to intend (have in mind)	мати наміри	['matɨ 'namirɨ]
wish	побажання (c)	[poba'ʒanʲa]
to wish (~ good luck)	побажати	[poba'ʒati]

surprise (astonishment)	здивування (c)	[zdɨwu'wanʲa]
to surprise (amaze)	дивувати	[dɨwu'wati]
to be surprised	дивуватись	[dɨwu'watisʲ]

to give (vt)	дати	['dati]
to take (get hold of)	взяти	['wzʲati]
to give back	повернути	[powɛr'nuti]
to return (give back)	віддати	[wid'dati]

to apologize (vi)	вибачатися	[wɨba'ʧatisʲa]
apology	вибачення (c)	['wɨbaʧɛnʲa]
to forgive (vt)	прощати	[pro'ɕati]

to talk (speak)	розмовляти	[rozmow'lʲati]
to listen (vi)	слухати	['sluhati]
to hear out	вислухати	['wɨsluhati]
to understand (vt)	зрозуміти	[zrozu'miti]

to show (to display)	показати	[poka'zati]
to look at …	дивитися	[dɨ'witisʲa]
to call (yell for sb)	покликати	[pok'lɨkati]
to disturb (vt)	заважати	[zawa'ʒati]
to pass (to hand sth)	передати	[pɛrɛ'dati]

demand (request)	прохання (c)	[pro'hanʲa]
to request (ask)	просити	[pro'sɨti]
demand (firm request)	вимога (ж)	[wɨ'mɔɦa]
to demand (request firmly)	вимагати	[wɨma'ɦati]

to tease (call names)	дражнити	[draʒ'nɨti]
to mock (make fun of)	насміхатися	[nasmi'hatisʲa]
mockery, derision	насмішка (ж)	[na'smiʃka]
nickname	прізвисько (c)	['prizwɨsʲko]

insinuation	натяк (ч)	['natʲak]
to insinuate (imply)	натякати	[natʲa'kati]
to mean (vt)	мати на увазі	['mati na u'wazi]

| description | опис (ч) | ['ɔpɨs] |
| to describe (vt) | описати | [opɨ'sati] |

| praise (compliments) | похвала (ж) | [pohwa'la] |
| to praise (vt) | похвалити | [pohwa'lɨti] |

disappointment	розчарування (c)	[rozʧaru'wanʲa]
to disappoint (vt)	розчарувати	[rozʧaru'wati]
to be disappointed	розчаруватися	[rozʧaru'watisʲa]

supposition	припущення (c)	[prɨ'puɕɛnʲa]
to suppose (assume)	припускати	[prɨpus'kati]
warning (caution)	застереження (c)	[zastɛ'rɛʒɛnʲa]
to warn (vt)	застерегти	[zastɛrɛɦ'ti]

64. Discussion, conversation. Part 3

to talk into (convince)	умовити	[u'mɔwiti]
to calm down (vt)	заспокоювати	[zaspo'kɔʲuwati]
silence (~ is golden)	мовчання (с)	[mow'tʃanʲa]
to be silent (not speaking)	мовчати	[mow'tʃati]
to whisper (vi, vt)	шепнути	[ʃɛp'nuti]
whisper	шепіт (ч)	['ʃɛpit]
frankly, sincerely (adv)	відверто	[wid'wɛrto]
in my opinion …	на мою думку …	[na mo'ʲu 'dumku]
detail (of the story)	подробиця (ж)	[pod'rɔbitsʲa]
detailed (adj)	докладний	[do'kladnij]
in detail (adv)	докладно	[do'kladno]
hint, clue	підказка (ж)	[pid'kazka]
to give a hint	підказувати	[pid'kazuwati]
look (glance)	погляд (ч)	['poɦlʲad]
to have a look	поглянути	[poɦ'lʲanuti]
fixed (look)	нерухомий	[nɛru'hɔmij]
to blink (vi)	кліпати	['klipati]
to wink (vi)	підморгнути	[pidmorɦ'nuti]
to nod (in assent)	кивнути	[kɨw'nuti]
sigh	зітхання (с)	[zit'hanʲa]
to sigh (vi)	зітхнути	[zith'nuti]
to shudder (vi)	здригатися	[zdri'ɦatisʲa]
gesture	жест (ч)	[ʒɛst]
to touch (one's arm, etc.)	доторкнутися	[dotor'knutisʲa]
to seize (e.g., ~ by the arm)	хапати	[ha'pati]
to tap (on the shoulder)	плескати	[plɛs'kati]
Look out!	Обережно!	[obɛ'rɛʒno]
Really?	Невже?	[nɛw'ʒɛ]
Are you sure?	Ти впевнений?	[tɨ 'wpɛwnɛnij]
Good luck!	Хай щастить!	[haj ɕas'titʲ]
I see!	Зрозуміло!	[zrozu'milo]
What a pity!	Шкода!	['ʃkɔda]

65. Agreement. Refusal

consent	згода (ж)	['zɦɔda]
to consent (vi)	погоджуватися	[po'ɦɔdʒuwatisʲa]
approval	схвалення (с)	[sh'walɛnʲa]
to approve (vt)	схвалити	[shwa'liti]
refusal	відмова (ж)	[wid'mɔwa]
to refuse (vi, vt)	відмовлятися	[widmow'lʲatisʲa]
Great!	Чудово!	[tʃu'dɔwo]
All right!	Добре!	['dɔbrɛ]

Okay! (I agree)	Згода!	['zɦɔda]
forbidden (adj)	заборонений	[zabo'rɔnɛnɨj]
it's forbidden	не можна	[nɛ 'mɔʒna]
it's impossible	неможливо	[nɛmɔʒ'lɨwo]
incorrect (adj)	помилковий	[pomɨl'kɔwɨj]

to reject (~ a demand)	відхилити	[widhɨ'lɨtɨ]
to support (cause, idea)	підтримати	[pid'trɨmatɨ]
to accept (~ an apology)	прийняти	[prɨj'nʲatɨ]

| to confirm (vt) | підтвердити | [pid'twɛrdɨtɨ] |
| confirmation | підтвердження (c) | [pid'twɛrdʒɛnʲa] |

permission	дозвіл (ч)	['dɔzwil]
to permit (vt)	дозволити	[doz'wɔlɨtɨ]
decision	рішення (c)	['riʃɛnʲa]
to say nothing (hold one's tongue)	промовчати	[promow'tʃatɨ]

condition (term)	умова (ж)	[u'mɔwa]
excuse (pretext)	відмовка (ж)	[wid'mɔwka]
praise (compliments)	похвала (ж)	[pohwa'la]
to praise (vt)	хвалити	[hwa'lɨtɨ]

66. Success. Good luck. Failure

success	успіх (ч)	['uspih]
successfully (adv)	успішно	[us'piʃno]
successful (adj)	успішний	[us'piʃnɨj]

| luck (good luck) | везіння (c) | [wɛ'zinʲa] |
| Good luck! | Хай щастить! | [haj ɕas'tɨtʲ] |

| lucky (e.g. ~ day) | вдалий | ['wdalɨj] |
| lucky (fortunate) | щасливий | [ɕas'lɨwɨj] |

failure	невдача (ж)	[nɛw'datʃa]
misfortune	невдача (ж)	[nɛw'datʃa]
bad luck	невезіння (c)	[nɛwɛ'zinʲa]

| unsuccessful (adj) | невдалий | [nɛw'dalɨj] |
| catastrophe | катастрофа (ж) | [kata'strɔfa] |

pride	гордість (ж)	['hɔrdistʲ]
proud (adj)	гордовитий	[hordo'wɨtɨj]
to be proud	пишатися	[pɨ'ʃatɨsʲa]

| winner | переможець (ч) | [pɛrɛ'mɔʒɛts] |
| to win (vi) | перемогти | [pɛrɛmoɦ'tɨ] |

to lose (not win)	програти	[proɦ'ratɨ]
try	спроба (ж)	['sprɔba]
to try (vi)	намагатися	[nama'ɦatɨsʲa]
chance (opportunity)	шанс (ч)	[ʃans]

67. Quarrels. Negative emotions

shout (scream)	крик (ч)	[krik]
to shout (vi)	кричати	[kri'tʃati]
to start to cry out	закричати	[zakri'tʃati]

quarrel	сварка (ж)	['swarka]
to quarrel (vi)	сваритися	[swa'ritisʲa]
fight (squabble)	скандал (ч)	[skan'dal]
to make a scene	сваритися	[swa'ritisʲa]
conflict	конфлікт (ч)	[kon'flikt]
misunderstanding	непорозуміння (с)	[nɛporozu'minʲa]

insult	образа (ж)	[ob'raza]
to insult (vt)	ображати	[obra'ʒati]
insulted (adj)	ображений	[ob'raʒɛnij]
resentment	образа (ж)	[ob'raza]
to offend (vt)	образити	[ob'raziti]
to take offence	образитись	[ob'razitisʲ]

indignation	обурення (с)	[o'burɛnʲa]
to be indignant	обурюватися	[o'burʲuwatisʲa]
complaint	скарга (ж)	['skarɦa]
to complain (vi, vt)	скаржитися	['skarʒitisʲa]

apology	вибачення (с)	['wibatʃɛnʲa]
to apologize (vi)	вибачатися	[wiba'tʃatisʲa]
to beg pardon	просити вибачення	[pro'siti 'wibatʃɛnʲa]

criticism	критика (ж)	['kritika]
to criticize (vt)	критикувати	[kritiku'wati]
accusation (charge)	обвинувачення (с)	[obwinu'watʃɛnʲa]
to accuse (vt)	звинувачувати	[zwinu'watʃuwati]

revenge	помста (ж)	['pomsta]
to avenge (get revenge)	мстити	['mstiti]
to pay back	помститися	[poms'titisʲa]

disdain	зневага (ж)	[znɛ'waɦa]
to despise (vt)	зневажати	[znɛwa'ʒati]
hatred, hate	ненависть (ж)	[nɛ'nawistʲ]
to hate (vt)	ненавидіти	[nɛna'widiti]

nervous (adj)	нервовий	[nɛr'wowij]
to be nervous	нервувати	[nɛrwu'wati]
angry (mad)	сердитий	[sɛr'ditij]
to make angry	розсердити	[roz'sɛrditi]

humiliation	приниження (с)	[pri'niʒɛnʲa]
to humiliate (vt)	принижувати	[pri'niʒuwati]
to humiliate oneself	принижуватись	[pri'niʒuwatisʲ]

shock	шок (ч)	[ʃok]
to shock (vt)	шокувати	[ʃoku'wati]
trouble (e.g. serious ~)	неприємність (ж)	[nɛpri'ɛmnistʲ]

unpleasant (adj)	неприємний	[nɛpriˈɛmnij]
fear (dread)	страх (ч)	[strah]
terrible (storm, heat)	страшний	[ˈstraʃnij]
scary (e.g. ~ story)	страшний	[ˈstraʃnij]
horror	жах (ч)	[ʒah]
awful (crime, news)	жахливий	[ʒahˈlïwïj]
to cry (weep)	плакати	[ˈplakati]
to start crying	заплакати	[zaˈplakati]
tear	сльоза (ж)	[slʲoˈza]
fault	вина (ж)	[wiˈna]
guilt (feeling)	провина (ж)	[proˈwina]
dishonor (disgrace)	ганьба (ж)	[ɦanʲˈba]
protest	протест (ч)	[proˈtɛst]
stress	стрес (ч)	[ˈstrɛs]
to disturb (vt)	заважати	[zawaˈʒati]
to be furious	лютувати	[lʲutuˈwati]
angry (adj)	злий	[ˈzlïj]
to end (~ a relationship)	припиняти	[pripiˈnʲati]
to swear (at sb)	лаятися	[ˈlaʲatisʲa]
to scare (become afraid)	лякатися	[lʲaˈkatisʲa]
to hit (strike with hand)	ударити	[uˈdariti]
to fight (street fight, etc.)	битися	[ˈbitisʲa]
to settle (a conflict)	урегулювати	[urɛɦulʲuˈwati]
discontented (adj)	незадоволений	[nɛzadoˈwɔlɛnij]
furious (adj)	розлючений	[rozˈlʲutʃɛnij]
It's not good!	Це недобре!	[ʦɛ nɛˈdɔbrɛ]
It's bad!	Це погано!	[ʦɛ poˈɦano]

Medicine

illness	хвороба (ж)	[hwo'rɔba]
to be ill	хворіти	[hwo'ritⁱ]
health	здоров'я (с)	[zdo'rɔwⁱa]
runny nose (coryza)	нежить (ч)	['nɛʒitⁱ]
tonsillitis	ангіна (ж)	[an'ɦina]
cold (illness)	застуда (ж)	[za'studa]
to catch a cold	застудитися	[zastu'ditisⁱa]
bronchitis	бронхіт (ч)	[bron'hit]
pneumonia	запалення (с) легенів	[za'palɛnja lɛ'ɦɛniw]
flu, influenza	грип (ч)	[ɦrip]
shortsighted (adj)	короткозорий	[korotko'zɔrij]
longsighted (adj)	далекозорий	[dalɛko'zɔrij]
strabismus (crossed eyes)	косоокість (ж)	[koso'ɔkistⁱ]
squint-eyed (adj)	косоокий	[koso'ɔkij]
cataract	катаракта (ж)	[kata'rakta]
glaucoma	глаукома (ж)	[ɦlau'kɔma]
stroke	інсульт (ч)	[in'sulⁱt]
heart attack	інфаркт (ч)	[in'farkt]
myocardial infarction	інфаркт (ч) міокарду	[in'farkt mio'kardu]
paralysis	параліч (ч)	[para'litʃ]
to paralyse (vt)	паралізувати	[paralizu'watⁱ]
allergy	алергія (ж)	[alɛr'ɦiⁱa]
asthma	астма (ж)	['astma]
diabetes	діабет (ч)	[dia'bɛt]
toothache	зубний біль (ч)	[zub'nⁱj bilⁱ]
caries	карієс (ч)	['kariɛs]
diarrhoea	діарея (ж)	[dia'rɛⁱa]
constipation	запор (ч)	[za'pɔr]
stomach upset	розлад (ч) шлунку	['rɔzlad 'ʃlunku]
food poisoning	отруєння (с)	[ot'ruɛnⁱa]
to get food poisoning	отруїтись	[otru'jitisⁱ]
arthritis	артрит (ч)	[art'rit]
rickets	рахіт (ч)	[ra'hit]
rheumatism	ревматизм (ч)	[rɛwma'tizm]
atherosclerosis	атеросклероз (ч)	[atɛrosklɛ'rɔz]
gastritis	гастрит (ч)	[hast'rit]
appendicitis	апендицит (ч)	[apɛndi'tsit]

| cholecystitis | холецистит (ч) | [holɛʦis'tit] |
| ulcer | виразка (ж) | ['wirazka] |

measles	кір (ч)	[kir]
rubella (German measles)	краснуха (ж)	[kras'nuha]
jaundice	жовтуха (ж)	[ʒow'tuha]
hepatitis	гепатит (ч)	[ɦɛpa'tit]

schizophrenia	шизофренія (ж)	[ʃizofrɛ'niʲa]
rabies (hydrophobia)	сказ (ч)	[skaz]
neurosis	невроз (ч)	[nɛw'rɔz]
concussion	струс (ч) мозку	['strus 'mɔzku]

cancer	рак (ч)	[rak]
sclerosis	склероз (ч)	[sklɛ'rɔz]
multiple sclerosis	розсіяний склероз (ч)	[roz'siʲanɨj sklɛ'rɔz]

alcoholism	алкоголізм (ч)	[alkoɦo'lizm]
alcoholic (n)	алкоголік (ч)	[alko'ɦɔlik]
syphilis	сифіліс (ч)	['siɦilis]
AIDS	СНІД (ч)	[snid]

tumour	пухлина (ж)	[puh'lɨna]
malignant (adj)	злоякісна	[zlo'ʲakisna]
benign (adj)	доброякісний	[dobro'ʲakisnij]

fever	гарячка (ж)	[ɦa'rʲatʃka]
malaria	малярія (ж)	[malʲa'riʲa]
gangrene	гангрена (ж)	[ɦan'ɦrɛna]
seasickness	морська хвороба (ж)	[morsʲ'ka hwo'rɔba]
epilepsy	епілепсія (ж)	[ɛpi'lɛpsiʲa]

epidemic	епідемія (ж)	[ɛpi'dɛmiʲa]
typhus	тиф (ч)	[tiɸ]
tuberculosis	туберкульоз (ч)	[tubɛrku'lʲoz]
cholera	холера (ж)	[ho'lɛra]
plague (bubonic ~)	чума (ж)	[ʧu'ma]

69. Symptoms. Treatments. Part 1

symptom	симптом (ч)	[simp'tɔm]
temperature	температура (ж)	[tɛmpɛra'tura]
high temperature (fever)	висока температура (ж)	[wi'sɔka tɛmpɛra'tura]
pulse (heartbeat)	пульс (ч)	[pulʲs]

dizziness (vertigo)	запаморочення (с)	[za'pamorotʃɛnʲa]
hot (adj)	гарячий	[ɦa'rʲatʃij]
shivering	озноб (ч)	[oz'nɔb]
pale (e.g. ~ face)	блідий	[bli'dij]

cough	кашель (ч)	['kaʃɛlʲ]
to cough (vi)	кашляти	['kaʃlʲati]
to sneeze (vi)	чхати	['ʧhati]
faint	непритомність (ж)	[nɛpri'tɔmnistʲ]

to faint (vi)	знепритомніти	[znɛpri'tɔmniti]
bruise (hématome)	синець (ч)	[si'nɛʦ]
bump (lump)	гуля (ж)	['hulʲa]
to bang (bump)	ударитись	[u'daritisʲ]
contusion (bruise)	забите місце (с)	[za'bitɛ 'misʦɛ]
to get a bruise	забитися	[za'bitisʲa]

to limp (vi)	кульгати	[kulʲ'hati]
dislocation	вивих (ч)	['wiwih]
to dislocate (vt)	вивихнути	['wiwihnuti]
fracture	перелом (ч)	[pɛrɛ'lɔm]
to have a fracture	дістати перелом	[dis'tati pɛrɛ'lɔm]

cut (e.g. paper ~)	поріз (ч)	[po'riz]
to cut oneself	порізатися	[po'rizatisʲa]
bleeding	кровотеча (ж)	[krowo'tɛʧa]

| burn (injury) | опік (ч) | ['ɔpik] |
| to get burned | обпектися | [obpɛk'tisʲa] |

to prick (vt)	уколоти	[uko'lɔti]
to prick oneself	уколотися	[uko'lɔtisʲa]
to injure (vt)	пошкодити	[poʃ'kɔditi]
injury	ушкодження (с)	[uʃ'kɔʤɛnʲa]
wound	рана (ж)	['rana]
trauma	травма (ж)	['trawma]

to be delirious	марити	['mariti]
to stutter (vi)	заїкатися	[zaji'katisʲa]
sunstroke	сонячний удар (ч)	['sɔnʲaʧnij u'dar]

70. Symptoms. Treatments. Part 2

| pain, ache | біль (ч) | [bilʲ] |
| splinter (in foot, etc.) | скалка (ж) | ['skalka] |

sweat (perspiration)	піт (ч)	[pit]
to sweat (perspire)	спітніти	[spit'niti]
vomiting	блювота (ж)	[blʲu'wota]
convulsions	судома (ж)	[su'dɔma]

pregnant (adj)	вагітна	[wa'hitna]
to be born	народитися	[naro'ditisʲa]
delivery, labour	пологи (мн)	[po'lɔhi]
to deliver (~ a baby)	народжувати	[na'rɔʤuwati]
abortion	аборт (ч)	[a'bɔrt]

breathing, respiration	дихання (с)	['dihanʲa]
in-breath (inhalation)	вдих (ч)	[wdih]
out-breath (exhalation)	видих (ч)	['widih]
to exhale (breathe out)	видихнути	['widihnuti]
to inhale (vi)	зробити вдих	[zro'biti wdih]
disabled person	інвалід (ч)	[inwa'lid]
cripple	каліка (ч)	[ka'lika]

drug addict	наркоман (ч)	[narko'man]
deaf (adj)	глухий (ч)	[ɦlu'hɨj]
mute (adj)	німий (ч)	[ni'mɨj]
deaf mute (adj)	глухонімий (ч)	[ɦluhoni'mɨj]

mad, insane (adj)	божевільний	[boʒɛ'wilʲnɨj]
madman (demented person)	божевільний (ч)	[boʒɛ'wilʲnɨj]
madwoman	божевільна (ж)	[boʒɛ'wilʲna]
to go insane	збожеволіти	[zboʒɛ'wɔliti]

gene	ген (ч)	[ɦɛn]
immunity	імунітет (ч)	[imuni'tɛt]
hereditary (adj)	спадковий	[spad'kɔwɨj]
congenital (adj)	вроджений	['wrɔdʒɛnɨj]

virus	вірус (ч)	['wirus]
microbe	мікроб (ч)	[mik'rɔb]
bacterium	бактерія (ж)	[bak'tɛriʲa]
infection	інфекція (ж)	[in'fɛktsiʲa]

71. Symptoms. Treatments. Part 3

| hospital | лікарня (ж) | [li'karnʲa] |
| patient | пацієнт (ч) | [patsi'ɛnt] |

diagnosis	діагноз (ч)	[di'aɦnoz]
cure	лікування (с)	[liku'wanʲa]
medical treatment	лікування (с)	[liku'wanʲa]
to get treatment	лікуватися	[liku'watisʲa]
to treat (~ a patient)	лікувати	[liku'wati]
to nurse (look after)	доглядати	[doɦlʲa'dati]
care (nursing ~)	догляд (ч)	['dɔɦlʲad]

operation, surgery	операція (ж)	[opɛ'ratsiʲa]
to bandage (head, limb)	перев'язати	[pɛrɛw'ʲa'zati]
bandaging	перев'язка (ж)	[pɛrɛ'w'ʲazka]

vaccination	щеплення (с)	['ɕɛplɛnʲa]
to vaccinate (vt)	робити щеплення	[ro'biti 'ɕɛplɛnʲa]
injection	ін'єкція (ж)	[i'n'ʲɛktsiʲa]
to give an injection	робити укол	[ro'biti u'kɔl]

amputation	ампутація (ж)	[ampu'tatsiʲa]
to amputate (vt)	ампутувати	[amputu'wati]
coma	кома (ж)	['kɔma]
to be in a coma	бути в комі	['buti w 'kɔmi]
intensive care	реанімація (ж)	[rɛani'matsiʲa]

to recover (~ from flu)	видужувати	[wɨ'duʒuwati]
condition (patient's ~)	стан (ч)	['stan]
consciousness	свідомість (ж)	[swi'dɔmistʲ]
memory (faculty)	пам'ять (ж)	['pam'ʲatʲ]
to pull out (tooth)	видалити	['wɨdaliti]

| filling | пломба (ж) | ['plɔmba] |
| to fill (a tooth) | пломбувати | [plombu'watɨ] |

| hypnosis | гіпноз (ч) | [ɦip'nɔz] |
| to hypnotize (vt) | гіпнотизувати | [ɦipnotɨzu'watɨ] |

72. Doctors

doctor	лікар (ч)	['likar]
nurse	медсестра (ж)	[mɛdsɛst'ra]
personal doctor	особистий лікар (ч)	[oso'bistɨj 'likar]

dentist	дантист (ч)	[dan'tist]
optician	окуліст (ч)	[oku'list]
general practitioner	терапевт (ч)	[tɛra'pɛwt]
surgeon	хірург (ч)	[hi'rurɦ]

psychiatrist	психіатр (ч)	[psɨhi'atr]
paediatrician	педіатр (ч)	[pɛdi'atr]
psychologist	психолог (ч)	[psɨ'ɦolɔɦ]
gynaecologist	гінеколог (ч)	[ɦinɛ'kɔlɔɦ]
cardiologist	кардіолог (ч)	[kardi'ɔlɔɦ]

73. Medicine. Drugs. Accessories

medicine, drug	ліки (мн)	['likɨ]
remedy	засіб (ч)	['zasib]
to prescribe (vt)	прописати	[propɨ'satɨ]
prescription	рецепт (ч)	[rɛ'tsɛpt]

tablet, pill	пігулка (ж)	[pi'ɦulka]
ointment	мазь (ж)	[mazʲ]
ampoule	ампула (ж)	['ampula]
mixture, solution	мікстура (ж)	[miks'tura]
syrup	сироп (ч)	[sɨ'rɔp]
capsule	пілюля (ж)	[pi'lʲulʲa]
powder	порошок (ч)	[poro'ʃɔk]

gauze bandage	бинт (ч)	[bɨnt]
cotton wool	вата (ж)	['wata]
iodine	йод (ч)	['jod]

plaster	лейкопластир (ч)	[lɛjko'plastɨr]
eyedropper	піпетка (ж)	[pi'pɛtka]
thermometer	градусник (ч)	['ɦradusnɨk]
syringe	шприц (ч)	[ʃprɨts]

| wheelchair | коляска (ж) | [ko'lʲaska] |
| crutches | милиці (мн) | ['mɨlɨtsi] |

| painkiller | знеболювальне (с) | [znɛ'bolʲuwalʲnɛ] |
| laxative | проносне (с) | [pronos'nɛ] |

spirits (ethanol)	спирт (ч)	[spɨrt]
medicinal herbs	трава (ж)	[traˈwa]
herbal (~ tea)	трав'яний	[trawʲaˈnɨj]

74. Smoking. Tobacco products

tobacco	тютюн (ч)	[tʲuˈtʲun]
cigarette	цигарка (ж)	[tsɨˈɦarka]
cigar	сигара (ж)	[sɨˈɦara]
pipe	люлька (ж)	[ˈlʲulʲka]
packet (of cigarettes)	пачка (ж)	[ˈpatʃka]

matches	сірники (мн)	[sirnɨˈkɨ]
matchbox	сірникова коробка (ж)	[sirnɨˈkɔwa koˈrɔbka]
lighter	запальничка (ж)	[zapalʲˈnɨtʃka]
ashtray	попільниця (ж)	[popilʲˈnɨtsʲa]
cigarette case	портсигар (ч)	[portsɨˈɦar]

| cigarette holder | мундштук (ч) | [mundˈʃtuk] |
| filter (cigarette tip) | фільтр (ч) | [ˈfilʲtr] |

to smoke (vi, vt)	палити	[paˈlɨti]
to light a cigarette	запалити	[zapaˈlɨti]
smoking	паління (с)	[paˈlinʲa]
smoker	курець (ч)	[kuˈrɛts]

cigarette end	недопалок (ч)	[nɛdoˈpalok]
smoke, fumes	дим (ч)	[dɨm]
ash	попіл (ч)	[ˈpɔpil]

HUMAN HABITAT

City

city, town	місто (с)	['misto]
capital city	столиця (ж)	[sto'litsʲa]
village	село (с)	[sɛ'lɔ]
city map	план (ч) міста	[plan 'mista]
city centre	центр (ч) міста	[tsɛntr 'mista]
suburb	передмістя (с)	[pɛrɛd'mistʲa]
suburban (adj)	приміський	[primisʲ'kij]
outskirts	околиця (ж)	[o'kɔlitsʲa]
environs (suburbs)	околиці (мн)	[o'kɔlitsi]
city block	квартал (ч)	[kwar'tal]
residential block (area)	житловий квартал (ч)	[ʒitlo'wij kwar'tal]
traffic	рух (ч)	[ruh]
traffic lights	світлофор (ч)	[switlo'fɔr]
public transport	міський транспорт (ч)	[misʲ'kij 'transport]
crossroads	перехрестя (с)	[pɛrɛh'rɛstʲa]
zebra crossing	перехід (ч)	[pɛrɛ'hid]
pedestrian subway	підземний перехід (ч)	[pi'dzɛmnij pɛrɛ'hid]
to cross (~ the street)	переходити	[pɛrɛ'hɔditi]
pedestrian	пішохід (ч)	[piʃo'hid]
pavement	тротуар (ч)	[trotu'ar]
bridge	міст (ч)	[mist]
embankment (river walk)	набережна (ж)	['nabɛrɛʒna]
fountain	фонтан (ч)	[fon'tan]
allée (garden walkway)	алея (ж)	[a'lɛʲa]
park	парк (ч)	[park]
boulevard	бульвар (ч)	[bulʲ'war]
square	площа (ж)	['plɔɕa]
avenue (wide street)	проспект (ч)	[pros'pɛkt]
street	вулиця (ж)	['wulitsʲa]
side street	провулок (ч)	[pro'wulok]
dead end	глухий кут (ч)	[ɦlu'hij kut]
house	будинок (ч)	[bu'dinok]
building	споруда (ж)	[spo'ruda]
skyscraper	хмарочос (ч)	[hmaro'tʃɔs]
facade	фасад (ч)	[fa'sad]
roof	дах (ч)	[dah]

window	вікно (c)	[wik'nɔ]
arch	арка (ж)	['arka]
column	колона (ж)	[ko'lɔna]
corner	ріг (ч)	[riɦ]

shop window	вітрина (ж)	[wi'trina]
signboard (store sign, etc.)	вивіска (ж)	['wiwiska]
poster (e.g., playbill)	афіша (ж)	[a'fiʃa]
advertising poster	рекламний плакат (ч)	[rɛk'lamnij pla'kat]
hoarding	рекламний щит (ч)	[rɛk'lamnij ɕit]

rubbish	сміття (c)	[smit'tʲa]
rubbish bin	урна (ж)	['urna]
to litter (vi)	смітити	[smi'titi]
rubbish dump	смітник (ч)	[smit'nik]

telephone box	телефонна будка (ж)	[tɛlɛ'fɔna 'budka]
lamppost	ліхтарний стовп (ч)	[liɦ'tarnij stowp]
bench (park ~)	лавка (ж)	['lawka]

police officer	поліцейський (ч)	[poli'tsɛjsʲkij]
police	поліція (ж)	[po'litsiʲa]
beggar	жебрак (ч)	[ʒɛb'rak]
homeless (n)	безпритульний (ч)	[bɛzpri'tulʲnij]

76. Urban institutions

shop	магазин (ч)	[maɦa'zin]
chemist, pharmacy	аптека (ж)	[ap'tɛka]
optician (spectacles shop)	оптика (ж)	['ɔptika]
shopping centre	торгівельний центр (ч)	[torɦi'wɛlʲnij 'tsɛntr]
supermarket	супермаркет (ч)	[supɛr'markɛt]

bakery	булочна (ж)	['bulotʃna]
baker	пекар (ч)	['pɛkar]
cake shop	кондитерська (ж)	[kon'ditɛrsʲka]
grocery shop	бакалія (ж)	[baka'liʲa]
butcher shop	м'ясний магазин (ч)	[mʲas'nij maɦa'zin]

| greengrocer | овочевий магазин (ч) | [owo'tʃɛwij maɦa'zin] |
| market | ринок (ч) | ['rinok] |

coffee bar	кав'ярня (ж)	[ka'wʲarnʲa]
restaurant	ресторан (ч)	[rɛsto'ran]
pub, bar	пивна (ж)	[piw'na]
pizzeria	піцерія (ж)	[pitsɛ'riʲa]

hairdresser	перукарня (ж)	[pɛru'karnʲa]
post office	пошта (ж)	['pɔʃta]
dry cleaners	хімчистка (ж)	[ɦim'tʃistka]
photo studio	фотоательє (c)	[fotoatɛ'ljɛ]

| shoe shop | взуттєвий магазин (ч) | [wzut'tɛwij maɦa'zin] |
| bookshop | книгарня (ж) | [kni'ɦarnʲa] |

sports shop	спортивний магазин (ч)	[spor'tiwnij maha'zin]
clothes repair shop	ремонт (ч) одягу	[rɛ'mɔnt 'ɔdʲahu]
formal wear hire	прокат (ч) одягу	[pro'kat 'ɔdʲahu]
video rental shop	прокат (ч) фільмів	[pro'kat 'filʲmiw]
circus	цирк (ч)	[ʦirk]
zoo	зоопарк (ч)	[zoo'park]
cinema	кінотеатр (ч)	[kinotɛ'atr]
museum	музей (ч)	[mu'zɛj]
library	бібліотека (ж)	[biblio'tɛka]
theatre	театр (ч)	[tɛ'atr]
opera (opera house)	опера (ж)	['ɔpɛra]
nightclub	нічний клуб (ч)	[nitʲ'nij klub]
casino	казино (с)	[kazi'nɔ]
mosque	мечеть (ж)	[mɛ'ʧɛtʲ]
synagogue	синагога (ж)	[sina'hɔha]
cathedral	собор (ч)	[so'bɔr]
temple	храм (ч)	[hram]
church	церква (ж)	['ʦɛrkwa]
college	інститут (ч)	[insti'tut]
university	університет (ч)	[uniwɛrsi'tɛt]
school	школа (ж)	['ʃkola]
prefecture	префектура (ж)	[prɛfɛk'tura]
town hall	мерія (ж)	['mɛriʲa]
hotel	готель (ч)	[ho'tɛlʲ]
bank	банк (ч)	[bank]
embassy	посольство (с)	[po'sɔlʲstwo]
travel agency	турагентство (с)	[tura'hɛntstwo]
information office	довідкове бюро (с)	[dowid'kowɛ bʲu'rɔ]
currency exchange	обмінний пункт (ч)	[ob'minij punkt]
underground, tube	метро (с)	[mɛt'rɔ]
hospital	лікарня (ж)	[li'karnʲa]
petrol station	бензоколонка (ж)	[bɛnzoko'lɔnka]
car park	стоянка (ж)	[sto'ʲanka]

77. Urban transport

bus, coach	автобус (ч)	[aw'tɔbus]
tram	трамвай (ч)	[tram'waj]
trolleybus	тролейбус (ч)	[tro'lɛjbus]
route (bus ~)	маршрут (ч)	[marʃ'rut]
number (e.g. bus ~)	номер (ч)	['nɔmɛr]
to go by ...	їхати на ...	['jihati na]
to get on (~ the bus)	сісти	['sisti]
to get off ...	зійти	[zij'ti]
stop (e.g. bus ~)	зупинка (ж)	[zu'pinka]

next stop	наступна зупинка (ж)	[na'stupna zu'pɨnka]
terminus	кінцева зупинка (ж)	[kin'tsɛwa zu'pɨnka]
timetable	розклад (ч)	['rɔzklad]
to wait (vt)	чекати	[ʧɛ'kati]

ticket	квиток (ч)	[kwɨ'tɔk]
fare	вартість (ж) квитка	['wartistʲ kwɨt'ka]

cashier (ticket seller)	касир (ч)	[ka'sɨr]
ticket inspection	контроль (ч)	[kon'trɔlʲ]
ticket inspector	контролер (ч)	[kontro'lɛr]

to be late (for ...)	запізнюватися	[za'pizɲʲuwatisʲa]
to miss (~ the train, etc.)	спізнитися	[spiz'nitisʲa]
to be in a hurry	поспішати	[pospi'ʃati]

taxi, cab	таксі (с)	[tak'si]
taxi driver	таксист (ч)	[tak'sɨst]
by taxi	на таксі	[na tak'si]
taxi rank	стоянка (с) таксі	[sto'ʲanka tak'si]
to call a taxi	викликати таксі	['wɨklikati tak'si]
to take a taxi	взяти таксі	['wzʲatɨ tak'si]

traffic	вуличний рух (ч)	['wulɨʧnɨj ruh]
traffic jam	пробка (ж)	['prɔbka]
rush hour	години (мн) пік	[ɦo'dɨnɨ pik]
to park (vi)	паркуватися	[parku'watisʲa]
to park (vt)	паркувати	[parku'watɨ]
car park	стоянка (ж)	[sto'ʲanka]

underground, tube	метро (с)	[mɛt'rɔ]
station	станція (ж)	['stantsiʲa]
to take the tube	їхати в метро	['jihatɨ w mɛt'rɔ]
train	поїзд (ч)	['pɔjizd]
train station	вокзал (ч)	[wok'zal]

78. Sightseeing

monument	пам'ятник (ч)	['pamʲʲatnɨk]
fortress	фортеця (ж)	[for'tɛtsʲa]
palace	палац (ч)	[pa'lats]
castle	замок (ч)	['zamok]
tower	вежа (ж)	['wɛʒa]
mausoleum	мавзолей (ч)	[mawzo'lɛj]

architecture	архітектура (ж)	[arhitɛk'tura]
medieval (adj)	середньовічний	[sɛrɛdnʲo'wiʧnɨj]
ancient (adj)	старовинний	[staro'wɨnɨj]
national (adj)	національний	[natsio'nalʲnɨj]
famous (monument, etc.)	відомий	[wi'dɔmɨj]

tourist	турист (ч)	[tu'rist]
guide (person)	гід (ч)	[ɦid]
excursion, sightseeing tour	екскурсія (ж)	[ɛks'kursiʲa]

| to show (vt) | показувати | [po'kazuwati] |
| to tell (vt) | розповідати | [rozpowi'dati] |

to find (vt)	знайти	[znaj'ti]
to get lost (lose one's way)	загубитися	[zaɦu'bitisʲa]
map (e.g. underground ~)	схема (ж)	['sɦɛma]
map (e.g. city ~)	план (ч)	[plan]

souvenir, gift	сувенір (ч)	[suwɛ'nir]
gift shop	магазин (ч) сувенірів	[maɦa'zin suwɛ'niriw]
to take pictures	фотографувати	[fotoɦrafu'wati]
to have one's picture taken	фотографуватися	[fotoɦrafu'watisʲa]

79. Shopping

to buy (purchase)	купляти	[kup'lʲati]
shopping	покупка (ж)	[po'kupka]
to go shopping	робити покупки	[ro'biti po'kupki]
shopping	шопінг (ч)	['ʃopinɦ]

| to be open (ab. shop) | працювати | [pratsʲu'wati] |
| to be closed | зачинитися | [zatʃi'nitisʲa] |

footwear, shoes	взуття (с)	[wzut'tʲa]
clothes, clothing	одяг (ч)	['odʲaɦ]
cosmetics	косметика (ж)	[kos'mɛtika]
food products	продукти (мн)	[pro'dukti]
gift, present	подарунок (ч)	[poda'runok]

| shop assistant (masc.) | продавець (ч) | [proda'wɛts] |
| shop assistant (fem.) | продавщиця (ж) | [prodaw'ɕitsʲa] |

cash desk	каса (ж)	['kasa]
mirror	дзеркало (с)	['dzɛrkalo]
counter (shop ~)	прилавок (ч)	[pri'lawok]
fitting room	примірочна (ж)	[pri'mirotʃna]

to try on	приміряти	[pri'mirʲati]
to fit (ab. dress, etc.)	пасувати	[pasu'wati]
to fancy (vt)	подобатися	[po'dobatisʲa]

price	ціна (ж)	[tsi'na]
price tag	цінник (ч)	['tsinik]
to cost (vt)	коштувати	['koʃtuwati]
How much?	Скільки?	['skilʲki]
discount	знижка (ж)	['zniʒka]

inexpensive (adj)	недорогий	[nɛdoro'ɦij]
cheap (adj)	дешевий	[dɛ'ʃɛwij]
expensive (adj)	дорогий	[doro'ɦij]
It's expensive	Це дорого.	[tsɛ 'doroɦo]

| hire (n) | прокат (ч) | [pro'kat] |
| to hire (~ a dinner jacket) | взяти напрокат | ['wzʲati napro'kat] |

| credit (trade credit) | кредит (ч) | [krɛ'dɪt] |
| on credit (adv) | в кредит (ч) | [w krɛ'dɪt] |

80. Money

money	гроші (мн)	['ɦrɔʃi]
currency exchange	обмін (ч)	['ɔbmin]
exchange rate	курс (ч)	[kurs]
cashpoint	банкомат (ч)	[banko'mat]
coin	монета (ж)	[mo'nɛta]

| dollar | долар (ч) | ['dɔlar] |
| euro | євро (ч) | ['ɛwro] |

lira	ліра (ж)	['lira]
Deutschmark	марка (ж)	['marka]
franc	франк (ч)	['frank]
pound sterling	фунт (ч)	['funt]
yen	ієна (ж)	[i'ɛna]

debt	борг (ч)	['bɔrɦ]
debtor	боржник (ч)	[borʒ'nɨk]
to lend (money)	позичити	[po'zɪtʃiti]
to borrow (vi, vt)	взяти в борг	['wzʲati w bɔrɦ]

bank	банк (ч)	[bank]
account	рахунок (ч)	[ra'hunok]
to deposit into the account	покласти на рахунок	[pok'lastɨ na ra'hunok]
to withdraw (vt)	зняти з рахунку	['znʲatɨ z ra'hunku]

credit card	кредитна картка (ж)	[krɛ'dɪtna 'kartka]
cash	готівка (ж)	[ɦo'tiwka]
cheque	чек (ч)	[tʃɛk]
to write a cheque	виписати чек	['wɨpɨsatɨ 'tʃɛk]
chequebook	чекова книжка (ж)	['tʃɛkowa 'knɨʒka]

wallet	гаманець (ч)	[ɦama'nɛts]
purse	гаманець (ч)	[ɦama'nɛts]
safe	сейф (ч)	[sɛjf]

heir	спадкоємець (ч)	[spadko'ɛmɛts]
inheritance	спадщина (с)	['spadɕina]
fortune (wealth)	статок (ч)	['statok]

lease	оренда (ж)	[o'rɛnda]
rent (money)	квартирна плата (ж)	[kwar'tɨrna 'plata]
to rent (sth from sb)	наймати	[naj'matɨ]

price	ціна (ж)	[tsi'na]
cost	вартість (ж)	['wartistʲ]
sum	сума (ж)	['suma]

| to spend (vt) | витрачати | [wɨtra'tʃatɨ] |
| expenses | витрати (мн) | ['wɨtratɨ] |

to economize (vi, vt)	економити	[ɛkoˈnɔmɨtɨ]
economical	економний	[ɛkoˈnɔmnɨj]

to pay (vi, vt)	платити	[plaˈtɨtɨ]
payment	оплата (ж)	[opˈlata]
change (give the ~)	решта (ж)	[ˈrɛʃta]

tax	податок (ч)	[poˈdatok]
fine	штраф (ч)	[ʃtraf]
to fine (vt)	штрафувати	[ʃtrafuˈwatɨ]

81. Post. Postal service

post office	пошта (ж)	[ˈpɔʃta]
post (letters, etc.)	пошта (ж)	[ˈpɔʃta]
postman	листоноша (ч)	[lɨstoˈnɔʃa]
opening hours	години (мн) роботи	[ɦoˈdɨnɨ roˈbɔtɨ]

letter	лист (ч)	[lɨst]
registered letter	рекомендований лист (ч)	[rɛkomɛnˈdɔwanɨj lɨst]
postcard	листівка (ж)	[lɨsˈtiwka]
telegram	телеграма (ж)	[tɛlɛˈɦrama]
parcel	посилка (ж)	[poˈsɨłka]
money transfer	грошовий переказ (ч)	[ɦroʃoˈwɨj pɛˈrɛkaz]

to receive (vt)	отримати	[otˈrɨmatɨ]
to send (vt)	відправити	[widˈprawɨtɨ]
sending	відправлення (с)	[widˈprawlɛnʲa]

address	адреса (ж)	[adˈrɛsa]
postcode	індекс (ч)	[ˈindɛks]
sender	відправник (ч)	[widˈprawnɨk]
receiver	одержувач (ч)	[oˈdɛrʒuwaʧ]

name (first name)	ім'я (с)	[iˈmʲʲa]
surname (last name)	прізвище (с)	[ˈprizwɨɕɛ]

postage rate	тариф (ч)	[taˈrɨf]
standard (adj)	звичайний	[zwɨˈʧajnɨj]
economical (adj)	економічний	[ɛkonoˈmiʧnɨj]

weight	вага (ж)	[waˈɦa]
to weigh (~ letters)	важити	[ˈwaʒɨtɨ]
envelope	конверт (ч)	[konˈwɛrt]
postage stamp	марка (ж)	[ˈmarka]

Dwelling. House. Home

82. House. Dwelling

house	будинок (ч)	[bu'dɨnok]
at home (adv)	вдома	['wdɔma]
yard	двір (ч)	[dwir]
fence (iron ~)	грати (мн)	['ɦratɨ]
brick (n)	цегла (ж)	['tsɛɦla]
brick (as adj)	цегляний	[tsɛɦlʲa'nɨj]
stone (n)	камінь (ч)	['kaminʲ]
stone (as adj)	кам'яний	[kamʔʲa'nɨj]
concrete (n)	бетон (ч)	[bɛ'tɔn]
concrete (as adj)	бетонний	[bɛ'tɔnʲij]
new (new-built)	новий	[no'wɨj]
old (adj)	старий	[sta'rɨj]
decrepit (house)	старий, ветхий	[sta'rɨj], ['wɛthɨj]
modern (adj)	сучасний	[su'tʃasnɨj]
multistorey (adj)	багатоповерховий	[ba'ɦato powɛr'hɔwɨj]
tall (~ building)	високий	[wɨ'sɔkɨj]
floor, storey	поверх (ч)	['powɛrh]
single-storey (adj)	одноповерховий	[odnopowɛr'hɔwɨj]
ground floor	нижній поверх (ч)	['nɨʒnij 'pɔwɛrh]
top floor	верхній поверх (ч)	['wɛrhnij 'pɔwɛrh]
roof	дах (ч)	[dah]
chimney	труба (ж)	[tru'ba]
roof tiles	черепиця (ж)	[tʃɛrɛ'pɨtsʲa]
tiled (adj)	черепичний	[tʃɛrɛ'pɨtʃnɨj]
loft (attic)	горище (c)	[ɦo'rɨçɛ]
window	вікно (c)	[wik'nɔ]
glass	скло (c)	['sklo]
window ledge	підвіконня (c)	[pidwi'kɔnʲa]
shutters	віконниці (мн)	[wi'kɔnɨtsi]
wall	стіна (ж)	[sti'na]
balcony	балкон (ч)	[bal'kɔn]
downpipe	ринва (ж)	['rɨnwa]
upstairs (to be ~)	нагорі	[naɦo'ri]
to go upstairs	підніматися	[pidni'matisʲa]
to come down (the stairs)	спускатися	[spus'katisʲa]
to move (to new premises)	переїздити	[pɛrɛjiz'dɨtɨ]

83.   House. Entrance. Lift

entrance	під'їзд (ч)	[pidˀjizd]
stairs (stairway)	сходи (мн)	['shɔdɨ]
steps	сходинки (мн)	['shɔdɨnkɨ]
banisters	поручча (мн)	[po'rutʃʲa]
lobby (hotel ~)	хол (ч)	[hol]
postbox	поштова скринька (ж)	[poʃ'tɔwa sk'rinʲka]
waste bin	бак (ч) для сміття	[bak dlʲa smit't'a]
refuse chute	сміттєпровід (ч)	[smittɛ'prɔwid]
lift	ліфт (ч)	[lift]
goods lift	вантажний ліфт (ч)	[wan'taʒnɨj lift]
lift cage	кабіна (ж)	[ka'bina]
to take the lift	їхати в ліфті	['jihatɨ w 'lifti]
flat	квартира (ж)	[kwar'tɨra]
residents (~ of a building)	мешканці (мн)	['mɛʃkanʦi]
neighbour (masc.)	сусід (ч)	[su'sid]
neighbour (fem.)	сусідка (ж)	[su'sidka]
neighbours	сусіди (мн)	[su'sidɨ]

84.   House. Doors. Locks

door	двері (мн)	['dwɛri]
gate (vehicle ~)	брама (ж)	['brama]
handle, doorknob	ручка (ж)	['rutʃka]
to unlock (unbolt)	відкрити	[wid'krɨtɨ]
to open (vt)	відкривати	[widkrɨ'watɨ]
to close (vt)	закривати	[zakrɨ'watɨ]
key	ключ (ч)	[klʲutʃ]
bunch (of keys)	в'язка (ж)	['wˀjazka]
to creak (door, etc.)	скрипіти	[skrɨ'pitɨ]
creak	скрипіння (с)	[skrɨ'pinʲa]
hinge (door ~)	петля (ж)	[pɛt'lʲa]
doormat	килимок (ч)	[kɨlɨ'mɔk]
door lock	замок (ч)	[za'mɔk]
keyhole	замкова щілина (ж)	[zam'kɔwa ɕi'lɨna]
crossbar (sliding bar)	засув (ч)	['zasuw]
door latch	засувка (ж)	['zasuwka]
padlock	навісний замок (ч)	[nawis'nɨj za'mɔk]
to ring (~ the door bell)	дзвонити	[ʣwo'nitɨ]
ringing (sound)	дзвінок (ч)	[ʣwi'nɔk]
doorbell	дзвінок (ч)	[ʣwi'nɔk]
doorbell button	кнопка (ж)	['knɔpka]
knock (at the door)	стукіт (ч)	['stukit]
to knock (vi)	стукати	['stukatɨ]

code	код (ч)	[kod]
combination lock	кодовий замок (ч)	['kɔdowij za'mɔk]
intercom	домофон (ч)	[domo'fɔn]
number (on the door)	номер (ч)	['nɔmɛr]
doorplate	табличка (ж)	[tab'litʃka]
peephole	вічко (с)	['witʃko]

85. Country house

village	село (с)	[sɛ'lɔ]
vegetable garden	город (ч)	[ɦo'rɔd]
fence	паркан (ч)	[par'kan]
picket fence	тин (ч)	[tin]
wicket gate	хвіртка (ж)	['hwirtka]

granary	комора (ж)	[ko'mɔra]
cellar	льох (ч)	[lʲoh]
shed (garden ~)	сарай (ч)	[sa'raj]
water well	криниця (ж)	[kri'nitsʲa]

stove (wood-fired ~)	піч (ж)	[pitʃ]
to stoke the stove	палити	[pa'liti]
firewood	дрова (мн)	['drɔwa]
log (firewood)	поліно (с)	[po'lino]

veranda	веранда (ж)	[wɛ'randa]
deck (terrace)	тераса (ж)	[tɛ'rasa]
stoop (front steps)	ганок (ч)	['ɦanok]
swing (hanging seat)	гойдалка (ж)	['ɦɔjdalka]

86. Castle. Palace

castle	замок (ч)	['zamok]
palace	палац (ч)	[pa'lats]
fortress	фортеця (ж)	[for'tɛtsʲa]

wall (round castle)	стіна (ж)	[sti'na]
tower	вежа (ж)	['wɛʒa]
keep, donjon	головна вежа (ж)	[ɦolow'na 'wɛʒa]

portcullis	підйомна брама (ж)	[pid'jɔmna 'brama]
subterranean passage	підземний хід (ч)	[pi'dzɛmnij hid]
moat	рів (ч)	[riw]

| chain | ланцюг (ч) | [lan'tsʲuɦ] |
| arrow loop | бійниця (ж) | [bij'nitsʲa] |

| magnificent (adj) | пишний | ['piʃnij] |
| majestic (adj) | величний | [wɛ'litʃnij] |

| impregnable (adj) | неприступний | [nɛpri'stupnij] |
| medieval (adj) | середньовічний | [sɛrɛdnʲo'witʃnij] |

87. Flat

flat	квартира (ж)	[kwar'tɨra]
room	кімната (ж)	[kim'nata]
bedroom	спальня (ж)	['spalʲnʲa]
dining room	їдальня (ж)	['jɨdalʲnʲa]
living room	вітальня (ж)	[wi'talʲnʲa]
study (home office)	кабінет (ч)	[kabi'nɛt]
entry room	передпокій (ч)	[pɛrɛd'pokij]
bathroom	ванна кімната (ж)	['wana kim'nata]
water closet	туалет (ч)	[tua'lɛt]
ceiling	стеля (ж)	['stɛlʲa]
floor	підлога (ж)	[pid'lɔɦa]
corner	куток (ч)	[ku'tɔk]

88. Flat. Cleaning

to clean (vi, vt)	прибирати	[prɨbɨ'ratɨ]
to put away (to stow)	прибирати	[prɨbɨ'ratɨ]
dust	пил (ч)	[pɨl]
dusty (adj)	курний	[kur'nɨj]
to dust (vt)	витирати пил	[wɨtɨ'ratɨ pɨl]
vacuum cleaner	пилосос (ч)	[pɨlo'sɔs]
to vacuum (vt)	пилососити	[pɨlo'sɔsɨtɨ]
to sweep (vi, vt)	підмітати	[pidmi'tatɨ]
sweepings	сміття (с)	[smit'tʲa]
order	лад (ч)	[lad]
disorder, mess	безлад (ч)	['bɛzlad]
mop	швабра (ж)	['ʃwabra]
duster	ганчірка (ж)	[ɦan'tʃirka]
short broom	віник (ч)	['winɨk]
dustpan	совок (ч) для сміття	[so'wɔk dlʲa smit'tʲa]

89. Furniture. Interior

furniture	меблі (мн)	['mɛbli]
table	стіл (ч)	[stil]
chair	стілець (ч)	[sti'lɛts]
bed	ліжко (с)	['liʒko]
sofa, settee	диван (ч)	[dɨ'wan]
armchair	крісло (с)	['krislo]
bookcase	шафа (ж)	['ʃafa]
shelf	полиця (ж)	[po'lɨtsʲa]
wardrobe	шафа (ж)	['ʃafa]
coat rack (wall-mounted ~)	вішалка (ж)	['wiʃalka]

coat stand	вішак (ч)	[wi'ʃak]
chest of drawers	комод (ч)	[ko'mɔd]
coffee table	журнальний столик (ч)	[ʒur'nalʲnij 'stɔlik]
mirror	дзеркало (с)	['dzɛrkalo]
carpet	килим (ч)	['kiɫim]
small carpet	килимок (ч)	[kiɫi'mɔk]
fireplace	камін (ч)	[ka'min]
candle	свічка (ж)	['switʃka]
candlestick	свічник (ч)	[switʃ'nik]
drapes	штори (мн)	['ʃtori]
wallpaper	шпалери (мн)	[ʃpa'lɛri]
blinds (jalousie)	жалюзі (мн)	['ʒalʲuzi]
table lamp	настільна лампа (ж)	[na'stilʲna 'lampa]
wall lamp (sconce)	світильник (ч)	[swi'tilʲnik]
standard lamp	торшер (ч)	[tor'ʃɛr]
chandelier	люстра (ж)	['lʲustra]
leg (of a chair, table)	ніжка (ж)	['niʒka]
armrest	підлокітник (ч)	[pidlo'kitnik]
back (backrest)	спинка (ж)	['spinka]
drawer	шухляда (ж)	[ʃuh'lʲada]

90. Bedding

bedclothes	білизна (ж)	[bi'ɫizna]
pillow	подушка (ж)	[po'duʃka]
pillowslip	наволочка (ж)	['nawolotʃka]
duvet	ковдра (ж)	['kɔwdra]
sheet	простирадло (с)	[prosti'radlo]
bedspread	покривало (с)	[pokri'walo]

91. Kitchen

kitchen	кухня (ж)	['kuhnʲa]
gas	газ (ч)	[ɦaz]
gas cooker	плита (ж) газова	[pɫi'ta 'ɦazowa]
electric cooker	плита (ж) електрична	[pɫi'ta ɛlɛkt'ritʃna]
oven	духовка (ж)	[du'hɔwka]
microwave oven	мікрохвильова піч (ж)	[mikrohwilʲo'wa pitʃ]
refrigerator	холодильник (ч)	[holo'dilʲnik]
freezer	морозильник (ч)	[moro'zilʲnik]
dishwasher	посудомийна машина (ж)	[posudo'mijna ma'ʃina]
mincer	м'ясорубка (ж)	[mʲʔaso'rubka]
juicer	соковижималка (ж)	[sokowiʒi'malka]
toaster	тостер (ч)	['tɔstɛr]
mixer	міксер (ч)	['miksɛr]

coffee machine	кавоварка (ж)	[kawo'warka]
coffee pot	кавник (ч)	[kaw'nɨk]
coffee grinder	кавомолка (ж)	[kawo'mɔlka]

kettle	чайник (ч)	['ʧajnɨk]
teapot	заварник (ч)	[za'warnɨk]
lid	кришка (ж)	['kriʃka]
tea strainer	ситечко (с)	['sɨtɛʧko]

spoon	ложка (ж)	['lɔʒka]
teaspoon	чайна ложка (ж)	['ʧajna 'lɔʒka]
soup spoon	столова ложка (ж)	[sto'lɔwa 'lɔʒka]
fork	виделка (ж)	[wɨ'dɛlka]
knife	ніж (ч)	[niʒ]

tableware (dishes)	посуд (ч)	['pɔsud]
plate (dinner ~)	тарілка (ж)	[ta'rilka]
saucer	блюдце (с)	['blʲudtsɛ]

shot glass	чарка (ж)	['ʧarka]
glass (tumbler)	склянка (ж)	['sklʲanka]
cup	чашка (ж)	['ʧaʃka]

sugar bowl	цукорниця (ж)	['tsukornɨtsʲa]
salt cellar	сільничка (ж)	[silʲ'nɨʧka]
pepper pot	перечниця (ж)	['pɛrɛʧnɨtsʲa]
butter dish	маслянка (ж)	['maslʲanka]

stock pot (soup pot)	каструля (ж)	[kas'trulʲa]
frying pan (skillet)	сковорідка (ж)	[skowo'ridka]
ladle	черпак (ч)	[ʧɛr'pak]
colander	друшляк (ч)	[druʃ'lʲak]
tray (serving ~)	піднос (ч)	[pid'nɔs]

bottle	пляшка (ж)	['plʲaʃka]
jar (glass)	банка (ж)	['banka]
tin (can)	банка (ж)	['banka]

bottle opener	відкривачка (ж)	[widkri'waʧka]
tin opener	відкривачка (ж)	[widkri'waʧka]
corkscrew	штопор (ч)	['ʃtopor]
filter	фільтр (ч)	['filʲtr]
to filter (vt)	фільтрувати	[filʲtru'watɨ]

| waste (food ~, etc.) | сміття (с) | [smit'tʲa] |
| waste bin (kitchen ~) | відро (с) для сміття | [wid'ro dlʲa smit'tʲa] |

92. Bathroom

bathroom	ванна кімната (ж)	['wana kim'nata]
water	вода (ж)	[wo'da]
tap	кран (ч)	[kran]
hot water	гаряча вода (ж)	[ɦa'rʲatʃa wo'da]
cold water	холодна вода (ж)	[ho'lɔdna wo'da]

| toothpaste | зубна паста (ж) | [zub'na 'pasta] |
| to clean one's teeth | чистити зуби | ['tʃistiti 'zubi] |

to shave (vi)	голитися	[ɦo'litisʲa]
shaving foam	піна (ж) для гоління	['pina dlʲa ɦo'linʲa]
razor	бритва (ж)	['britwa]

to wash (one's hands, etc.)	мити	['miti]
to have a bath	митися	['mitisʲa]
shower	душ (ч)	[duʃ]
to have a shower	приймати душ	[prij'mati duʃ]

bath	ванна (ж)	['wana]
toilet (toilet bowl)	унітаз (ч)	[uni'taz]
sink (washbasin)	раковина (ж)	['rakowina]

| soap | мило (с) | ['milo] |
| soap dish | мильниця (ж) | ['milʲnitsʲa] |

sponge	губка (ж)	['ɦubka]
shampoo	шампунь (ч)	[ʃam'punʲ]
towel	рушник (ч)	[ruʃ'nik]
bathrobe	халат (ч)	[ha'lat]

laundry (laundering)	прання (с)	[pra'nʲa]
washing machine	пральна машина (ж)	['pralʲna ma'ʃina]
to do the laundry	прати білизну	['prati bi'liznu]
washing powder	пральний порошок (ч)	['pralʲnij poro'ʃok]

93. Household appliances

TV, telly	телевізор (ч)	[tɛlɛ'wizor]
tape recorder	магнітофон (ч)	[maɦnito'fon]
video	відеомагнітофон (ч)	['widɛo maɦnito'fon]
radio	приймач (ч)	[prij'matʃ]
player (CD, MP3, etc.)	плеєр (ч)	['plɛɛr]

video projector	відеопроектор (ч)	['widɛo pro'ɛktor]
home cinema	домашній кінотеатр (ч)	[do'maʃnij kinotɛ'atr]
DVD player	програвач (ч) DVD	[proɦra'watʃ diwi'di]
amplifier	підсилювач (ч)	[pid'silʲuwatʃ]
video game console	гральна приставка (ж)	['ɦralʲna pri'stawka]

video camera	відеокамера (ж)	['widɛo 'kamɛra]
camera (photo)	фотоапарат (ч)	[fotoapa'rat]
digital camera	цифровий фотоапарат (ч)	[tsifro'wij fotoapa'rat]

vacuum cleaner	пилосос (ч)	[pilo'sɔs]
iron (e.g. steam ~)	праска (ж)	['praska]
ironing board	дошка (ж) для прасування	['dɔʃka dlʲa prasu'wanʲa]

telephone	телефон (ч)	[tɛlɛ'fon]
mobile phone	мобільний телефон (ч)	[mo'bilʲnij tɛlɛ'fon]
typewriter	машинка (ж)	[ma'ʃinka]

sewing machine	швейна машинка (ж)	['ʃwɛjna ma'ʃinka]
microphone	мікрофон (ч)	[mikro'fɔn]
headphones	навушники (мн)	[na'wuʃnikɨ]
remote control (TV)	пульт (ч)	[pulʲt]

CD, compact disc	CD-диск (ч)	[si'di dɨsk]
cassette, tape	касета (ж)	[ka'sɛta]
vinyl record	платівка (ж)	[pla'tiwka]

94. Repairs. Renovation

renovations	ремонт (ч)	[rɛ'mɔnt]
to renovate (vt)	робити ремонт	[ro'bitɨ rɛ'mɔnt]
to repair, to fix (vt)	ремонтувати	[rɛmontu'watɨ]
to put in order	привести до ладу	[pri'wɛstɨ do 'ladu]
to redo (do again)	перeробляти	[pɛrɛrob'lʲatɨ]

paint	фарба (ж)	['farba]
to paint (~ a wall)	фарбувати	[farbu'watɨ]
house painter	маляр (ж)	['malʲar]
paintbrush	щітка (ж)	['ɕitka]

| whitewash | побілка (ж) | [po'bilka] |
| to whitewash (vt) | білити | [bi'litɨ] |

wallpaper	шпалери (мн)	[ʃpa'lɛrɨ]
to wallpaper (vt)	поклеїти шпалерами	[pok'lɛjitɨ ʃpa'lɛramɨ]
varnish	лак (ч)	[lak]
to varnish (vt)	покривати лаком	[pokrɨ'watɨ 'lakom]

95. Plumbing

water	вода (ж)	[wo'da]
hot water	гаряча вода (ж)	[ha'rʲatʃa wo'da]
cold water	холодна вода (ж)	[ho'lɔdna wo'da]
tap	кран (ч)	[kran]

drop (of water)	крапля (ж)	['kraplʲa]
to drip (vi)	крапати	['krapatɨ]
to leak (ab. pipe)	текти	[tɛk'tɨ]
leak (pipe ~)	теча (ж)	['tɛtʃa]
puddle	калюжа (ж)	[ka'lʲuʒa]

pipe	труба (ж)	[tru'ba]
valve (e.g., ball ~)	вентиль (ч)	['wɛntɨlʲ]
to be clogged up	забитись	[za'bɨtɨsʲ]

tools	інструменти (мн)	[instru'mɛntɨ]
adjustable spanner	розвідний ключ (ч)	[roz'widnɨj klʲutʃ]
to unscrew (lid, filter, etc.)	відкрутити	[widkru'tɨtɨ]
to screw (tighten)	закручувати	[za'krutʃuwatɨ]
to unclog (vt)	прочищати	[protʃi'ɕatɨ]

plumber	сантехнік (ч)	[san'tɛhnik]
basement	підвал (ч)	[pid'wal]
sewerage (system)	каналізація (ж)	[kanali'zatsiˈa]

96. Fire. Conflagration

fire (accident)	вогонь (ч)	[wo'hɔnˈ]
flame	полум'я (с)	['pɔlumˈa]
spark	іскра (ж)	['iskra]
smoke (from fire)	дим (ч)	[dɨm]
torch (flaming stick)	смолоскип (ч)	[smolos'kɨp]
campfire	багаття (с)	[ba'hattˈa]

petrol	бензин (ч)	[bɛn'zɨn]
paraffin	керосин (ч)	[kɛro'sɨn]
flammable (adj)	горючий	[ho'rˈutʃɨj]
explosive (adj)	вибухонебезпечний	[wɨbuhonɛbɛz'pɛtʃnɨj]
NO SMOKING	ПАЛИТИ ЗАБОРОНЕНО	[pa'lɨtɨ zabo'rɔnɛno]

safety	безпека (ж)	[bɛz'pɛka]
danger	небезпека (ж)	[nɛbɛz'pɛka]
dangerous (adj)	небезпечний	[nɛbɛz'pɛtʃnɨj]

to catch fire	загорітися	[zaho'rɨtɨsˈa]
explosion	вибух (ч)	['wɨbuh]
to set fire	підпалити	[pidpa'lɨtɨ]
arsonist	підпалювач (ч)	[pid'palˈuwatʃ]
arson	підпал (ч)	['pidpal]

to blaze (vi)	палати	[pa'latɨ]
to burn (be on fire)	горіти	[ho'rɨtɨ]
to burn down	згоріти	[zho'rɨtɨ]

firefighter, fireman	пожежник (ч)	[po'ʒɛʒnɨk]
fire engine	пожежна машина (ж)	[po'ʒɛʒna ma'ʃɨna]
fire brigade	пожежна команда (ж)	[po'ʒɛʒna ko'manda]
fire engine ladder	драбина (ж)	[dra'bɨna]

fire hose	шланг (ч)	[ʃlanh]
fire extinguisher	вогнегасник (ч)	[wohnɛ'hasnɨk]
helmet	каска (ж)	['kaska]
siren	сирена (ж)	[sɨ'rɛna]

to cry (for help)	кричати	[krɨ'tʃatɨ]
to call for help	кликати на допомогу	['klɨkatɨ na dopo'mɔhu]
rescuer	рятувальник (ч)	[rˈatu'walˈnɨk]
to rescue (vt)	рятувати	[rˈatu'watɨ]

to arrive (vi)	приїхати	[prɨ'jihatɨ]
to extinguish (vt)	тушити	[tu'ʃɨtɨ]
water	вода (ж)	[wo'da]
sand	пісок (ч)	[pi'sɔk]
ruins (destruction)	руїни (мн)	[ru'jinɨ]
to collapse (building, etc.)	повалитися	[powa'lɨtɨsˈa]

| to fall down (vi) | обвалитися | [obwalitisʲa] |
| to cave in (ceiling, floor) | завалитися | [zawaˈlitisʲa] |

| piece of debris | уламок (ч) | [uˈlamok] |
| ash | попіл (ч) | [ˈpopil] |

| to suffocate (die) | задихнутися | [zadihˈnutisʲa] |
| to be killed (perish) | загинути | [zaˈɦinuti] |

HUMAN ACTIVITIES

Job. Business. Part 1

97. Banking

bank	банк (ч)	[bank]
branch (of a bank)	відділення (с)	[wid'dilɛnʲa]
consultant	консультант (ч)	[konsulʲ'tant]
manager (director)	управляючий (ч)	[upraw'lʲaʲutʃij]
bank account	рахунок (ч)	[ra'hunok]
account number	номер (ч) рахунка	['nɔmɛr ra'hunka]
current account	поточний рахунок (ч)	[po'tɔtʃnij ra'hunok]
deposit account	накопичувальний рахунок (ч)	[nako'pitʃuwalʲnij ra'hunok]
to open an account	відкрити рахунок	[wid'kriti ra'hunok]
to close the account	закрити рахунок	[za'kriti ra'hunok]
to deposit into the account	покласти на рахунок	[pok'lasti na ra'hunok]
to withdraw (vt)	зняти з рахунку	['znʲati z ra'hunku]
deposit	внесок (ч)	['wnɛsok]
to make a deposit	зробити внесок	[zro'biti 'wnɛsok]
wire transfer	переказ (ч)	[pɛ'rɛkaz]
to wire, to transfer	зробити переказ	[zro'biti pɛ'rɛkaz]
sum	сума (ж)	['suma]
How much?	Скільки?	['skilʲki]
signature	підпис (ч)	['pidpis]
to sign (vt)	підписати	[pidpi'sati]
credit card	кредитна картка (ж)	[krɛ'ditna 'kartka]
code (PIN code)	код (ч)	[kod]
credit card number	номер (ч) кредитної картки	['nɔmɛr krɛ'ditnoji 'kartki]
cashpoint	банкомат (ч)	[banko'mat]
cheque	чек (ч)	[tʃɛk]
to write a cheque	виписати чек	['wipisati 'tʃɛk]
chequebook	чекова книжка (ж)	['tʃɛkowa 'kniʒka]
loan (bank ~)	кредит (ч)	[krɛ'dit]
to apply for a loan	звертатися за кредитом	[zwɛr'tatisʲa za krɛ'ditom]
to get a loan	брати кредит	['brati krɛ'dit]
to give a loan	надавати кредит	[nada'wati krɛ'dit]
guarantee	застава (ж)	[za'stawa]

98.   Telephone. Phone conversation

telephone	телефон (ч)	[tɛlɛ'fɔn]
mobile phone	мобільний телефон (ч)	[mo'bilʲnij tɛlɛ'fɔn]
answerphone	автовідповідач (ч)	[awtowidpowi'datʃ]
to call (by phone)	телефонувати	[tɛlɛfonu'wati]
call, ring	дзвінок (ч)	[dzwi'nɔk]
to dial a number	набрати номер	[nab'ratɨ 'nɔmɛr]
Hello!	Алло!	[a'lɔ]
to ask (vt)	запитати	[zapɨ'tatɨ]
to answer (vi, vt)	відповісти	[widpo'wistɨ]
to hear (vt)	чути	['tʃutɨ]
well (adv)	добре	['dɔbrɛ]
not well (adv)	погано	[po'ɦano]
noises (interference)	перешкоди (мн)	[pɛrɛʃ'kɔdɨ]
receiver	трубка (ж)	['trubka]
to pick up (~ the phone)	зняти трубку	['znʲatɨ 'trubku]
to hang up (~ the phone)	покласти трубку	[pok'lastɨ t'rubku]
busy (engaged)	зайнятий	['zajnʲatɨj]
to ring (ab. phone)	дзвонити	[dzwo'nɨtɨ]
telephone book	телефонна книга (ж)	[tɛlɛ'fɔna 'kniɦa]
local (adj)	місцевий	[mis'tsɛwɨj]
local call	місцевий зв'язок (ч)	[mis'tsɛwɨj 'zwʲazok]
trunk (e.g. ~ call)	міжміський	[miʒmis'ʲkij]
trunk call	міжміський зв'язок (ч)	[miʒmis'ʲkij 'zwʲazok]
international (adj)	міжнародний	[miʒna'rɔdnɨj]
international call	міжнародний зв'язок (ч)	[miʒna'rɔdnɨj 'zwʲazok]

99.   Mobile telephone

mobile phone	мобільний телефон (ч)	[mo'bilʲnij tɛlɛ'fɔn]
display	дисплей (ч)	[dɨs'plɛj]
button	кнопка (ж)	['knɔpka]
SIM card	SIM-карта (ж)	[sim 'karta]
battery	батарея (ж)	[bata'rɛʲa]
to be flat (battery)	розрядитися	[rozrʲa'dɨtɨsʲa]
charger	зарядний пристрій (ч)	[za'rʲadnɨj 'pristrij]
menu	меню (с)	[mɛ'nʲu]
settings	настройки (мн)	[na'strɔjki]
tune (melody)	мелодія (ж)	[mɛ'lɔdiʲa]
to select (vt)	вибрати	['wɨbratɨ]
calculator	калькулятор (ч)	[kalʲku'lʲator]
voice mail	автовідповідач (ч)	[awtowidpowi'datʃ]
alarm clock	будильник (ч)	[bu'dɨlʲnɨk]

contacts	телефонна книга (ж)	[tɛlɛ'fɔna 'knɨɦa]
SMS (text message)	SMS-повідомлення (с)	[ɛsɛ'mɛs powi'dɔmlɛnʲa]
subscriber	абонент (ч)	[abo'nɛnt]

100. Stationery

| ballpoint pen | авторучка (ж) | [awto'ruʧka] |
| fountain pen | ручка-перо (с) | ['ruʧka pɛ'rɔ] |

pencil	олівець (ч)	[oli'wɛts]
highlighter	маркер (ч)	['markɛr]
felt-tip pen	фломастер (ч)	[flo'mastɛr]

| notepad | блокнот (ч) | [blok'nɔt] |
| diary | щоденник (ч) | [ɕo'dɛnɨk] |

ruler	лінійка (ж)	[li'nijka]
calculator	калькулятор (ч)	[kalʲku'lʲator]
rubber	гумка (ж)	['ɦumka]
drawing pin	кнопка (ж)	['knɔpka]
paper clip	скріпка (ж)	['skripka]

glue	клей (ч)	[klɛj]
stapler	степлер (ч)	['stɛplɛr]
hole punch	діркопробивач (ч)	[dirkoprobɨ'waʧ]
pencil sharpener	стругачка (ж)	[stru'ɦaʧka]

Job. Business. Part 2

101. Mass Media

newspaper	газета (ж)	[ɦa'zɛta]
magazine	журнал (ч)	[ʒur'nal]
press (printed media)	преса (ж)	['prɛsa]
radio	радіо (с)	['radio]
radio station	радіостанція (ж)	[radios'tantsi'a]
television	телебачення (с)	[tɛlɛ'batʃɛniˈa]
presenter, host	ведучий (ч)	[wɛ'dutʃij]
newsreader	диктор (ч)	['diktor]
commentator	коментатор (ч)	[komɛn'tator]
journalist	журналіст (ч)	[ʒurna'list]
correspondent (reporter)	кореспондент (ч)	[korɛspon'dɛnt]
press photographer	фотокореспондент (ч)	['foto korɛspon'dɛnt]
reporter	репортер (ч)	[rɛpor'tɛr]
editor	редактор (ч)	[rɛ'daktor]
editor-in-chief	головний редактор (ч)	[ɦolow'nij rɛ'daktor]
to subscribe (to …)	передплатити	[pɛrɛdpla'titi]
subscription	передплата (ж)	[pɛrɛdp'lata]
subscriber	передплатник (ч)	[pɛrɛdp'latnik]
to read (vi, vt)	читати	[tʃi'tati]
reader	читач (ч)	[tʃi'tatʃ]
circulation (of a newspaper)	наклад (ч)	['naklad]
monthly (adj)	щомісячний	[ɕo'misiatʃnij]
weekly (adj)	щотижневий	[ɕotiʒ'nɛwij]
issue (edition)	номер (ч)	['nɔmɛr]
new (~ issue)	свіжий	['swiʒij]
headline	заголовок (ч)	[zaɦo'lowok]
short article	замітка (ж)	[za'mitka]
column (regular article)	рубрика (ж)	['rubrika]
article	стаття (ж)	[stat'tˈa]
page	сторінка (ж)	[sto'rinka]
reportage, report	репортаж (ч)	[rɛpor'taʒ]
event (happening)	подія (ж)	[po'diˈa]
sensation (news)	сенсація (ж)	[sɛn'satsiˈa]
scandal	скандал (ч)	[skan'dal]
scandalous (adj)	скандальний	[skan'dalˈnij]
great (~ scandal)	гучний	[ɦutʃ'nij]
programme (e.g. cooking ~)	передача (ж)	[pɛrɛ'datʃa]
interview	інтерв'ю (с)	[intɛr'wˀiu]

| live broadcast | пряма трансляція (ж) | [pr'a'ma trans'l'atsi'a] |
| channel | канал (ч) | [ka'nal] |

102. Agriculture

agriculture	сільське господарство (с)	[sil's'k'kɛ ɦospo'darstwo]
peasant (masc.)	селянин (ч)	[sɛl'a'nin]
peasant (fem.)	селянка (ж)	[sɛ'l'anka]
farmer	фермер (ч)	['fɛrmɛr]

| tractor | трактор (ч) | ['traktor] |
| combine, harvester | комбайн (ч) | [kom'bajn] |

plough	плуг (ч)	[pluɦ]
to plough (vi, vt)	орати	[o'rati]
ploughland	рілля (ж)	[ri'l'a]
furrow (in field)	борозна (ж)	[boroz'na]

to sow (vi, vt)	сіяти	['si'ati]
seeder	сівалка (ж)	[si'walka]
sowing (process)	посів (ч)	[po'siw]

| scythe | коса (ж) | [ko'sa] |
| to mow, to scythe | косити | [ko'siti] |

| spade (tool) | лопата (ж) | [lo'pata] |
| to till (vt) | копати | [ko'pati] |

hoe	сапка (ж)	['sapka]
to hoe, to weed	полоти	[po'loti]
weed (plant)	бур'ян (ч)	[bu'r'jan]

watering can	лійка (ж)	['lijka]
to water (plants)	поливати	[poli'wati]
watering (act)	поливання (с)	[poli'wan'a]

| pitchfork | вила (мн) | ['wila] |
| rake | граблі (мн) | [ɦra'bli] |

fertiliser	добриво (с)	['dobriwo]
to fertilise (vt)	удобрювати	[u'dobr'uwati]
manure (fertiliser)	гній (ч)	[ɦnij]

field	поле (с)	['polɛ]
meadow	лука (ж)	['luka]
vegetable garden	город (ч)	[ɦo'rod]
orchard (e.g. apple ~)	сад (ч)	[sad]

to graze (vt)	пасти	['pasti]
herdsman	пастух (ч)	[pas'tuh]
pasture	пасовище (с)	[paso'wiɕɛ]

| cattle breeding | тваринництво (с) | [twa'rinitstwo] |
| sheep farming | вівчарство (с) | [wiw'ʧarstwo] |

plantation	плантація (ж)	[plan'tatsiʲa]
row (garden bed ~s)	грядка (ж)	['ɦrʲadka]
hothouse	парник (ч)	[par'nɨk]

| drought (lack of rain) | посуха (ж) | ['pɔsuha] |
| dry (~ summer) | посушливий | [po'suʃlɨwɨj] |

| cereal crops | зернові (мн) | [zɛrno'wi] |
| to harvest, to gather | збирати | [zbɨ'ratɨ] |

miller (person)	мірошник (ч)	[mi'rɔʃnɨk]
mill (e.g. gristmill)	млин (ч)	[mlɨn]
to grind (grain)	молотити зерно	[molo'tɨtɨ zɛr'nɔ]
flour	борошно (с)	['bɔroʃno]
straw	солома (ж)	[so'lɔma]

103. Building. Building process

building site	будівництво (с)	[budiw'nɨtstwo]
to build (vt)	будувати	[budu'watɨ]
building worker	будівельник (ч)	[budi'wɛlʲnɨk]

project	проект (ч)	[pro'ɛkt]
architect	архітектор (ч)	[arhi'tɛktor]
worker	робочий (ч)	[ro'bɔʧij]

foundations (of a building)	фундамент (ч)	[fun'damɛnt]
roof	дах (ч)	[dah]
foundation pile	паля (ж)	['palʲa]
wall	стіна (ж)	[sti'na]

| reinforcing bars | арматура (ж) | [arma'tura] |
| scaffolding | риштування (мн) | [riʃtu'wanʲa] |

concrete	бетон (ч)	[bɛ'tɔn]
granite	граніт (ч)	[ɦra'nit]
stone	камінь (ч)	['kaminʲ]
brick	цегла (ж)	['ʦɛɦla]

sand	пісок (ч)	[pi'sɔk]
cement	цемент (ч)	[ʦɛ'mɛnt]
plaster (for walls)	штукатурка (ж)	[ʃtuka'turka]
to plaster (vt)	штукатурити	[ʃtuka'turitɨ]

paint	фарба (ж)	['farba]
to paint (~ a wall)	фарбувати	[farbu'watɨ]
barrel	бочка (ж)	['bɔʧka]

crane	кран (ч)	[kran]
to lift, to hoist (vt)	піднімати	[pidni'matɨ]
to lower (vt)	опускати	[opus'katɨ]

| bulldozer | бульдозер (ч) | [bulʲ'dɔzɛr] |
| excavator | екскаватор (ч) | [ɛkska'wator] |

scoop, bucket	ківш (ч)	[kiwʃ]
to dig (excavate)	копати	[ko'pati]
hard hat	каска (ж)	['kaska]

Professions and occupations

job	робота (ж)	[ro'bota]
staff (work force)	колектив, штат (ч)	[kolɛk'tiw], [ʃtat]
personnel	персонал (ч)	[pɛrso'nal]
career	кар'єра (ж)	[ka'r²ɛra]
prospects (chances)	перспектива (ж)	[pɛrspɛk'tiwa]
skills (mastery)	майстерність (ж)	[majs'tɛrnistʲ]
selection (screening)	підбір (ч)	[pid'bir]
employment agency	кадрове агентство (с)	['kadrowɛ a'ɦɛntstwo]
curriculum vitae, CV	резюме (с)	[rɛzʲu'mɛ]
job interview	співбесіда (ж)	[spiw'bɛsida]
vacancy	вакансія (ж)	[wa'kansiʲa]
salary, pay	зарплатня (ж)	[zarplat'nʲa]
fixed salary	оклад (ч)	[ok'lad]
pay, compensation	оплата (ж)	[op'lata]
position (job)	посада (ж)	[po'sada]
duty (of an employee)	обов'язок (ч)	[o'bow²ʲazok]
range of duties	коло (с)	['kolo]
busy (I'm ~)	зайнятий	['zajnʲatij]
to fire (dismiss)	звільнити	[zwilʲ'niti]
dismissal	звільнення (с)	['zwilʲnɛnʲa]
unemployment	безробіття (с)	[bɛzro'bittʲa]
unemployed (n)	безробітний (ч)	[bɛzro'bitnij]
retirement	пенсія (ж)	['pɛnsiʲa]
to retire (from job)	вийти на пенсію	['wijti na 'pɛnsiʲu]

director	директор (ч)	[di'rɛktor]
manager (director)	управляючий (ч)	[upraw'lʲaʲutʃij]
boss	керівник (ч)	[kɛriw'nik]
superior	начальник (ч)	[na'tʃalʲnik]
superiors	керівництво (с)	[kɛriw'nitstwo]
president	президент (ч)	[prɛzi'dɛnt]
chairman	голова (ч)	[ɦolo'wa]
deputy (substitute)	заступник (ч)	[za'stupnik]
assistant	помічник (ч)	[pomitʃ'nik]

| secretary | секретар (ч) | [sɛkrɛ'tar] |
| personal assistant | особистий секретар (ч) | [oso'bistij sɛkrɛ'tar] |

businessman	бізнесмен (ч)	[biznɛs'mɛn]
entrepreneur	підприємець (ч)	[pidpri'ɛmɛts]
founder	засновник (ч)	[zas'nɔwnik]
to found (vt)	заснувати	[zasnu'wati]

founding member	фундатор (ч)	[fun'dator]
partner	партнер (ч)	[part'nɛr]
shareholder	акціонер (ч)	[aktsio'nɛr]

millionaire	мільйонер (ч)	[miljo'nɛr]
billionaire	мільярдер (ч)	[miljar'dɛr]
owner, proprietor	власник (ч)	['wlasnik]
landowner	землевласник (ч)	[zɛmlɛw'lasnik]

client	клієнт (ч)	[kli'ɛnt]
regular client	постійний клієнт (ч)	[pos'tijnij kli'ɛnt]
buyer (customer)	покупець (ч)	[poku'pɛts]
visitor	відвідувач (ч)	[wid'widuwatʃ]

professional (n)	професіонал (ч)	[profɛsio'nal]
expert	експерт (ч)	[ɛks'pɛrt]
specialist	фахівець (ч)	[fahi'wɛts]

| banker | банкір (ч) | [ba'nkir] |
| broker | брокер (ч) | ['brɔkɛr] |

cashier	касир (ч)	[ka'sir]
accountant	бухгалтер (ч)	[buh'haltɛr]
security guard	охоронник (ч)	[oho'ronik]

investor	інвестор (ч)	[in'wɛstor]
debtor	боржник (ч)	[borʒ'nik]
creditor	кредитор (ч)	[krɛdi'tor]
borrower	боржник (ч)	[borʒ'nik]

| importer | імпортер (ч) | [impor'tɛr] |
| exporter | експортер (ч) | [ɛkspor'tɛr] |

manufacturer	виробник (ч)	[wirob'nik]
distributor	дистриб'ютор (ч)	[distri'b'jutor]
middleman	посередник (ч)	[posɛ'rɛdnik]

consultant	консультант (ч)	[konsul'tant]
sales representative	представник (ч)	[prɛdstaw'nik]
agent	агент (ч)	[a'hɛnt]
insurance agent	страховий агент (ч)	[straho'wij a'hɛnt]

106. Service professions

| cook | кухар (ч) | ['kuhar] |
| chef (kitchen chef) | шеф-кухар (ч) | [ʃɛf 'kuhar] |

baker	пекар (ч)	['pɛkar]
barman	бармен (ч)	[bar'mɛn]
waiter	офіціант (ч)	[ofitsi'ant]
waitress	офіціантка (ж)	[ofitsi'antka]

lawyer, barrister	адвокат (ч)	[adwo'kat]
lawyer (legal expert)	юрист (ч)	[ʲu'rist]
notary public	нотаріус (ч)	[no'tarius]

electrician	електрик (ч)	[ɛ'lɛktrik]
plumber	сантехнік (ч)	[san'tɛhnik]
carpenter	тесля (ч)	['tɛslʲa]

masseur	масажист (ч)	[masa'ʒist]
masseuse	масажистка (ж)	[masa'ʒistka]
doctor	лікар (ч)	['likar]

taxi driver	таксист (ч)	[tak'sist]
driver	шофер (ч)	[ʃo'fɛr]
delivery man	кур'єр (ч)	[ku'rʲɛr]

chambermaid	покоївка (ж)	[poko'ʲiwka]
security guard	охоронник (ч)	[oho'ronik]
flight attendant (fem.)	стюардеса (ж)	[stʲuar'dɛsa]

schoolteacher	вчитель (ч)	['wtʃitɛlʲ]
librarian	бібліотекар (ч)	[biblio'tɛkar]
translator	перекладач (ч)	[pɛrɛkla'datʃ]
interpreter	перекладач (ч)	[pɛrɛkla'datʃ]
guide	гід (ч)	[ɦid]

hairdresser	перукар (ч)	[pɛru'kar]
postman	листоноша (ч)	[listo'noʃa]
salesman (store staff)	продавець (ч)	[proda'wɛts]

gardener	садівник (ч)	[sadiw'nik]
domestic servant	слуга (ч)	[slu'ɦa]
maid (female servant)	служниця (ж)	[sluʒ'nitsʲa]
cleaner (cleaning lady)	прибиральниця (ж)	[pribiʲralʲnitsʲa]

107. Military professions and ranks

private	рядовий (ч)	[rʲado'wij]
sergeant	сержант (ч)	[sɛr'ʒant]
lieutenant	лейтенант (ч)	[lɛjtɛ'nant]
captain	капітан (ч)	[kapi'tan]

major	майор (ч)	[ma'ʲɔr]
colonel	полковник (ч)	[pol'kɔwnik]
general	генерал (ч)	[ɦɛnɛ'ral]
marshal	маршал (ч)	['marʃal]
admiral	адмірал (ч)	[admi'ral]
military (n)	військовий (ч)	[wijsʲʲkɔwij]
soldier	солдат (ч)	[sol'dat]

| officer | офіцер (ч) | [ofi'tsɛr] |
| commander | командир (ч) | [koman'dɨr] |

border guard	прикордонник (ч)	[prɨkor'dɔnɨk]
radio operator	радист (ч)	[ra'dɨst]
scout (searcher)	розвідник (ч)	[roz'widnɨk]
pioneer (sapper)	сапер (ч)	[sa'pɛr]
marksman	стрілок (ч)	[stri'lɔk]
navigator	штурман (ч)	['ʃturman]

108. Officials. Priests

| king | король (ч) | [ko'rɔlʲ] |
| queen | королева (ж) | [koro'lɛwa] |

| prince | принц (ч) | [prɨnts] |
| princess | принцеса (ж) | [prɨn'tsɛsa] |

| czar | цар (ч) | [tsar] |
| czarina | цариця (ж) | [tsa'rɨtsʲa] |

president	президент (ч)	[prɛzɨ'dɛnt]
Secretary (minister)	міністр (ч)	[mi'nistr]
prime minister	прем'єр-міністр (ч)	[prɛ'mʲɛr mi'nistr]
senator	сенатор (ч)	[sɛ'nator]

diplomat	дипломат (ч)	[dɨplo'mat]
consul	консул (ч)	['kɔnsul]
ambassador	посол (ч)	[po'sɔl]
counselor (diplomatic officer)	радник (ч)	['radnɨk]

official, functionary (civil servant)	чиновник (ч)	[tʃɨ'nɔwnɨk]
prefect	префект (ч)	[prɛ'fɛkt]
mayor	мер (ч)	[mɛr]

| judge | суддя (ч) | [sud'dʲa] |
| prosecutor | прокурор (ч) | [proku'rɔr] |

missionary	місіонер (ч)	[misio'nɛr]
monk	чернець (ч)	[tʃɛr'nɛts]
abbot	абат (ч)	[a'bat]
rabbi	рабин (ч)	[ra'bɨn]

vizier	візир (ч)	[wi'zɨr]
shah	шах (ч)	[ʃah]
sheikh	шейх (ч)	[ʃɛjh]

109. Agricultural professions

| beekeeper | пасічник (ч) | ['pasitʃnɨk] |
| shepherd | пастух (ч) | [pas'tuh] |

agronomist	агроном (ч)	[afiro'nɔm]
cattle breeder	тваринник (ч)	[twa'rinik]
veterinary surgeon	ветеринар (ч)	[wɛtɛri'nar]

farmer	фермер (ч)	['fɛrmɛr]
winemaker	винороб (ч)	[wino'rɔb]
zoologist	зоолог (ч)	[zo'ɔlɔfi]
cowboy	ковбой (ч)	[kow'bɔj]

110. Art professions

| actor | актор (ч) | [ak'tɔr] |
| actress | акторка (ж) | [ak'tɔrka] |

| singer (masc.) | співак (ч) | [spi'wak] |
| singer (fem.) | співачка (ж) | [spi'watʃka] |

| dancer (masc.) | танцюрист (ч) | [tantsʲu'rist] |
| dancer (fem.) | танцюристка (ж) | [tantsʲu'ristka] |

| performer (masc.) | артист (ч) | [ar'tist] |
| performer (fem.) | артистка (ж) | [ar'tistka] |

musician	музикант (ч)	[muzi'kant]
pianist	піаніст (ч)	[pia'nist]
guitar player	гітарист (ч)	[fiita'rist]

conductor (orchestra ~)	диригент (ч)	[diri'fiɛnt]
composer	композитор (ч)	[kompo'zitor]
impresario	імпресаріо (ч)	[imprɛ'sario]

film director	режисер (ч)	[rɛʒi'sɛr]
producer	продюсер (ч)	[pro'dʲusɛr]
scriptwriter	сценарист (ч)	[stsɛna'rist]
critic	критик (ч)	['kritik]

writer	письменник (ч)	[pisʲ'mɛnik]
poet	поет (ч)	[po'ɛt]
sculptor	скульптор (ч)	['skulʲptor]
artist (painter)	художник (ч)	[hu'dɔʒnik]

juggler	жонглер (ч)	[ʒonfi'lɛr]
clown	клоун (ч)	['klɔun]
acrobat	акробат (ч)	[akro'bat]
magician	фокусник (ч)	['fɔkusnik]

111. Various professions

doctor	лікар (ч)	['likar]
nurse	медсестра (ж)	[mɛdsɛst'ra]
psychiatrist	психіатр (ч)	[psihi'atr]
dentist	стоматолог (ч)	[stoma'tɔlofi]

surgeon	хірург (ч)	[hi'rurɦ]
astronaut	астронавт (ч)	[astro'nawt]
astronomer	астроном (ч)	[astro'nɔm]

driver (of a taxi, etc.)	водій (ч)	[wo'dij]
train driver	машиніст (ч)	[maʃi'nist]
mechanic	механік (ч)	[mɛ'hanik]

miner	шахтар (ч)	[ʃah'tar]
worker	робочий (ч)	[ro'bɔʧij]
locksmith	слюсар (ч)	['slʲusar]
joiner (carpenter)	столяр (ч)	['stɔlʲar]
turner (lathe operator)	токар (ч)	['tɔkar]
building worker	будівельник (ч)	[budi'wɛlʲnik]
welder	зварник (ч)	['zwarnik]

professor (title)	професор (ч)	[pro'fɛsor]
architect	архітектор (ч)	[arhi'tɛktor]
historian	історик (ч)	[is'tɔrik]
scientist	вчений (ч)	['wʧɛnij]
physicist	фізик (ч)	['fizik]
chemist (scientist)	хімік (ч)	['himik]

archaeologist	археолог (ч)	[arhɛ'ɔloɦ]
geologist	геолог (ч)	[ɦɛ'ɔloɦ]
researcher (scientist)	дослідник (ч)	[do'slidnik]

| babysitter | няня (ж) | ['nʲanʲa] |
| teacher, educator | педагог (ч) | [pɛda'ɦɔɦ] |

editor	редактор (ч)	[rɛ'daktor]
editor-in-chief	головний редактор (ч)	[ɦolow'nij rɛ'daktor]
correspondent	кореспондент (ч)	[korɛspon'dɛnt]
typist (fem.)	машиністка (ж)	[maʃi'nistka]

designer	дизайнер (ч)	[di'zajnɛr]
computer expert	комп'ютерник (ч)	[kom'pʲiutɛrnik]
programmer	програміст (ч)	[proɦ'ramist]
engineer (designer)	інженер (ч)	[inʒɛ'nɛr]

sailor	моряк (ч)	[mo'rʲak]
seaman	матрос (ч)	[mat'rɔs]
rescuer	рятувальник (ч)	[rʲatu'walʲnik]

firefighter	пожежник (ч)	[po'ʒɛʒnik]
police officer	поліцейський (ч)	[poli'tsɛjsʲkij]
watchman	сторож (ч)	['stɔroʒ]
detective	сищик (ч)	['siɕik]

customs officer	митник (ч)	['mitnik]
bodyguard	охоронець (ч)	[oho'rɔnɛts]
prison officer	доглядач (ч)	[doɦlʲa'daʧ]
inspector	інспектор (ч)	[ins'pɛktor]

| sportsman | спортсмен (ч) | [sports'mɛn] |
| trainer, coach | тренер (ч) | ['trɛnɛr] |

butcher	м'ясник (ч)	[mʔjasˈnik]
cobbler (shoe repairer)	чоботар (ч)	[ʧoboˈtar]
merchant	комерсант (ч)	[komɛrˈsant]
loader (person)	вантажник (ч)	[wanˈtaʒnik]

| fashion designer | модельєр (ч) | [modɛˈljɛr] |
| model (fem.) | модель (ж) | [modɛlʲ] |

112. Occupations. Social status

| schoolboy | школяр (ч) | [ʃkoˈlʲar] |
| student (college ~) | студент (ч) | [stuˈdɛnt] |

philosopher	філософ (ч)	[fiˈlɔsof]
economist	економіст (ч)	[ɛkonoˈmist]
inventor	винахідник (ч)	[winaˈhidnik]

unemployed (n)	безробітний (ч)	[bɛzroˈbitnij]
retiree, pensioner	пенсіонер (ч)	[pɛnsioˈnɛr]
spy, secret agent	шпигун (ч)	[ʃpiˈhun]

prisoner	в'язень (ч)	[ˈwʔjazɛnʲ]
striker	страйкар (ч)	[strajˈkar]
bureaucrat	бюрократ (ч)	[bʲuroˈkrat]
traveller (globetrotter)	мандрівник (ч)	[mandriwˈnik]

| gay, homosexual (n) | гомосексуаліст (ч) | [homosɛksuaˈlist] |
| hacker | хакер (ч) | [ˈhakɛr] |

bandit	бандит (ч)	[banˈdit]
hit man, killer	найманий вбивця (ч)	[ˈnajmanij ˈwbiwʦʲa]
drug addict	наркоман (ч)	[narkoˈman]
drug dealer	наркоторгівець (ч)	[narkotorˈhiwɛʦ]
prostitute (fem.)	проститутка (ж)	[prostiˈtutka]
pimp	сутенер (ч)	[sutɛˈnɛr]

sorcerer	чаклун (ч)	[ʧakˈlun]
sorceress (evil ~)	чаклунка (ж)	[ʧakˈlunka]
pirate	пірат (ч)	[piˈrat]
slave	раб (ч)	[rab]
samurai	самурай (ч)	[samuˈraj]
savage (primitive)	дикун (ч)	[diˈkun]

Sports

sportsman	спортсмен (ч)	[sporʦ'mɛn]
kind of sport	вид спорту (ч)	[wɨd 'sportu]
basketball	баскетбол (ч)	[baskɛt'bɔl]
basketball player	баскетболіст (ч)	[baskɛtbo'list]
baseball	бейсбол (ч)	[bɛjs'bɔl]
baseball player	бейсболіст (ч)	[bɛjsbo'list]
football	футбол (ч)	[fut'bɔl]
football player	футболіст (ч)	[futbo'list]
goalkeeper	воротар (ч)	[woro'tar]
ice hockey	хокей (ч)	[ho'kɛj]
ice hockey player	хокеїст (ч)	[hokɛ'jist]
volleyball	волейбол (ч)	[wolɛj'bɔl]
volleyball player	волейболіст (ч)	[wolɛjbo'list]
boxing	бокс (ч)	[boks]
boxer	боксер (ч)	[bok'sɛr]
wrestling	боротьба (ж)	[boroti'ba]
wrestler	борець (ч)	[bo'rɛʦ]
karate	карате (с)	[kara'tɛ]
karate fighter	каратист (ч)	[kara'tist]
judo	дзюдо (с)	[dzʲu'dɔ]
judo athlete	дзюдоїст (ч)	[dzʲudo'jist]
tennis	теніс (ч)	['tɛnis]
tennis player	тенісист (ч)	[tɛni'sist]
swimming	плавання (с)	['plawanʲa]
swimmer	плавець (ч)	[pla'wɛʦ]
fencing	фехтування (с)	[fɛhtu'wanʲa]
fencer	фехтувальник (ч)	[fɛhtu'walʲnɨk]
chess	шахи (мн)	['ʃahɨ]
chess player	шахіст (ч)	[ʃa'hist]
alpinism	альпінізм (ч)	[alʲpi'nizm]
alpinist	альпініст (ч)	[alʲpi'nist]
running	біг (ч)	[biɦ]

runner	бігун (ч)	[bi'ɦun]
athletics	легка атлетика (ж)	[lɛɦ'ka at'lɛtika]
athlete	атлет (ч)	[at'lɛt]
horse riding	кінний спорт (ч)	['kinij 'spɔrt]
horse rider	наїзник (ч)	[na'jiznik]
figure skating	фігурне катання (с)	[fi'ɦurnɛ ka'tanʲa]
figure skater (masc.)	фігурист (ч)	[fiɦu'rist]
figure skater (fem.)	фігуристка (ж)	[fiɦu'ristka]
powerlifting	важка атлетика (ж)	[waʒ'ka at'lɛtika]
car racing	автогонки (мн)	[awto'ɦonki]
racer (driver)	гонщик (ч)	['ɦonɕik]
cycling	велоспорт (ч)	[wɛlo'spɔrt]
cyclist	велосипедист (ч)	[wɛlosipɛ'dist]
long jump	стрибки (мн) в довжину	[strib'ki w dowʒi'nu]
pole vaulting	стрибки (мн) з жердиною	[strib'ki z ʒɛr'dinoʲu]
jumper	стрибун (ч)	[stri'bun]

114. Kinds of sports. Miscellaneous

American football	американський футбол (ч)	[amɛri'kansʲkij fut'bol]
badminton	бадмінтон (ч)	[badmin'tɔn]
biathlon	біатлон (ч)	[biat'lɔn]
billiards	більярд (ч)	[bi'ljard]
bobsleigh	бобслей (ч)	[bob'slɛj]
bodybuilding	бодібілдинг (ч)	[bodi'bildinɦ]
water polo	водне поло (с)	['wɔdnɛ 'pɔlo]
handball	гандбол (ч)	[ɦand'bɔl]
golf	гольф (ч)	[ɦolʲf]
rowing	гребля (ч)	['ɦrɛblʲa]
scuba diving	дайвінг (ч)	['dajwinɦ]
cross-country skiing	лижні гонки (мн)	['liʒni 'ɦonki]
table tennis (ping-pong)	настільний теніс (ч)	[na'stilʲnij 'tɛnis]
sailing	парусний спорт (ч)	['parusnij sport]
rally	ралі (с)	['rali]
rugby	регбі (с)	['rɛɦbi]
snowboarding	сноуборд (ч)	[snou'bɔrd]
archery	стрільба (ж) з луку	[strilʲ'ba z 'luku]

115. Gym

barbell	штанга (ж)	['ʃtanɦa]
dumbbells	гантелі (мн)	[ɦan'tɛli]
training machine	тренажер (ч)	[trɛna'ʒɛr]
exercise bicycle	велотренажер (ч)	[wɛlotrɛna'ʒɛr]

treadmill	бігова доріжка (ж)	[biɦo'wa do'riʒka]
horizontal bar	перекладина (ж)	[pɛrɛk'ladina]
parallel bars	бруси (мн)	['brusi]
vault (vaulting horse)	кінь (ч)	[kinʲ]
mat (exercise ~)	мат (ч)	[mat]
aerobics	аеробіка (ж)	[aɛ'rɔbika]
yoga	йога (ж)	['jɔɦa]

116. Sports. Miscellaneous

Olympic Games	Олімпійські ігри (мн)	[olim'pijsʲki 'iɦri]
winner	переможець (ч)	[pɛrɛ'mɔʒɛts]
to be winning	перемагати	[pɛrɛma'ɦati]
to win (vi)	виграти	['wiɦrati]
leader	лідер (ч)	['lidɛr]
to lead (vi)	лідирувати	[li'diruwati]
first place	перше місце (с)	['pɛrʃɛ 'mistsɛ]
second place	друге місце (с)	['druɦɛ 'mistsɛ]
third place	третє місце (с)	['trɛtɛ 'mistsɛ]
medal	медаль (ж)	[mɛ'dalʲ]
trophy	трофей (ч)	[tro'fɛj]
prize cup (trophy)	кубок (ч)	['kubok]
prize (in game)	приз (ч)	[priz]
main prize	головний приз (ч)	[ɦolow'nij priz]
record	рекорд (ч)	[rɛ'kord]
to set a record	встановлювати рекорд	[wsta'nɔwlʲuwati rɛ'kord]
final	фінал (ч)	[fi'nal]
final (adj)	фінальний	[fi'nalʲnij]
champion	чемпіон (ч)	[tʃɛmpi'ɔn]
championship	чемпіонат (ч)	[tʃɛmpio'nat]
stadium	стадіон (ч)	[stadi'ɔn]
terrace	трибуна (ж)	[tri'buna]
fan, supporter	уболівальник (ч)	[uboli'walʲnik]
opponent, rival	супротивник (ч)	[supro'tiwnik]
start (start line)	старт (ч)	[start]
finish line	фініш (ч)	['finiʃ]
defeat	поразка (ж)	[po'razka]
to lose (not win)	програти	[proɦ'rati]
referee	суддя (ч)	[sud'dʲa]
jury (judges)	журі (с)	[ʒu'ri]
score	рахунок (ч)	[ra'ɦunok]
draw	нічия (ж)	[nitʃi'a]
to draw (vi)	зіграти внічию	[zi'ɦrati wnitʃi'u]

point	**очко** (c)	[oʧ'kɔ]
result (final score)	**результат** (ч)	[rɛzulʲ'tat]
half-time	**перерва** (ж)	[pɛ'rɛrwa]
doping	**допінг** (ч)	['dɔpinɦ]
to penalise (vt)	**штрафувати**	[ʃtrafu'watɨ]
to disqualify (vt)	**дискваліфікувати**	[dɨskwalifiku'watɨ]
apparatus	**снаряд** (ч)	[sna'rʲad]
javelin	**спис** (ч)	[spɨs]
shot (metal ball)	**ядро** (c)	[jad'rɔ]
ball (snooker, etc.)	**куля** (ж)	['kulʲa]
aim (target)	**ціль** (ж)	[ʦilʲ]
target	**мішень** (ж)	[mi'ʃɛnʲ]
to shoot (vi)	**стріляти**	[stri'lʲatɨ]
accurate (~ shot)	**влучний**	['wluʧnɨj]
trainer, coach	**тренер** (ч)	['trɛnɛr]
to train (sb)	**тренувати**	[trɛnu'watɨ]
to train (vi)	**тренуватися**	[trɛnu'watɨsʲa]
training	**тренування** (c)	[trɛnu'wanʲa]
gym	**спортзал** (ч)	[sport'zal]
exercise (physical)	**вправа** (ж)	['wprawa]
warm-up (athlete ~)	**розминка** (ж)	[roz'mɨnka]

Education

school	школа (ж)	['ʃkɔla]
headmaster	директор (ч) школи	[diˈrɛktor ˈʃkɔli]
student (m)	учень (ч)	[ˈutʃɛnʲ]
student (f)	учениця (ж)	[utʃɛˈnitsʲa]
schoolboy	школяр (ч)	[ʃkoˈlʲar]
schoolgirl	школярка (ж)	[ʃkoˈlʲarka]
to teach (sb)	вчити	[ˈwtʃiti]
to learn (language, etc.)	вчити	[ˈwtʃiti]
to learn by heart	вчити напам'ять	[ˈwtʃiti naˈpamʲatʲ]
to learn (~ to count, etc.)	вчитися	[ˈwtʃitisʲa]
to be at school	вчитися	[ˈwtʃitisʲa]
to go to school	йти до школи	[jti do ʃkoli]
alphabet	алфавіт (ч)	[alfaˈwit]
subject (at school)	предмет (ч)	[prɛdˈmɛt]
classroom	клас (ч)	[klas]
lesson	урок (ч)	[uˈrɔk]
playtime, break	перерва (ж)	[pɛˈrɛrwa]
school bell	дзвінок (ч)	[dzwiˈnɔk]
school desk	парта (ж)	[ˈparta]
blackboard	дошка (ж)	[ˈdɔʃka]
mark	відмітка (ж)	[widˈmitka]
good mark	добра оцінка (ж)	[ˈdɔbra oˈtsinka]
bad mark	погана оцінка (ж)	[poˈɦana oˈtsinka]
to give a mark	ставити оцінку	[ˈstawiti oˈtsinku]
mistake, error	помилка (ж)	[poˈmilka]
to make mistakes	робити помилки	[roˈbiti ˈpomilki]
to correct (an error)	виправляти	[wiprawˈlʲati]
crib	шпаргалка (ж)	[ʃparˈɦalka]
homework	домашнє завдання (с)	[doˈmaʃnɛ zawˈdanʲa]
exercise (in education)	вправа (ж)	[ˈwprawa]
to be present	бути присутнім	[ˈbuti priˈsutnim]
to be absent	бути відсутнім	[ˈbuti widˈsutnim]
to punish (vt)	покарати	[pokaˈrati]
punishment	покарання (с)	[pokaˈranʲa]
conduct (behaviour)	поведінка (ж)	[powɛˈdinka]
school report	щоденник (ч)	[ɕoˈdɛnik]

pencil	олівець (ч)	[oli'wɛts]
rubber	гумка (ж)	['ɦumka]
chalk	крейда (ж)	['krɛjda]
pencil case	пенал (ч)	[pɛ'nal]

schoolbag	портфель (ч)	[port'fɛlʲ]
pen	ручка (ж)	['rutʃka]
exercise book	зошит (ч)	['zɔʃit]
textbook	підручник (ч)	[pid'rutʃnik]
compasses	циркуль (ч)	['tsirkulʲ]

| to make technical drawings | креслити | ['krɛsliti] |
| technical drawing | креслення (с) | ['krɛslɛnʲa] |

poem	вірш (ч)	[wirʃ]
by heart (adv)	напам'ять	[na'pamʲatʲ]
to learn by heart	вчити напам'ять	['wtʃiti na'pamʲatʲ]

| school holidays | канікули (мн) | [ka'nikulɨ] |
| to be on holiday | бути на канікулах | ['butɨ na ka'nikulah] |

test (at school)	контрольна робота (ж)	[kon'trolʲna ro'bɔta]
essay (composition)	твір (ч)	[twir]
dictation	диктант (ч)	[dik'tant]

exam (examination)	іспит (ч)	['ispɨt]
to do an exam	складати іспити	[skla'datɨ 'ispiti]
experiment (e.g., chemistry ~)	досвід (ч)	['dɔswid]

118. College. University

academy	академія (ж)	[aka'dɛmiʲa]
university	університет (ч)	[uniwɛrsɨ'tɛt]
faculty (e.g., ~ of Medicine)	факультет (ч)	[fakulʲ'tɛt]

student (masc.)	студент (ч)	[stu'dɛnt]
student (fem.)	студентка (ж)	[stu'dɛntka]
lecturer (teacher)	викладач (ч)	[wikla'datʃ]

| lecture hall, room | аудиторія (ж) | [audɨ'tɔriʲa] |
| graduate | випускник (ч) | [wɨpusk'nik] |

| diploma | диплом (ч) | [dip'lɔm] |
| dissertation | дисертація (ж) | [disɛr'tatsiʲa] |

| study (report) | дослідження (с) | [do'slidʒɛnʲa] |
| laboratory | лабораторія (ж) | [labora'tɔriʲa] |

| lecture | лекція (ж) | ['lɛktsiʲa] |
| coursemate | однокурсник (ч) | [odno'kursnik] |

| scholarship, bursary | стипендія (ж) | [stɨ'pɛndiʲa] |
| academic degree | вчений ступінь (ч) | ['wtʃɛnij 'stupinʲ] |

119. Sciences. Disciplines

mathematics	математика (ж)	[matε'matika]
algebra	алгебра (ж)	['alħεbra]
geometry	геометрія (ж)	[ħεo'mεtriˈa]

astronomy	астрономія (ж)	[astro'nɔmiˈa]
biology	біологія (ж)	[bio'lɔħiˈa]
geography	географія (ж)	[ħεo'ħrafiˈa]
geology	геологія (ж)	[ħεo'lɔħiˈa]
history	історія (ж)	[is'tɔriˈa]

medicine	медицина (ж)	[mεdiˈtsina]
pedagogy	педагогіка (ж)	[pεda'ħɔħika]
law	право (с)	['prawo]

physics	фізика (ж)	['fizika]
chemistry	хімія (ж)	['himiˈa]
philosophy	філософія (ж)	[filo'sɔfiˈa]
psychology	психологія (ж)	[psiho'lɔħiˈa]

120. Writing system. Orthography

grammar	граматика (ж)	[ħra'matika]
vocabulary	лексика (ж)	['lεksika]
phonetics	фонетика (ж)	[fo'nεtika]

noun	іменник (ч)	[i'mεnik]
adjective	прикметник (ч)	[prik'mεtnik]
verb	дієслово (с)	[diε'slowo]
adverb	прислівник (ч)	[pris'liwnik]

pronoun	займенник (ч)	[zaj'mεnik]
interjection	вигук (ч)	['wiħuk]
preposition	прийменник (ч)	[prij'mεnik]

root	корінь (ч) слова	['korinˈ 'slɔwa]
ending	закінчення (с)	[za'kintʃεnˈa]
prefix	префікс (ч)	['prεfiks]
syllable	склад (ч)	['sklad]
suffix	суфікс (ч)	['sufiks]

| stress mark | наголос (ч) | ['naħolos] |
| apostrophe | апостроф (ч) | [a'pɔstrof] |

full stop	крапка (ж)	['krapka]
comma	кома (ж)	['kɔma]
semicolon	крапка (ж) з комою	['krapka z 'kɔmoˈu]
colon	двокрапка (ж)	[dwo'krapka]
ellipsis	крапки (мн)	[krap'ki]

| question mark | знак (ч) питання | [znak pi'tanˈa] |
| exclamation mark | знак (ч) оклику | [znak 'ɔkliku] |

inverted commas	лапки (мн)	[lap'kɨ]
in inverted commas	в лапках	[w lap'kah]
parenthesis	дужки (мн)	[duʒ'kɨ]
in parenthesis	в дужках	[w duʒ'kah]

hyphen	дефіс (ч)	[dɛ'fis]
dash	тире (с)	[ti'rɛ]
space (between words)	пробіл (ч)	[pro'bil]

| letter | літера (ж) | ['litɛra] |
| capital letter | велика літера (ж) | [wɛ'lɨka 'litɛra] |

| vowel (n) | голосний звук (ч) | [ɦolos'nɨj zwuk] |
| consonant (n) | приголосний (ч) | ['priɦolosnɨj] |

sentence	речення (с)	['rɛʧɛnʲa]
subject	підмет (ч)	['pidmɛt]
predicate	присудок (ч)	['prisudok]

line	рядок (ч)	[rʲa'dɔk]
on a new line	с нової стрічки (ж)	[s no'wɔjɨ 'striʧki]
paragraph	абзац (ч)	[ab'zats]

word	слово (с)	['slɔwo]
group of words	словосполучення (с)	[slowospo'luʧɛnʲa]
expression	вислів (ч)	['wisliw]
synonym	синонім (ч)	[sɨ'nɔnim]
antonym	антонім (ч)	[an'tɔnim]

rule	правило (с)	['prawɨlo]
exception	виняток (ч)	['winʲatok]
correct (adj)	вірний	['wirnɨj]

conjugation	дієвідміна (ж)	[diɛwid'mina]
declension	відміна (ж)	[wid'mina]
nominal case	відмінок (ч)	[wid'minok]
question	питання (с)	[pi'tanʲa]
to underline (vt)	підкреслити	[pid'krɛslɨtɨ]
dotted line	пунктир (ч)	[punk'tɨr]

121. Foreign languages

language	мова (ж)	['mɔwa]
foreign language	іноземна мова (ж)	[ino'zɛmna 'mɔwa]
to study (vt)	вивчати	[wiw'ʧatɨ]
to learn (language, etc.)	вчити	['wʧitɨ]

to read (vi, vt)	читати	[ʧi'tatɨ]
to speak (vi, vt)	розмовляти	[rozmow'lʲatɨ]
to understand (vt)	розуміти	[rozu'mitɨ]
to write (vt)	писати	[pi'satɨ]

| fast (adv) | швидко | ['ʃwɨdko] |
| slowly (adv) | повільно | [po'wilʲno] |

fluently (adv)	вільно	['wiľno]
rules	правила (мн)	['prawiła]
grammar	граматика (ж)	[ɦra'matika]
vocabulary	лексика (ж)	['lɛksika]
phonetics	фонетика (ж)	[fo'nɛtika]
textbook	підручник (ч)	[pid'rutʃnik]
dictionary	словник (ч)	[slow'nik]
teach-yourself book	самовчитель (ч)	[samow'tʃitɛľ]
phrasebook	розмовник (ч)	[roz'mɔwnik]
cassette, tape	касета (ж)	[ka'sɛta]
videotape	відеокасета (ж)	['widɛo ka'sɛta]
CD, compact disc	CD-диск (ч)	[si'di disk]
DVD	DVD (ч)	[diwi'di]
alphabet	алфавіт (ч)	[alfa'wit]
to spell (vt)	говорити по буквах	[ɦowo'riti po 'bukwah]
pronunciation	вимова (ж)	[wi'mɔwa]
accent	акцент (ч)	[ak'tsɛnt]
with an accent	з акцентом	[z ak'tsɛntom]
without an accent	без акценту (ч)	[bɛz ak'tsɛntu]
word	слово (с)	['slɔwo]
meaning	сенс (ч)	[sɛns]
course (e.g. a French ~)	курси (мн)	['kursi]
to sign up	записатися	[zapi'satisʲa]
teacher	викладач (ч)	[wikla'datʃ]
translation (process)	переклад (ч)	[pɛ'rɛklad]
translation (text, etc.)	переклад (ч)	[pɛ'rɛklad]
translator	перекладач (ч)	[pɛrɛkla'datʃ]
interpreter	перекладач (ч)	[pɛrɛkla'datʃ]
polyglot	поліглот (ч)	[poliɦ'lɔt]
memory	пам'ять (ж)	['pamʲatʲ]

122. Fairy tale characters

Father Christmas	Санта Клаус (ч)	['santa 'klaus]
mermaid	русалка (ж)	[ru'salka]
magician, wizard	чарівник (ч)	[tʃariw'nik]
fairy	чарівниця (ж)	[tʃariw'nitsʲa]
magic (adj)	чарівний	[tʃariw'nij]
magic wand	чарівна паличка (ж)	[tʃa'riwna 'palitʃka]
fairy tale	казка (ж)	['kazka]
miracle	диво (с)	['diwo]
dwarf	гном (ч)	[ɦnom]
to turn into ...	перетворитися на	[pɛrɛtwo'ritisʲa na]
ghost	привид (ч)	['priwid]

phantom	примара (ж)	[pri'mara]
monster	чудовисько (с)	[ʧu'dɔwisko]
dragon	дракон (ч)	[dra'kɔn]
giant	велетень (ч)	['wɛlɛtɛnʲ]

123. Zodiac Signs

Aries	Овен (ч)	['ɔwɛn]
Taurus	Тілець (ч)	[ti'lɛts]
Gemini	Близнюки (мн)	[bliznʲu'kɨ]
Cancer	Рак (ч)	[rak]
Leo	Лев (ч)	[lɛw]
Virgo	Діва (ж)	['diwa]

Libra	Терези (мн)	[tɛrɛ'zɨ]
Scorpio	Скорпіон (ч)	[skorpi'ɔn]
Sagittarius	Стрілець (ч)	[stri'lɛts]
Capricorn	Козерог (ч)	[kozɛ'rɔɦ]
Aquarius	Водолій (ч)	[wodo'lij]
Pisces	Риби (мн)	['rɨbɨ]

character	характер (ч)	[ha'raktɛr]
character traits	риси (мн) характеру	['rɨsɨ ha'raktɛru]
behaviour	поведінка (ж)	[powɛ'dinka]
to tell fortunes	ворожити	[woro'ʒɨtɨ]
fortune-teller	гадалка (ж)	[ɦa'dalka]
horoscope	гороскоп (ч)	[ɦoro'skɔp]

Arts

theatre	театр (ч)	[tɛ'atr]
opera	опера (ж)	['ɔpɛra]
operetta	оперета (ж)	[opɛ'rɛta]
ballet	балет (ч)	[ba'lɛt]
theatre poster	афіша (ж)	[a'fiʃa]
theatre company	трупа (ж)	['trupa]
tour	гастролі (мн)	[ɦa'strɔli]
to be on tour	гастролювати	[ɦastrolʲu'wati]
to rehearse (vi, vt)	репетирувати	[rɛpɛ'tiruwati]
rehearsal	репетиція (ж)	[rɛpɛ'titsiʲa]
repertoire	репертуар (ч)	[rɛpɛrtu'ar]
performance	вистава (ж)	[wis'tawa]
theatrical show	спектакль (ч)	[spɛk'taklʲ]
play	п'єса (ж)	['p'ɛsa]
ticket	квиток (ч)	[kwi'tɔk]
booking office	квиткова каса (ж)	[kwit'kowa 'kasa]
lobby, foyer	хол (ч)	[hol]
coat check (cloakroom)	гардероб (ж)	[ɦardɛ'rɔb]
cloakroom ticket	номерок (ч)	[nomɛ'rɔk]
binoculars	бінокль (ч)	[bi'nɔklʲ]
usher	контролер (ч)	[kontro'lɛr]
stalls (orchestra seats)	партер (ч)	[par'tɛr]
balcony	балкон (ч)	[bal'kɔn]
dress circle	бельетаж (ч)	[bɛlʲʲɛ'taʒ]
box	ложа (ж)	['lɔʒa]
row	ряд (ч)	[rʲad]
seat	місце (с)	['mistsɛ]
audience	публіка (ж)	['publika]
spectator	глядач (ч)	[ɦlʲa'datʃ]
to clap (vi, vt)	плескати	[plɛs'kati]
applause	аплодисменти (мн)	[aplodis'mɛnti]
ovation	овації (мн)	[o'watsiji]
stage	сцена (ж)	['stsɛna]
curtain	завіса (ж)	[za'wisa]
scenery	декорація (ж)	[dɛko'ratsiʲa]
backstage	куліси (мн)	[ku'lisi]
scene (e.g. the last ~)	дія (ж)	['diʲa]
act	акт (ч)	[akt]
interval	антракт (ч)	[an'trakt]

125. Cinema

actor	актор (ч)	[ak'tɔr]
actress	акторка (ж)	[ak'tɔrka]
film	кіно (с)	[ki'nɔ]
episode	серія (ж)	['sɛriʲa]
detective film	детектив (ч)	[dɛtɛk'tiw]
action film	бойовик (ч)	[boʲo'wik]
adventure film	пригодницький фільм (ч)	[pri'ɦɔdnitskij filʲm]
science fiction film	фантастичний фільм (ч)	[fantas'titʃnij filʲm]
horror film	фільм (ч) жахів	[filʲm 'ʒahiw]
comedy film	кінокомедія (ж)	[kinoko'mɛdiʲa]
melodrama	мелодрама (ж)	[mɛlod'rama]
drama	драма (ж)	['drama]
fictional film	художній фільм (ч)	[hu'dɔʒnij filʲm]
documentary	документальний фільм (ч)	[dokumɛn'talʲnij filʲm]
cartoon	мультфільм (ч)	[mulʲt'filʲm]
silent films	німе кіно (с)	[ni'mɛ ki'nɔ]
role (part)	роль (ж)	[rolʲ]
leading role	головна роль (ж)	[ɦolow'na rolʲ]
to play (vi, vt)	грати	['ɦrati]
film star	кінозірка (ж)	[kino'zirka]
well-known (adj)	відомий	[wi'dɔmij]
famous (adj)	відомий	[wi'dɔmij]
popular (adj)	популярний	[popu'lʲarnij]
script (screenplay)	сценарій (ч)	[stsɛ'narij]
scriptwriter	сценарист (ч)	[stsɛna'rist]
film director	режисер (ч)	[rɛʒi'sɛr]
producer	продюсер (ч)	[pro'dʲusɛr]
assistant	асистент (ч)	[asis'tɛnt]
cameraman	оператор (ч)	[opɛ'rator]
stuntman	каскадер (ч)	[kaska'dɛr]
to shoot a film	знімати фільм	[zni'mati filʲm]
audition, screen test	проби (мн)	['prɔbi]
shooting	зйомки (мн)	['zʲɔmki]
film crew	знімальна група (ж)	[zni'malʲna 'ɦrupa]
film set	знімальний майданчик (ч)	[zni'malʲnij maj'dantʃik]
camera	кінокамера (ж)	[kino'kamɛra]
cinema	кінотеатр (ч)	[kinotɛ'atr]
screen (e.g. big ~)	екран (ч)	[ɛk'ran]
to show a film	показувати фільм	[po'kazuwati filʲm]
soundtrack	звукова доріжка (ж)	[zwuko'wa do'riʒka]
special effects	спеціальні ефекти (мн)	[spɛtsi'alʲni ɛ'fɛkti]
subtitles	субтитри (мн)	[sub'titri]
credits	титри (мн)	['titri]
translation	переклад (ч)	[pɛ'rɛklad]

126. Painting

art	мистецтво (c)	[mis'tɛtstwo]
fine arts	образотворчі мистецтва (мн)	[obrazot'wortʃi mis'tɛtstwa]
art gallery	галерея (ж)	[ɦalɛ'rɛʲa]
art exhibition	виставка (ж) картин	['wistawka kar'tin]
painting (art)	живопис (ч)	[ʒi'wopis]
graphic art	графіка (ж)	['ɦrafika]
abstract art	абстракціонізм (ч)	[abstraktsio'nizm]
impressionism	імпресіонізм (ч)	[imprɛsio'nizm]
picture (painting)	картина (ж)	[kar'tina]
drawing	малюнок (ч)	[ma'lʲunok]
poster	плакат (ч)	[pla'kat]
illustration (picture)	ілюстрація (ж)	[ilʲust'ratsiʲa]
miniature	мініатюра (ж)	[minia'tʲura]
copy (of painting, etc.)	копія (ж)	['kopiʲa]
reproduction	репродукція (ж)	[rɛpro'duktsiʲa]
mosaic	мозаїка (ж)	[mo'zajika]
stained glass window	вітраж (ч)	[wit'raʒ]
fresco	фреска (ж)	['frɛska]
engraving	гравюра (ж)	[ɦra'wʲura]
bust (sculpture)	бюст (ч)	[bʲust]
sculpture	скульптура (ж)	[skulʲp'tura]
statue	статуя (ж)	['statuʲa]
plaster of Paris	гіпс (ч)	[ɦips]
plaster (as adj)	з гіпсу	[z 'ɦipsu]
portrait	портрет (ч)	[port'rɛt]
self-portrait	автопортрет (ч)	[awtopor'trɛt]
landscape painting	пейзаж (ч)	[pɛj'zaʒ]
still life	натюрморт (ч)	[natʲur'mort]
caricature	карикатура (ж)	[karika'tura]
sketch	нарис (ч)	['naris]
paint	фарба (ж)	['farba]
watercolor paint	акварель (ж)	[akwa'rɛlʲ]
oil (paint)	масло (c)	['maslo]
pencil	олівець (ч)	[oli'wɛts]
Indian ink	туш (ж)	[tuʃ]
charcoal	вугілля (c)	[wu'ɦilʲa]
to draw (vi, vt)	малювати	[malʲu'wati]
to paint (vi, vt)	малювати	[malʲu'wati]
to pose (vi)	позувати	[pozu'wati]
artist's model (masc.)	натурник (ч)	[na'turnik]
artist's model (fem.)	натурниця (ж)	[na'turnitsʲa]
artist (painter)	художник (ч)	[hu'doʒnik]
work of art	витвір (ч)	['witwir]

| masterpiece | шедевр (ч) | [ʃɛ'dɛwr] |
| studio (artist's workroom) | майстерня (ж) | [majs'tɛrnʲa] |

canvas (cloth)	полотно (с)	[polot'nɔ]
easel	мольберт (ч)	[molʲ'bɛrt]
palette	палітра (ж)	[pa'litra]

frame (picture ~, etc.)	рама (ж)	['rama]
restoration	реставрація (ж)	[rɛstaw'ratsiʲa]
to restore (vt)	реставрувати	[rɛstawru'watɨ]

127. Literature & Poetry

literature	література (ж)	[litɛra'tura]
author (writer)	автор (ч)	['awtor]
pseudonym	псевдонім (ч)	[psɛwdo'nim]

book	книга (ж)	['knɨɦa]
volume	видання (с)	[wɨda'nʲa]
table of contents	зміст (ч)	[zmist]
page	сторінка (ж)	[sto'rinka]
main character	головний герой (ч)	[ɦolow'nɨj ɦɛ'rɔj]
autograph	автограф (ч)	[aw'tɔɦraf]

short story	оповідання (с)	[opowi'danʲa]
story (novella)	повість (ж)	['pɔwistʲ]
novel	роман (ч)	[ro'man]
work (writing)	твір (ч)	[twir]
fable	байка (ж)	['bajka]
detective novel	детектив (ч)	[dɛtɛk'tɨw]

poem (verse)	вірш (ч)	[wirʃ]
poetry	поезія (ж)	[po'ɛziʲa]
poem (epic, ballad)	поема (ж)	[po'ɛma]
poet	поет (ч)	[po'ɛt]

fiction	белетристика (ж)	[bɛlɛt'rɨstɨka]
science fiction	наукова фантастика (ж)	[nau'kɔwa fan'tastɨka]
adventures	пригоди (мн)	[prɨ'ɦɔdɨ]
educational literature	учбова література (ж)	[utʃ'bɔwa litɛra'tura]
children's literature	дитяча література (ж)	[dɨ'tʲatʃa litɛra'tura]

128. Circus

circus	цирк (ч)	[tsɨrk]
travelling circus	цирк-шапіто (ч)	[tsɨrk ʃapi'tɔ]
programme	програма (ж)	[proɦ'rama]
performance	вистава (ж)	[wɨs'tawa]

act (circus ~)	номер (ч)	['nɔmɛr]
circus ring	арена (ж)	[a'rɛna]
pantomime (act)	пантоміма (ж)	[panto'mima]

clown	клоун (ч)	['kloun]
acrobat	акробат (ч)	[akro'bat]
acrobatics	акробатика (ж)	[akro'batika]
gymnast	гімнаст (ч)	[ɦim'nast]
acrobatic gymnastics	гімнастика (ж)	[ɦim'nastika]
somersault	сальто (с)	['salʲto]
strongman	атлет (ч)	[at'lɛt]
tamer (e.g., lion ~)	приборкувач (ч)	[prɨ'borkuwatʃ]
rider (circus horse ~)	наїзник (ч)	[na'jiznɨk]
assistant	асистент (ч)	[asɨs'tɛnt]
stunt	трюк (ч)	[trʲuk]
magic trick	фокус (ч)	['fokus]
conjurer, magician	фокусник (ч)	['fokusnɨk]
juggler	жонглер (ч)	[ʒonɦ'lɛr]
to juggle (vi, vt)	жонглювати	[ʒonɦlʲu'watɨ]
animal trainer	дресирувальник (ч)	[drɛsiru'walʲnɨk]
animal training	дресура (ж)	[drɛ'sura]
to train (animals)	дресирувати	[drɛsiru'watɨ]

129. Music. Pop music

music	музика (ж)	['muzɨka]
musician	музикант (ч)	[muzi'kant]
musical instrument	музичний інструмент (ч)	[mu'zɨtʃnɨj instru'mɛnt]
to play …	грати на …	['ɦratɨ na]
guitar	гітара (ж)	[ɦi'tara]
violin	скрипка (ж)	['skrɨpka]
cello	віолончель (ж)	[wiolon'tʃɛlʲ]
double bass	контрабас (ч)	[kontra'bas]
harp	арфа (ж)	['arfa]
piano	піаніно (с)	[pia'nino]
grand piano	рояль (ч)	[ro'ʲalʲ]
organ	орган (ч)	[or'ɦan]
wind instruments	духові інструменти (мн)	[duho'wi instru'mɛnti]
oboe	гобой (ч)	[ɦo'boj]
saxophone	саксофон (ч)	[sakso'fon]
clarinet	кларнет (ч)	[klar'nɛt]
flute	флейта (ж)	['flɛjta]
trumpet	труба (ж)	[tru'ba]
accordion	акордеон (ч)	[akordɛ'on]
drum	барабан (ч)	[bara'ban]
duo	дует (ч)	[du'ɛt]
trio	тріо (с)	['trio]
quartet	квартет (ч)	[kwar'tɛt]
choir	хор (ч)	[hor]
orchestra	оркестр (ч)	[or'kɛstr]

pop music	поп-музика (ж)	[pop 'muzɨka]
rock music	рок-музика (ж)	[rok 'muzɨka]
rock group	рок-група (ж)	[rok 'ɦrupa]
jazz	джаз (ч)	[dʒaz]

| idol | кумир (ч) | [ku'mɨr] |
| admirer, fan | шанувальник (ч) | [ʃanu'walʲnik] |

concert	концерт (ч)	[kon'ʦɛrt]
symphony	симфонія (ж)	[sɨm'fɔniʲa]
composition	твір (ч)	[twir]
to compose (write)	створити	[stwo'rɨtɨ]

singing (n)	спів (ч)	[spiw]
song	пісня (ж)	['pisnʲa]
tune (melody)	мелодія (ж)	[mɛ'lɔdiʲa]
rhythm	ритм (ч)	[rɨtm]
blues	блюз (ч)	[blʲuz]

sheet music	ноти (мн)	['nɔtɨ]
baton	паличка (ж)	['palɨʧka]
bow	смичок (ч)	[smɨ'ʧɔk]
string	струна (ж)	[stru'na]
case (e.g. guitar ~)	футляр (ч)	[fut'lʲar]

Rest. Entertainment. Travel

130. Trip. Travel

tourism, travel	туризм (ч)	[tu'rizm]
tourist	турист (ч)	[tu'rist]
trip, voyage	мандрівка (ж)	[mand'riwka]
adventure	пригода (ж)	[pri'ɦɔda]
trip, journey	поїздка (ж)	[po'jizdka]
holiday	відпустка (ж)	[wid'pustka]
to be on holiday	бути у відпустці	['butɨ u wid'pusttsi]
rest	відпочинок (ч)	[widpo'tʃɨnok]
train	поїзд (ч)	['pɔjizd]
by train	поїздом	['pɔjizdom]
aeroplane	літак (ч)	[li'tak]
by aeroplane	літаком	[lita'kɔm]
by car	автомобілем	[awtomo'bilɛm]
by ship	кораблем	[korab'lɛm]
luggage	багаж (ч)	[ba'ɦaʒ]
suitcase	валіза (ж)	[wa'liza]
luggage trolley	візок (ч) для багажу	[wi'zɔk dlʲa baɦa'ʒu]
passport	паспорт (ч)	['pasport]
visa	віза (ж)	['wiza]
ticket	квиток (ч)	[kwi'tɔk]
air ticket	авіаквиток (ч)	[awiakwi'tɔk]
guidebook	путівник (ч)	[putiw'nik]
map (tourist ~)	карта (ж)	['karta]
area (rural ~)	місцевість (ж)	[mis'tsɛwistʲ]
place, site	місце (с)	['mistsɛ]
exotica (n)	екзотика (ж)	[ɛk'zɔtika]
exotic (adj)	екзотичний	[ɛkzo'titʃnij]
amazing (adj)	дивовижний	['diwowiʒnij]
group	група (ж)	['ɦrupa]
excursion, sightseeing tour	екскурсія (ж)	[ɛks'kursiʲa]
guide (person)	екскурсовод (ч)	[ɛkskurso'wɔd]

131. Hotel

hotel	готель (ч)	[ɦo'tɛlʲ]
motel	мотель (ч)	[mo'tɛlʲ]
three-star (~ hotel)	три зірки	[tri 'zirkɨ]

five-star	п'ять зірок	[pˀjatˌ ziˈrɔk]
to stay (in a hotel, etc.)	зупинитися	[zupiˈnitisˌa]
room	номер (ч)	[ˈnɔmɛr]
single room	одномісний номер (ч)	[odnoˈmisnij nomɛr]
double room	двомісний номер (ч)	[dwoˈmisnij ˈnɔmɛr]
to book a room	резервувати номер	[rɛzɛrwuˈwatɪ ˈnɔmɛr]
half board	напівпансіон (ч)	[napiwpansiˈɔn]
full board	повний пансіон (ч)	[ˈpownij pansiˈɔn]
with bath	з ванною	[z ˈwanoˌu]
with shower	з душем	[z ˈduʃɛm]
satellite television	супутникове телебачення (с)	[suˈputnɪkowɛ tɛlɛˈbatʃɛnˌa]
air-conditioner	кондиціонер (ч)	[kondɪtsioˈnɛr]
towel	рушник (ч)	[ruʃˈnɪk]
key	ключ (ч)	[klˌutʃ]
administrator	адміністратор (ч)	[adminiˈstrator]
chambermaid	покоївка (ж)	[pokoˈjiwka]
porter	носильник (ч)	[noˈsɪlˌnɪk]
doorman	портьє (ч)	[porˈtˌɛ]
restaurant	ресторан (ч)	[rɛstoˈran]
pub, bar	бар (ч)	[bar]
breakfast	сніданок (ч)	[sniˈdanok]
dinner	вечеря (ж)	[wɛˈtʃɛrˌa]
buffet	шведський стіл (ч)	[ˈʃwɛdsˌkij stil]
lobby	вестибюль (ч)	[wɛstiˈbˌulˌ]
lift	ліфт (ч)	[lift]
DO NOT DISTURB	НЕ ТУРБУВАТИ	[nɛ turbuˈwatɪ]
NO SMOKING	ПАЛИТИ ЗАБОРОНЕНО	[paˈlɪtɪ zaboˈrɔnɛno]

132. Books. Reading

book	книга (ж)	[ˈknɪɦa]
author	автор (ч)	[ˈawtor]
writer	письменник (ч)	[pɪsˌˈmɛnɪk]
to write (~ a book)	написати	[napɪˈsatɪ]
reader	читач (ч)	[tʃiˈtatʃ]
to read (vi, vt)	читати	[tʃiˈtati]
reading (activity)	читання (с)	[tʃiˈtanˌa]
silently (to oneself)	про себе	[pro ˈsɛbɛ]
aloud (adv)	вголос	[ˈwɦɔlos]
to publish (vt)	видавати	[wɪdaˈwatɪ]
publishing (process)	примірник (ч)	[prɪˈmirnɪk]
publisher	видавець (ч)	[wɪdaˈwɛts]
publishing house	видавництво (с)	[wɪdawˈnɪtstwo]

to come out (be released)	вийти	['wijti]
release (of a book)	вихід (ч)	['wihid]
print run	наклад (ч)	['naklad]
bookshop	книгарня (ж)	[kni'harnʲa]
library	бібліотека (ж)	[biblio'tɛka]
story (novella)	повість (ж)	['powistʲ]
short story	оповідання (с)	[opowi'danʲa]
novel	роман (ч)	[ro'man]
detective novel	детектив (ч)	[dɛtɛk'tiw]
memoirs	мемуари (мн)	[mɛmu'ari]
legend	легенда (ж)	[lɛ'hɛnda]
myth	міф (ч)	[mif]
poetry, poems	вірші (мн)	['wirʃi]
autobiography	автобіографія (ж)	[awtobio'hrafiʲa]
selected works	вибране (с)	['wibranɛ]
science fiction	фантастика (ж)	[fan'tastika]
title	назва (ж)	['nazwa]
introduction	вступ (ч)	[wstup]
title page	титульна сторінка (ж)	['titulʲna sto'rinka]
chapter	розділ (ч)	['rɔzdil]
extract	уривок (ч)	[u'riwok]
episode	епізод (ч)	[ɛpi'zɔd]
plot (storyline)	сюжет (ч)	[sʲu'ʒɛt]
contents	зміст (ч)	[zmist]
table of contents	зміст (ч)	[zmist]
main character	головний герой (ч)	[holow'nij hɛ'rɔj]
volume	том (ч)	[tom]
cover	обкладинка (ж)	[ob'kladinka]
binding	палітура (ж)	[pali'tura]
bookmark	закладка (ж)	[za'kladka]
page	сторінка (ж)	[sto'rinka]
to page through	гортати	[hor'tati]
margins	поля (мн)	[po'lʲa]
annotation (marginal note, etc.)	позначка (ж)	['pɔznatʃka]
footnote	примітка (ж)	[pri'mitka]
text	текст (ч)	[tɛkst]
type, fount	шрифт (ч)	[ʃrift]
misprint, typo	помилка (ж)	[po'milka]
translation	переклад (ч)	[pɛ'rɛklad]
to translate (vt)	перекладати	[pɛrɛkla'dati]
original (n)	оригінал (ч)	[orihi'nal]
famous (adj)	відомий	[wi'dɔmij]
unknown (not famous)	невідомий	[nɛwi'dɔmij]

| interesting (adj) | цікавий | [tsi'kawij] |
| bestseller | бестселер (ч) | [bɛst'sɛlɛr] |

dictionary	словник (ч)	[slow'nik]
textbook	підручник (ч)	[pid'rutʃnik]
encyclopedia	енциклопедія (ж)	[ɛntsiklo'pɛdi'a]

133. Hunting. Fishing

hunting	полювання (с)	[pol'u'wan'a]
to hunt (vi, vt)	полювати	[pol'u'wati]
hunter	мисливець (ч)	[mis'liwɛts]

to shoot (vi)	стріляти	[stri'l'ati]
rifle	рушниця (ж)	[ruʃ'nits'a]
bullet (shell)	патрон (ч)	[pat'rɔn]
shot (lead balls)	шріт (ч)	[ʃrit]

steel trap	капкан (ч)	[kap'kan]
snare (for birds, etc.)	пастка (ж)	['pastka]
to lay a steel trap	ставити пастку	['stawiti 'pastku]

poacher	браконьєр (ч)	[brako'n'ɛr]
game (in hunting)	дичина (ж)	[ditʃi'na]
hound dog	мисливський пес (ч)	[mis'liws'kij pɛs]
safari	сафарі (с)	[sa'fari]
mounted animal	опудало (с)	[o'pudalo]

fisherman	рибалка (ч)	[ri'balka]
fishing (angling)	риболовля (ж)	[ribo'lowl'a]
to fish (vi)	ловити рибу	[lo'witi 'ribu]

fishing rod	вудочка (ж)	['wudotʃka]
fishing line	волосінь (ж)	[wolo'sin']
hook	гачок (ч)	[ɦa'tʃok]
float	поплавець (ч)	[popla'wɛts]
bait	наживка (ж)	[na'ʒiwka]

| to cast a line | закинути вудочку | [za'kinuti 'wudotʃku] |
| to bite (ab. fish) | клювати | [kl'u'wati] |

| catch (of fish) | улов (ч) | [u'lɔw] |
| ice-hole | ополонка (ж) | [opo'lɔnka] |

fishing net	сітка (ж)	['sitka]
boat	човен (ч)	['tʃɔwɛn]
to net (to fish with a net)	ловити	[lo'witi]

| to cast[throw] the net | закидати сіті | [zaki'dati 'siti] |
| to haul the net in | витягати сіті | [wit'a'ɦati 'siti] |

whaler (person)	китобій (ч)	[kito'bij]
whaleboat	китобійне судно (с)	[kito'bijnɛ 'sudno]
harpoon	гарпун (ч)	[ɦar'pun]

134. Games. Billiards

billiards	більярд (ч)	[bi'ljard]
billiard room, hall	більярдна (ж)	[bi'ljardna]
ball (snooker, etc.)	більярдна куля (ж)	[bi'ljardna 'kulʲa]
to pocket a ball	загнати кулю	[za'ɦnatɨ 'kulʲu]
cue	кий (ч)	[kɨj]
pocket	луза (ж)	['luza]

135. Games. Playing cards

diamonds	бубни (мн)	['bubnɨ]
spades	піки (мн)	['pikɨ]
hearts	черви (мн)	['tʃɛrwɨ]
clubs	трефи (мн)	['trɛfɨ]
ace	туз (ч)	[tuz]
king	король (ч)	[ko'rɔlʲ]
queen	дама (ж)	['dama]
jack, knave	валет (ч)	[wa'lɛt]
playing card	карта (ж)	['karta]
cards	карти (мн)	['kartɨ]
trump	козир (ч)	['kɔzɨr]
pack of cards	колода (ж)	[ko'lɔda]
to deal (vi, vt)	здавати	[zda'watɨ]
to shuffle (cards)	тасувати	[tasu'watɨ]
lead, turn (n)	хід (ч)	[hid]
cardsharp	шулер (ч)	['ʃulɛr]

136. Rest. Games. Miscellaneous

to stroll (vi, vt)	прогулюватися	[pro'ɦulʲuwatɨsʲa]
stroll (leisurely walk)	прогулянка (ж)	[pro'ɦulʲanka]
car ride	поїздка (ж)	[po'jizdka]
adventure	пригода (ж)	[pri'ɦɔda]
picnic	пікнік (ч)	[pik'nik]
game (chess, etc.)	гра (ж)	[ɦra]
player	гравець (ч)	[ɦra'wɛts]
game (one ~ of chess)	партія (ж)	['partiʲa]
collector (e.g. philatelist)	колекціонер (ч)	[kolɛktsio'nɛr]
to collect (stamps, etc.)	колекціонувати	[kolɛktsionu'watɨ]
collection	колекція (ж)	[ko'lɛktsiʲa]
crossword puzzle	кросворд (ч)	[kros'wɔrd]
racecourse (hippodrome)	іподром (ч)	[ipod'rɔm]
disco (discotheque)	дискотека (ж)	[dɨsko'tɛka]

| sauna | сауна (ж) | ['sauna] |
| lottery | лотерея (ж) | [lotɛ'rɛʲa] |

camping trip	похід (ч)	[po'hid]
camp	табір (ч)	['tabir]
tent (for camping)	намет (ч)	[na'mɛt]
compass	компас (ч)	['kɔmpas]
camper	турист (ч)	[tu'rist]

to watch (film, etc.)	дивитися	[di'witisʲa]
viewer	телеглядач (ч)	[tɛlɛhlʲa'datʃ]
TV show (TV program)	телепередача (ж)	['tɛlɛ pɛrɛ'datʃa]

137. Photography

| camera (photo) | фотоапарат (ч) | [fotoapa'rat] |
| photo, picture | фото (с) | ['fɔto] |

photographer	фотограф (ч)	[fo'tɔhraf]
photo studio	фотостудія (ж)	[foto'studiʲa]
photo album	фотоальбом (ч)	[fotoalʲ'bɔm]

camera lens	об'єктив (ч)	[ob'ɛk'tiw]
telephoto lens	телеоб'єктив (ч)	[tɛlɛob'ɛk'tiw]
filter	фільтр (ч)	['filʲtr]
lens	лінза (ж)	['linza]

optics (high-quality ~)	оптика (ж)	['ɔptika]
diaphragm (aperture)	діафрагма (ж)	[dia'frahma]
exposure time (shutter speed)	витримка (ж)	['witrimka]
viewfinder	видошукач (ч)	[widoʃu'katʃ]

digital camera	цифрова камера (ж)	[tsifro'wa 'kamɛra]
tripod	штатив (ч)	[ʃta'tiw]
flash	спалах (ч)	['spalah]

to photograph (vt)	фотографувати	[fotohrafu'wati]
to take pictures	знімати	[zni'mati]
to have one's picture taken	фотографуватися	[fotohrafu'watisʲa]

focus	різкість (ж)	['rizkistʲ]
to focus	наводити різкість	[na'woditi 'rizkistʲ]
sharp, in focus (adj)	різкий	[riz'kij]
sharpness	різкість (ж)	['rizkistʲ]

| contrast | контраст (ч) | [kon'trast] |
| contrast (as adj) | контрастний | [kon'trastnij] |

picture (photo)	знімок (ч)	['znimok]
negative (n)	негатив (ч)	[nɛha'tiw]
film (a roll of ~)	фотоплівка (ж)	[foto'pliwka]
frame (still)	кадр (ч)	[kadr]
to print (photos)	друкувати	[druku'wati]

138. Beach. Swimming

beach	пляж (ч)	[pl'aʒ]
sand	пісок (ч)	[pi'sɔk]
deserted (beach)	пустельний	[pus'tɛl'nij]
suntan	засмага (ж)	[zas'maɦa]
to get a tan	засмагати	[zasma'ɦati]
tanned (adj)	засмаглий	[zas'maɦlij]
sunscreen	крем (ч) для засмаги	[krɛm dl'a zas'maɦi]
bikini	бікіні (мн)	[bi'kini]
swimsuit, bikini	купальник (ч)	[ku'pal'nik]
swim trunks	плавки (мн)	['plawki]
swimming pool	басейн (ч)	[ba'sɛjn]
to swim (vi)	плавати	['plawati]
shower	душ (ч)	[duʃ]
to change (one's clothes)	перевдягатися	[pɛrɛwd'a'ɦatis'a]
towel	рушник (ч)	[ruʃ'nik]
boat	човен (ч)	['ʧɔwɛn]
motorboat	катер (ч)	['katɛr]
water ski	водяні лижі (мн)	[wod'a'ni 'liʒi]
pedalo	водяний велосипед (ч)	[wod'a'nij wɛlosi'pɛd]
surfing	серфінг (ч)	['sɛrfinɦ]
surfer	серфінгіст (ч)	[sɛrfi'nɦist]
scuba set	акваланг (ч)	[akwa'lanɦ]
flippers (swim fins)	ласти (мн)	['lasti]
mask (diving ~)	маска (ж)	['maska]
diver	нирець (ч)	[ni'rɛʦ]
to dive (vi)	пірнати	[pir'nati]
underwater (adv)	під водою	[pid wo'dɔ'u]
beach umbrella	парасолька (ж)	[para'sɔl'ka]
beach chair (sun lounger)	шезлонг (ч)	[ʃɛz'lonɦ]
sunglasses	окуляри (мн)	[oku'l'ari]
air mattress	плавальний матрац (ч)	['plawal'nij mat'raʦ]
to play (amuse oneself)	грати	['ɦrati]
to go for a swim	купатися	[ku'patis'a]
beach ball	м'яч (ч)	[mʔ'aʧ]
to inflate (vt)	надувати	[nadu'wati]
inflatable, air (adj)	надувний	[naduw'nij]
wave	хвиля (ж)	['hwil'a]
buoy (line of ~s)	буй (ч)	[buj]
to drown (ab. person)	тонути	[to'nuti]
to save, to rescue	рятувати	[r'atu'wati]
life jacket	рятувальний жилет (ч)	[r'atu'wal'nij ʒi'lɛt]
to observe, to watch	спостерігати	[spostɛri'ɦati]
lifeguard	рятувальник (ч)	[r'atu'wal'nik]

TECHNICAL EQUIPMENT. TRANSPORT

Technical equipment

139. Computer

computer	комп'ютер (ч)	[kom'p'utɛr]
notebook, laptop	ноутбук (ч)	[nout'buk]
to turn on	увімкнути	[uwimk'nutɨ]
to turn off	вимкнути	['wɨmknutɨ]
keyboard	клавіатура (ж)	[klawia'tura]
key	клавіша (ж)	['klawiʃa]
mouse	миша (ж)	['mɨʃa]
mouse mat	килимок (ч)	[kɨɫɨ'mɔk]
button	кнопка (ж)	['knɔpka]
cursor	курсор (ч)	[kur'sɔr]
monitor	монітор (ч)	[moni'tɔr]
screen	екран (ч)	[ɛk'ran]
hard disk	жорсткий диск (ч)	[ʒor'stkɨj dɨsk]
hard disk capacity	об'єм (ч)	[o'bʼɛm]
memory	пам'ять (ж)	['pam'at']
random access memory	оперативна пам'ять (ж)	[opɛra'tɨwna 'pam'at']
file	файл (ч)	[fajl]
folder	`папка (ж)	['papka]
to open (vt)	відкрити файл	[wid'krɨtɨ 'fajl]
to close (vt)	закрити файл	[za'krɨtɨ 'fajl]
to save (vt)	зберегти	[zbɛrɛɦ'tɨ]
to delete (vt)	видалити	['wɨdalɨtɨ]
to copy (vt)	скопіювати	[skopiʲu'watɨ]
to sort (vt)	сортувати	[sortu'watɨ]
to transfer (copy)	переписати	[pɛrɛpɨ'satɨ]
programme	програма (ж)	[proɦ'rama]
software	програмне забезпечення (с)	[proɦ'ramnɛ zabɛz'pɛʧɛnʲa]
programmer	програміст (ч)	[proɦ'ramist]
to program (vt)	програмувати	[proɦramu'watɨ]
hacker	хакер (ч)	['ɦakɛr]
password	пароль (ч)	[pa'rɔlʲ]
virus	вірус (ч)	['wirus]
to find, to detect	виявити	['wɨjawɨtɨ]

byte	байт (ч)	[bajt]
megabyte	мегабайт (ч)	[mɛɦaˈbajt]
data	дані (мн)	[ˈdani]
database	база (ж) даних	[ˈbaza ˈdanɨɦ]
cable (USB, etc.)	кабель (ч)	[ˈkabɛlʲ]
to disconnect (vt)	від'єднати	[widˀɛdˈnatɨ]
to connect (sth to sth)	під'єднати	[pidˀɛdˈnatɨ]

140. Internet. E-mail

Internet	інтернет (ч)	[intɛrˈnɛt]
browser	браузер (ч)	[ˈbrauzɛr]
search engine	пошуковий ресурс (ч)	[poʃuˈkɔwɨj rɛˈsurs]
provider	провайдер (ч)	[proˈwajdɛr]
webmaster	веб-майстер (ч)	[wɛb ˈmajstɛr]
website	веб-сайт (ч)	[wɛb ˈsajt]
web page	веб-сторінка (ж)	[wɛb stoˈrinka]
address (e-mail ~)	адреса (ж)	[adˈrɛsa]
address book	адресна книга (ж)	[ˈadrɛsna ˈknɨɦa]
postbox	поштова скринька (ж)	[poʃˈtɔwa skˈrinʲka]
post	пошта (ж)	[ˈpɔʃta]
message	повідомлення (с)	[powiˈdɔmlɛnʲa]
sender	відправник (ч)	[widˈprawnɨk]
to send (vt)	відправити	[widˈprawɨtɨ]
sending (of mail)	відправлення (с)	[widˈprawlɛnʲa]
receiver	одержувач (ч)	[oˈdɛrʒuwatʃ]
to receive (vt)	отримати	[otˈrimatɨ]
correspondence	листування (с)	[lʲistuˈwanʲa]
to correspond (vi)	листуватися	[lʲistuˈwatisʲa]
file	файл (ч)	[fajl]
to download (vt)	скачати	[skaˈtʃatɨ]
to create (vt)	створити	[stwoˈritɨ]
to delete (vt)	видалити	[ˈwidalitɨ]
deleted (adj)	видалений	[ˈwidalɛnɨj]
connection (ADSL, etc.)	зв'язок (ч)	[zwˀjaˈzɔk]
speed	швидкість (ж)	[ˈʃwidkistʲ]
modem	модем (ч)	[moˈdɛm]
access	доступ (ч)	[ˈdɔstup]
port (e.g. input ~)	порт (ч)	[port]
connection (make a ~)	підключення (с)	[pidˈklʲutʃɛnʲa]
to connect to ... (vi)	підключитися	[pidklʲuˈtʃitisʲa]
to select (vt)	вибрати	[ˈwibratɨ]
to search (for ...)	шукати	[ʃuˈkatɨ]

Transport

aeroplane	літак (ч)	[li'tak]
air ticket	авіаквиток (ч)	[awiakwi'tɔk]
airline	авіакомпанія (ж)	[awiakom'paniˈa]
airport	аеропорт (ч)	[aɛro'pɔrt]
supersonic (adj)	надзвуковий	[nadzwuko'wij]
captain	командир (ч) корабля	[koman'dɨr korab'lʲa]
crew	екіпаж (ч)	[ɛki'paʒ]
pilot	пілот (ч)	[pi'lɔt]
stewardess	стюардеса (ж)	[stʲuar'dɛsa]
navigator	штурман (ч)	['ʃturman]
wings	крила (мн)	['krɨla]
tail	хвіст (ч)	[hwist]
cockpit	кабіна (ж)	[ka'bina]
engine	двигун (ч)	[dwɨ'ɦun]
undercarriage (landing gear)	шасі (с)	[ʃa'si]
turbine	турбіна (ж)	[tur'bina]
propeller	пропелер (ч)	[pro'pɛlɛr]
black box	чорна скринька (ж)	['tʃorna 'skrinʲka]
yoke (control column)	штурвал (ч)	[ʃtur'wal]
fuel	пальне (с)	[palʲ'nɛ]
safety card	інструкція (ж)	[inst'ruktsiˈa]
oxygen mask	киснева маска (ж)	['kɨsnɛwa 'maska]
uniform	уніформа (ж)	[uni'forma]
lifejacket	рятувальний жилет (ч)	[rʲatu'walʲnɨj ʒɨ'lɛt]
parachute	парашут (ч)	[para'ʃut]
takeoff	зліт (ч)	[zlit]
to take off (vi)	злітати	[zli'tati]
runway	злітна смуга (ж)	['zlitna 'smuɦa]
visibility	видимість (ж)	['wɨdɨmistʲ]
flight (act of flying)	політ (ч)	[po'lit]
altitude	висота (ж)	[wɨso'ta]
air pocket	повітряна яма (ж)	[po'witrʲana 'jama]
seat	місце (с)	['mistsɛ]
headphones	навушники (мн)	[na'wuʃnɨkɨ]
folding tray (tray table)	відкидний столик (ч)	[widkɨd'nɨj 'stɔlɨk]
airplane window	ілюмінатор (ч)	[ilʲumi'nator]
aisle	прохід (ч)	[pro'hid]

142. Train

train	поїзд (ч)	['pɔjizd]
commuter train	електропоїзд (ч)	[ɛlɛktro'pɔjizd]
express train	швидкий поїзд (ч)	[ʃwid'kij 'pɔjizd]
diesel locomotive	тепловоз (ч)	[tɛplo'wɔz]
steam locomotive	паровоз (ч)	[paro'wɔz]
coach, carriage	вагон (ч)	[wa'hɔn]
buffet car	вагон-ресторан (ч)	[wa'hɔn rɛsto'ran]
rails	рейки (мн)	['rɛjkɨ]
railway	залізниця (ж)	[zaliz'nɨtsʲa]
sleeper (track support)	шпала (ж)	['ʃpala]
platform (railway ~)	платформа (ж)	[plat'fɔrma]
platform (~ 1, 2, etc.)	колія (ж)	['kɔliʲa]
semaphore	семафор (ч)	[sɛma'fɔr]
station	станція (ж)	['stantsʲiʲa]
train driver	машиніст (ч)	[maʃi'nist]
porter (of luggage)	носильник (ч)	[no'sɨlʲnɨk]
carriage attendant	провідник (ч)	[prowid'nɨk]
passenger	пасажир (ч)	[pasa'ʒɨr]
ticket inspector	контролер (ч)	[kontro'lɛr]
corridor (in train)	коридор (ч)	[kori'dɔr]
emergency brake	стоп-кран (ч)	[stop kran]
compartment	купе (с)	[ku'pɛ]
berth	полиця (ж)	[po'lɨtsʲa]
upper berth	полиця (ж) верхня	[po'lɨtsʲa 'wɛrhnʲa]
lower berth	полиця (ж) нижня	[po'lɨtsʲa 'nɨʒnʲa]
bed linen, bedding	білизна (ж)	[bi'lɨzna]
ticket	квиток (ч)	[kwɨ'tɔk]
timetable	розклад (ч)	['rɔzklad]
information display	табло (с)	[tab'lɔ]
to leave, to depart	відходити	[wid'hɔdɨtɨ]
departure (of a train)	відправлення (с)	[wid'prawlɛnʲa]
to arrive (ab. train)	прибувати	[prɨbu'watɨ]
arrival	прибуття (с)	[prɨbut'tʲa]
to arrive by train	приїхати поїздом	[prɨ'jihatɨ 'pɔjizdom]
to get on the train	сісти на поїзд	['sistɨ na 'pɔjizd]
to get off the train	зійти з поїзду	[zij'tɨ z 'pɔjizdu]
train crash	катастрофа (ж)	[kata'strɔfa]
steam locomotive	паровоз (ч)	[paro'wɔz]
stoker, fireman	кочегар (ч)	[kotʃɛ'har]
firebox	топка (ж)	['tɔpka]
coal	вугілля (с)	[wu'hilʲa]

143. Ship

ship	корабель (ч)	[kora'bɛlʲ]
vessel	судно (с)	['sudno]
steamship	пароплав (ч)	[paro'plaw]
riverboat	теплохід (ч)	[tɛplo'hid]
cruise ship	лайнер (ч)	['lajnɛr]
cruiser	крейсер (ч)	['krɛjsɛr]
yacht	яхта (ж)	['ʲahta]
tugboat	буксир (ч)	[buk'sɨr]
barge	баржа (ж)	['barʒa]
ferry	паром (ч)	[pa'rɔm]
sailing ship	вітрильник (ч)	[wi'trilʲnɨk]
brigantine	бригантина (ж)	[brɨɦan'tɨna]
ice breaker	криголам (ч)	[krɨɦo'lam]
submarine	човен (ч) підводний	['tʃɔwɛn pid'wɔdnɨj]
boat (flat-bottomed ~)	човен (ч)	['tʃɔwɛn]
dinghy (lifeboat)	шлюпка (ж)	['ʃlʲupka]
lifeboat	шлюпка (ж) рятувальна	['ʃlʲupka rʲatu'walʲna]
motorboat	катер (ч)	['katɛr]
captain	капітан (ч)	[kapi'tan]
seaman	матрос (ч)	[mat'rɔs]
sailor	моряк (ч)	[mo'rʲak]
crew	екіпаж (ч)	[ɛki'paʒ]
boatswain	боцман (ч)	['bɔtsman]
ship's boy	юнга (ч)	['ʲunɦa]
cook	кок (ч)	[kok]
ship's doctor	судновий лікар (ч)	['sudnowɨj 'likar]
deck	палуба (ж)	['paluba]
mast	щогла (ж)	['ɕɔɦla]
sail	вітрило (с)	[wi'trɨɫo]
hold	трюм (ч)	[trʲum]
bow (prow)	ніс (ч)	[nis]
stern	корма (ж)	[kor'ma]
oar	весло (с)	[wɛs'lɔ]
screw propeller	гвинт (ч)	[ɦwint]
cabin	каюта (ж)	[ka'ʲuta]
wardroom	кают-компанія (ж)	[ka'ʲut kom'paniʲa]
engine room	машинне відділення (с)	[ma'ʃɨnɛ wid'dilɛnʲa]
bridge	капітанський місток (ч)	[kapi'tansʲkij mis'tɔk]
radio room	радіорубка (ж)	[radio'rubka]
wave (radio)	хвиля (ж)	['hwilʲa]
logbook	судновий журнал (ч)	['sudnowɨj ʒur'nal]
spyglass	підзорна труба (ж)	[pi'dzɔrna tru'ba]
bell	дзвін (ч)	[dzwin]

flag	прапор (ч)	['prapor]
hawser (mooring ~)	канат (ч)	[ka'nat]
knot (bowline, etc.)	вузол (ч)	['wuzol]

| deckrails | поручень (ч) | ['pɔrutʃɛnʲ] |
| gangway | трап (ч) | [trap] |

anchor	якір (ч)	['ʲakir]
to weigh anchor	підняти якір	[pidˈnʲatɨ ˈjakir]
to drop anchor	кинути якір	['kɨnutɨ ˈjakir]
anchor chain	якірний ланцюг (ч)	[ˈʲakirnɨj lanˈtsʲuɦ]

port (harbour)	порт (ч)	[port]
quay, wharf	причал (ч)	[priˈtʃal]
to berth (moor)	причалювати	[priˈtʃalʲuwatɨ]
to cast off	відчалювати	[widˈtʃalʲuwatɨ]

trip, voyage	подорож (ж)	['pɔdorɔʒ]
cruise (sea trip)	круїз (ч)	[kruˈjɨz]
course (route)	курс (ч)	[kurs]
route (itinerary)	маршрут (ч)	[marˈʃrut]

fairway (safe water channel)	фарватер (ч)	[farˈwatɛr]
shallows	мілина (ж)	[miliˈna]
to run aground	сісти на мілину	['sistɨ na miliˈnu]

storm	буря (ж)	['burʲa]
signal	сигнал (ч)	[siɦˈnal]
to sink (vi)	тонути	[toˈnutɨ]
SOS (distress signal)	SOS	[sos]
ring buoy	рятувальний круг (ч)	[rʲatuˈwalʲnɨj ˈkruɦ]

144. Airport

airport	аеропорт (ч)	[aɛroˈpɔrt]
aeroplane	літак (ч)	[liˈtak]
airline	авіакомпанія (ж)	[awiakomˈpaniʲa]
air traffic controller	диспетчер (ч)	[dɨsˈpɛtʃɛr]

departure	виліт (ч)	['wɨlit]
arrival	приліт (ч)	[priˈlit]
to arrive (by plane)	прилетіти	[priˈlɛtiti]

| departure time | час (ч) вильоту | [tʃas ˈwɨlʲotu] |
| arrival time | час (ч) прильоту | [tʃas prɨlʲotu] |

| to be delayed | затримуватися | [zaˈtrɨmuwatɨsʲa] |
| flight delay | затримка (ж) вильоту | [zaˈtrɨmka ˈwɨlʲotu] |

information board	інформаційне табло (с)	[informaˈtsijnɛ tabˈlɔ]
information	інформація (ж)	[inforˈmatsiʲa]
to announce (vt)	оголошувати	[oɦoˈlɔʃuwatɨ]
flight (e.g. next ~)	рейс (ч)	[rɛjs]
customs	митниця (ж)	['mɨtnɨtsʲa]

customs officer	митник (ч)	['mitnik]
customs declaration	декларація (ж)	[dɛklaˈratsiʲa]
to fill in (vt)	заповнити	[zaˈpowniti]
to fill in the declaration	заповнити декларацію	[zaˈpowniti dɛklaˈratsiʲu]
passport control	паспортний контроль (ч)	['pasportnij konˈtrolʲ]
luggage	багаж (ч)	[baˈɦaʒ]
hand luggage	ручний вантаж (ж)	[ruʧˈnij wanˈtaʒ]
luggage trolley	візок (ч) для багажу	[wiˈzok dlʲa baɦaˈʒu]
landing	посадка (ж)	[poˈsadka]
landing strip	посадкова смуга (ж)	[poˈsadkowa ˈsmuɦa]
to land (vi)	сідати	[siˈdati]
airstair (passenger stair)	трап (ч)	[trap]
check-in	реєстрація (ж)	[rɛɛˈstratsiʲa]
check-in counter	реєстрація (ж)	[rɛɛˈstratsiʲa]
to check-in (vi)	зареєструватися	[zarɛɛstruˈwatisʲa]
boarding card	посадковий талон (ч)	[poˈsadkowij taˈlɔn]
departure gate	вихід (ч)	['wihid]
transit	транзит (ч)	[tranˈzit]
to wait (vt)	чекати	[ʧɛˈkati]
departure lounge	зал (ч) очікування	['zal oˈʧikuwanʲa]
to see off	проводжати	[prowoˈdʒati]
to say goodbye	прощатися	[proˈɕatisʲa]

145. Bicycle. Motorcycle

bicycle	велосипед (ч)	[wɛlosiˈpɛd]
scooter	моторолер (ч)	[motoˈrolɛr]
motorbike	мотоцикл (ч)	[motoˈʦikl]
to go by bicycle	їхати на велосипеді	['jihati na wɛlosiˈpɛdi]
handlebars	кермо (с)	[kɛrˈmɔ]
pedal	педаль (ж)	[pɛˈdalʲ]
brakes	гальма (мн)	['ɦalʲma]
bicycle seat (saddle)	сідло (с)	[sidˈlɔ]
pump	помпа (ж)	['pɔmpa]
pannier rack	багажник (ч)	[baˈɦaʒnik]
front lamp	ліхтар (ч)	[lihˈtar]
helmet	шолом (ч)	[ʃoˈlɔm]
wheel	колесо (с)	['kɔlɛso]
mudguard	крило (с)	[kriˈlɔ]
rim	обвід (ч)	['ɔbwid]
spoke	спиця (ж)	['spiʦʲa]

Cars

car	автомобіль (ч)	[awtomo'bilʲ]
sports car	спортивний автомобіль (ч)	[spor'tiwnij awtomo'bilʲ]
limousine	лімузин (ч)	[limu'zin]
off-road vehicle	позадорожник (ч)	[pozado'rɔʒnik]
drophead coupé (convertible)	кабріолет (ч)	[kabrio'lɛt]
minibus	мікроавтобус (ч)	[mikroaw'tɔbus]
ambulance	швидка допомога (ж)	[ʃwid'ka dopo'mɔɦa]
snowplough	снігоприбиральна машина (ж)	[sniɦopribi'ralʲna ma'ʃina]
lorry	вантажівка (ж)	[wanta'ʒiwka]
road tanker	бензовоз (ч)	[bɛnzo'wɔz]
van (small truck)	фургон (ч)	[fur'ɦɔn]
tractor unit	тягач (ч)	[tʲa'ɦatʃ]
trailer	причіп (ч)	[pri'tʃip]
comfortable (adj)	комфортабельний	[komfor'tabɛlʲnij]
used (adj)	вживаний	['wʒiwanij]

bonnet	капот (ч)	[ka'pɔt]
wing	крило (с)	[kri'lɔ]
roof	дах (ч)	[dah]
windscreen	вітрове скло (с)	[witro'wɛ 'sklo]
rear-view mirror	дзеркало (с) заднього виду	['dzɛrkalo 'zadnʲoɦo 'widu]
windscreen washer	омивач (ч)	[omi'watʃ]
windscreen wipers	склоочисники (мн)	[skloo'tʃisniki]
side window	бічне скло (с)	['bitʃnɛ 'sklo]
electric window	склопідіймач (ч)	[sklopidij'matʃ]
aerial	антена (ж)	[an'tɛna]
sunroof	люк (ч)	[lʲuk]
bumper	бампер (ч)	['bampɛr]
boot	багажник (ч)	[ba'ɦaʒnik]
door	дверцята (мн)	[dwɛr'tsʲata]
door handle	ручка (ж)	['rutʃka]
door lock	замок (ч)	[za'mɔk]

number plate	номер (ч)	['nɔmɛr]
silencer	глушник (ч)	[ɦluʃ'nɨk]
petrol tank	бензобак (ч)	[bɛnzo'bak]
exhaust pipe	вихлопна труба (ж)	[wɨhlop'na tru'ba]

accelerator	газ (ч)	[ɦaz]
pedal	педаль (ж)	[pɛ'dalʲ]
accelerator pedal	педаль (ж) газу	[pɛ'dalʲ 'ɦazu]

brake	гальмо (с)	[ɦalʲ'mɔ]
brake pedal	педаль (ж) гальма	[pɛ'dalʲ ɦalʲ'ma]
to brake (use the brake)	гальмувати	[ɦalʲmu'watɨ]
handbrake	стоянкове гальмо (с)	[sto'ⁱankowɛ ɦalʲ'mɔ]

clutch	зчеплення (с)	['ztʃɛplɛnʲa]
clutch pedal	педаль (ж) зчеплення	[pɛ'dalʲ 'ztʃɛplɛnʲa]
clutch disc	диск (ч) зчеплення	['dɨsk 'ztʃɪplɛnʲa]
shock absorber	амортизатор (ч)	[amortɨ'zator]

wheel	колесо (с)	['kɔlɛso]
spare tyre	запасне колесо (с)	[zapas'nɛ 'kɔlɛso]
wheel cover (hubcap)	ковпак (ч)	[kow'pak]

driving wheels	ведучі колеса (мн)	[wɛ'dutʃi ko'lɛsa]
front-wheel drive (as adj)	передньоприводний	[pɛrɛdnʲop'rɨwidnɨj]
rear-wheel drive (as adj)	задньоприводний	[zadnʲoprɨwid'nɨj]
all-wheel drive (as adj)	повноприводний	[pownop'rɨwidnɨj]

gearbox	коробка (ж) передач	[ko'rɔbka pɛrɛ'datʃ]
automatic (adj)	автоматичний	[awtoma'titʃnɨj]
mechanical (adj)	механічний	[mɛha'nitʃnɨj]
gear lever	важіль (ч) коробки передач	['waʒilʲ ko'rɔbkɨ pɛrɛ'datʃ]

| headlamp | фара (ж) | ['fara] |
| headlights | фари (мн) | ['farɨ] |

dipped headlights	ближнє світло (с)	['blɨʒnɛ 'switlo]
full headlights	дальнє світло (с)	['dalʲnɛ 'switlo]
brake light	стоп-сигнал (ч)	[stop sɨɦ'nal]

sidelights	габаритні вогні (мн)	[ɦaba'rɨtni woɦ'ni]
hazard lights	аварійні вогні (мн)	[awa'rijni woɦ'ni]
fog lights	протитуманні фари (мн)	[protɨtu'mani 'farɨ]
turn indicator	поворотник (ч)	[powo'rɔtnɨk]
reversing light	задній хід (ч)	['zadnɨj hid]

148. Cars. Passenger compartment

car interior	салон (ч)	[sa'lɔn]
leather (as adj)	шкіряний	[ʃkir'a'nɨj]
velour (as adj)	велюровий	[wɛ'lʲurowɨj]
upholstery	оббивка (ж)	[ob'bɨwka]
instrument (gage)	прилад (ч)	['prɨlad]

dashboard	приладовий щиток (ч)	['priladowij ɕi'tɔk]
speedometer	спідометр (ч)	[spi'dɔmɛtr]
needle (pointer)	стрілка (ж)	['strilka]
mileometer	лічильник (ч)	[li'tʃiliniк]
indicator (sensor)	датчик (ч)	['datʃik]
level	рівень (ч)	['riwɛnʲ]
warning light	лампочка (ж)	['lampotʃka]
steering wheel	кермо (с)	[kɛr'mɔ]
horn	сигнал (ч)	[siɦ'nal]
button	кнопка (ж)	['knɔpka]
switch	перемикач (ч)	[pɛrɛmi'katʃ]
seat	сидіння (с)	[si'dinʲa]
backrest	спинка (ж)	['spinka]
headrest	підголівник (ч)	[pidɦo'liwnik]
seat belt	ремінь (ч) безпеки	['rɛminʲ bɛz'pɛki]
to fasten the belt	пристебнути ремінь	[pristɛb'nuti 'rɛminʲ]
adjustment (of seats)	регулювання (с)	[rɛɦulʲu'wanʲa]
airbag	повітряна подушка (ж)	[po'witrʲana po'duʃka]
air-conditioner	кондиціонер (ч)	[kondiʦio'nɛr]
radio	радіо (с)	['radio]
CD player	CD-програвач (ч)	[si'di proɦra'watʃ]
to turn on	увімкнути	[uwimk'nuti]
aerial	антена (ж)	[an'tɛna]
glove box	бардачок (ч)	[barda'tʃok]
ashtray	попільниця (ж)	[popilʲ'niʦʲa]

149. Cars. Engine

engine	двигун (ч)	[dwi'ɦun]
motor	мотор (ч)	[mo'tɔr]
diesel (as adj)	дизельний	['dizɛlʲnij]
petrol (as adj)	бензиновий	[bɛn'zinowij]
engine volume	об'єм (ч) двигуна	[o'bʲɛm dwiɦu'na]
power	потужність (ж)	[po'tuʒnistʲ]
horsepower	кінська сила (ж)	['kinsʲka 'sila]
piston	поршень (ч)	['pɔrʃɛnʲ]
cylinder	циліндр (ч)	[ʦi'lindr]
valve	клапан (ч)	['klapan]
injector	інжектор (ч)	[in'ʒɛktor]
generator (alternator)	генератор (ч)	[ɦɛnɛ'rator]
carburettor	карбюратор (ч)	[karbʲu'rator]
motor oil	масло (с) моторне	['maslo mo'tɔrnɛ]
radiator	радіатор (ч)	[radi'ator]
coolant	охолоджувальна рідина (ж)	[oho'lɔdʒuwalʲna ridi'na]
cooling fan	вентилятор (ч)	[wɛnti'lʲator]

battery (accumulator)	акумулятор (ч)	[akumu'lʲator]
starter	стартер (ч)	['startɛr]
ignition	запалювання (с)	[za'palʲuwanʲa]
sparking plug	свічка (ж) запалювання	['switʃka za'palʲuwanʲa]
terminal (battery ~)	клема (ж)	['klɛma]
positive terminal	плюс (ч)	[plʲus]
negative terminal	мінус (ч)	['minus]
fuse	запобіжник (ч)	[zapo'biʒnɪk]
air filter	повітряний фільтр (ч)	[po'witrʲanɪj 'filʲtr]
oil filter	масляний фільтр (ч)	['maslʲanɪj 'filʲtr]
fuel filter	паливний фільтр (ч)	['palɪwnɪj 'filʲtr]

150. Cars. Crash. Repair

car crash	аварія (ж)	[a'warʲiʲa]
traffic accident	дорожня пригода (ж)	[do'rɔʒnʲa prɪ'ɦɔda]
to crash (into the wall, etc.)	врізатися	['wrizatɪsʲa]
to get smashed up	розбитися	[roz'bitɪsʲa]
damage	пошкодження (с)	[poʃ'kɔdʒɛnʲa]
intact (unscathed)	цілий	[tsi'lʲij]
to break down (vi)	зламатися	[zla'matɪsʲa]
towrope	буксирний трос (ч)	[buk'sɪrnɪj tros]
puncture	прокол (ч)	[pro'kɔl]
to have a puncture	спустити	[spus'tɪtɪ]
to pump up	накачати	[naka'tʃatɪ]
pressure	тиск (ч)	[tɪsk]
to check (to examine)	перевірити	[pɛrɛ'wirɪtɪ]
repair	ремонт (ч)	[rɛ'mɔnt]
garage (auto service shop)	ремонтна майстерня (ж)	[rɛ'mɔntna majs'tɛrnʲa]
spare part	запчастина (ж)	[zaptʃas'tɪna]
part	деталь (ж)	[dɛ'talʲ]
bolt (with nut)	болт (ч)	[bolt]
screw (fastener)	гвинт (ч)	[ɦwɪnt]
nut	гайка (ж)	['ɦajka]
washer	шайба (ж)	['ʃajba]
bearing (e.g. ball ~)	підшипник (ч)	[pid'ʃɪpnɪk]
tube	трубка (ж)	['trubka]
gasket (head ~)	прокладка (ж)	[prok'ladka]
cable, wire	провід (ч)	['prɔwid]
jack	домкрат (ч)	[domk'rat]
spanner	ключ (ч)	[klʲutʃ]
hammer	молоток (ч)	[molo'tɔk]
pump	помпа (ж)	['pɔmpa]
screwdriver	викрутка (ж)	['wɪkrutka]
fire extinguisher	вогнегасник (ч)	[woɦnɛ'ɦasnɪk]
warning triangle	аварійний трикутник (ч)	[awa'rijnɪj trɪ'kutnɪk]

to stall (vi)	глохнути	['ɦlɔhnutɨ]
stall (n)	зупинка (ж)	[zu'pɨnka]
to be broken	бути зламаним	['butɨ 'zlamanɨm]
to overheat (vi)	перегрітися	[pɛrɛɦ'rɨtɨsʲa]
to freeze up (pipes, etc.)	замерзнути	[za'mɛrznutɨ]
to burst (vi, ab. tube)	лопнути	['lɔpnutɨ]
pressure	тиск (ч)	[tɨsk]
level	рівень (ч)	['riwɛnʲ]
slack (~ belt)	слабкий	[slab'kɨj]
dent	вм'ятина (ж)	['wmʲatɨna]
knocking noise (engine)	стукіт (ч)	['stukit]
crack	тріщина (ж)	['triçɨna]
scratch	подряпина (ж)	[pod'rʲapɨna]

151. Cars. Road

road	дорога (ж)	[do'rɔɦa]
motorway	автомагістраль (ж)	[awtomaɦi'stralʲ]
highway	шосе (с)	[ʃo'sɛ]
direction (way)	напрямок (ч)	['naprʲamok]
distance	відстань (ж)	['widstanʲ]
bridge	міст (ч)	[mist]
car park	паркінг (ч)	['parkinɦ]
square	площа (ж)	['plɔça]
road junction	розв'язка (ж)	[roz'wʲazka]
tunnel	тунель (ч)	[tu'nɛlʲ]
petrol station	автозаправка (ж)	[awtoza'prawka]
car park	автостоянка (ж)	[awtosto'ʲanka]
petrol pump	бензоколонка (ж)	[bɛnzoko'lɔnka]
auto repair shop	гараж (ч)	[ɦa'raʒ]
to fill up	заправити	[za'prawɨtɨ]
fuel	паливо (с)	['palɨwo]
jerrycan	каністра (ж)	[ka'nistra]
asphalt, tarmac	асфальт (ч)	[as'falʲt]
road markings	розмітка (ж)	[roz'mitka]
kerb	бордюр (ч)	[bor'dʲur]
crash barrier	огорожа (ж)	[oɦo'rɔʒa]
ditch	кювет (ч)	[kʲu'wɛt]
roadside (shoulder)	узбіччя (с)	[uz'bitʲʲa]
lamppost	стовп (ч)	[stowp]
to drive (a car)	вести	['wɛstɨ]
to turn (e.g., ~ left)	повертати	[powɛr'tatɨ]
to make a U-turn	розвертатися	[rozwɛr'tatɨsʲa]
reverse (~ gear)	задній хід (ч)	['zadnij hid]
to honk (vi)	сигналити	[sɨɦ'nalɨtɨ]
honk (sound)	звуковий сигнал (ч)	[zwuko'wɨj sɨɦ'nal]

to get stuck (in the mud, etc.)	**застрягти**	[zaˈstrʲaɦti]
to spin the wheels	**буксувати**	[buksuˈwati]
to cut, to turn off (vt)	**глушити**	[ɦluˈʃiti]

speed	**швидкість** (ж)	[ˈʃwidkistʲ]
to exceed the speed limit	**перевищити швидкість**	[pɛrɛˈwiçiti ˈʃwidkistʲ]
to give a ticket	**штрафувати**	[ʃtrafuˈwati]
traffic lights	**світлофор** (ч)	[switloˈfɔr]
driving licence	**посвідчення** (с) **водія**	[posˈwidtʃɛnja wodiˈʲa]

level crossing	**переїзд** (ч)	[pɛrɛˈjizd]
crossroads	**перехрестя** (с)	[pɛrɛhˈrɛstʲa]
zebra crossing	**пішохідний перехід** (ч)	[piʃoˈhidnij pɛrɛˈhid]
bend, curve	**поворот** (ч)	[powoˈrɔt]
pedestrian precinct	**пішохідна зона** (ж)	[piʃoˈhidna ˈzɔna]

PEOPLE. LIFE EVENTS

152. Holidays. Event

celebration, holiday	свято (с)	['swʲato]
national day	національне свято (с)	[natsio'nalʲnɛ 'swʲato]
public holiday	святковий день (ч)	[swʲat'kɔwɨj dɛnʲ]
to commemorate (vt)	святкувати	[swʲatku'watɨ]
event (happening)	подія (ж)	[po'dʲiʲa]
event (organized activity)	захід (ч)	['zahid]
banquet (party)	бенкет (ч)	[bɛ'nkɛt]
reception (formal party)	прийом (ч)	[prɨ'jɔm]
feast	бенкет (ч)	[bɛ'nkɛt]
anniversary	річниця (ж)	[ritʃ'nɨtsʲa]
jubilee	ювілей (ч)	[ʲuwi'lɛj]
to celebrate (vt)	відмітити	[wid'mititɨ]
New Year	Новий рік (ч)	[no'wɨj rik]
Happy New Year!	З Новим Роком!	[z no'wɨm 'rɔkom]
Christmas	Різдво (с)	[rizd'wɔ]
Merry Christmas!	Щасливого Різдва!	[ɕas'lɨwoɦo rizd'wa]
Christmas tree	Новорічна ялинка (ж)	[nowo'ritʃna ja'lɨnka]
fireworks (fireworks show)	салют (ч)	[sa'lʲut]
wedding	весілля (с)	[wɛ'silʲa]
groom	наречений (ч)	[narɛ'tʃɛnɨj]
bride	наречена (ж)	[narɛ'tʃɛna]
to invite (vt)	запрошувати	[za'prɔʃuwatɨ]
invitation card	запрошення (с)	[za'prɔʃɛnʲa]
guest	гість (ч)	[ɦistʲ]
to visit (~ your parents, etc.)	йти в гості	[jtɨ w 'ɦɔsti]
to meet the guests	зустрічати гостей	[zustri'tʃatɨ ɦos'tɛj]
gift, present	подарунок (ч)	[poda'runok]
to give (sth as present)	дарувати	[daru'watɨ]
to receive gifts	отримувати подарунки	[ot'rɨmuwatɨ poda'runkɨ]
bouquet (of flowers)	букет (ч)	[bu'kɛt]
congratulations	привітання (с)	[prɨwi'tanʲa]
to congratulate (vt)	вітати	[wi'tatɨ]
greetings card	вітальна листівка (ж)	[wi'talʲna lɨs'tiwka]
to send a postcard	надіслати листівку	[nadi'slatɨ lɨs'tiwku]
to get a postcard	отримати листівку	[ot'rɨmatɨ lɨs'tiwku]
toast	тост (ч)	[tost]

| to offer (a drink, etc.) | пригощати | [priɦoˈɕati] |
| champagne | шампанське (c) | [ʃamˈpansʲkɛ] |

to enjoy oneself	веселитися	[wɛsɛˈlitisʲa]
merriment (gaiety)	веселощі (мн)	[wɛˈsɛloɕi]
joy (emotion)	радість (ж)	[ˈradistʲ]

| dance | танець (ч) | [ˈtanɛʦ] |
| to dance (vi, vt) | танцювати | [tanʦʲuˈwati] |

| waltz | вальс (ч) | [walʲs] |
| tango | танго (c) | [ˈtanɦo] |

153. Funerals. Burial

cemetery	цвинтар (ч)	[ˈʦwintar]
grave, tomb	могила (ж)	[moˈɦila]
cross	хрест (ч)	[hrɛst]
gravestone	нагробок (ч)	[naˈɦrobok]
fence	огорожа (ж)	[oɦoˈrɔʒa]
chapel	каплиця (ж)	[kapˈlitsʲa]

death	смерть (ж)	[smɛrtʲ]
to die (vi)	померти	[poˈmɛrti]
the deceased	покійник (ч)	[poˈkijnik]
mourning	траур (ч)	[ˈtraur]

to bury (vt)	ховати	[hoˈwati]
undertakers	похоронне бюро (c)	[pohoˈrɔnɛ bʲuro]
funeral	похорон (ч)	[ˈpɔhoron]

wreath	вінок (ч)	[wiˈnɔk]
coffin	труна (ж)	[truˈna]
hearse	катафалк (ч)	[kataˈfalk]
shroud	саван (ч)	[saˈwan]

| funerary urn | урна (ж) | [ˈurna] |
| crematorium | крематорій (ч) | [krɛmaˈtɔrij] |

obituary	некролог (ч)	[nɛkroˈlɔɦ]
to cry (weep)	плакати	[ˈplakati]
to sob (vi)	ридати	[riˈdati]

154. War. Soldiers

platoon	взвод (ч)	[wzwod]
company	рота (ж)	[ˈrota]
regiment	полк (ч)	[polk]
army	армія (ж)	[ˈarmiʲa]
division	дивізія (ж)	[diˈwiziʲa]
section, squad	загін (ч)	[zaˈɦin]
host (army)	військо (c)	[ˈwijsʲko]

| soldier | солдат (ч) | [sol'dat] |
| officer | офіцер (ч) | [ofi'tsɛr] |

private	рядовий (ч)	[rʲado'wij]
sergeant	сержант (ч)	[sɛr'ʒant]
lieutenant	лейтенант (ч)	[lɛjtɛ'nant]
captain	капітан (ч)	[kapi'tan]
major	майор (ч)	[ma'jɔr]
colonel	полковник (ч)	[pol'kɔwnɪk]
general	генерал (ч)	[ɦɛnɛ'ral]

sailor	моряк (ч)	[mo'rʲak]
captain	капітан (ч)	[kapi'tan]
boatswain	боцман (ч)	['bɔtsman]

artilleryman	артилерист (ч)	[artilɛ'rist]
paratrooper	десантник (ч)	[dɛ'santnɪk]
pilot	льотчик (ч)	[lʲotʃik]
navigator	штурман (ч)	['ʃturman]
mechanic	механік (ч)	[mɛ'hanik]

pioneer (sapper)	сапер (ч)	[sa'pɛr]
parachutist	парашутист (ч)	[paraʃu'tist]
reconnaissance scout	розвідник (ч)	[roz'widnɪk]
sniper	снайпер (ч)	['snajpɛr]

patrol (group)	патруль (ч)	[pat'rulʲ]
to patrol (vt)	патрулювати	[patrulʲu'wati]
sentry, guard	вартовий (ч)	[warto'wij]

warrior	воїн (ч)	['wɔjin]
patriot	патріот (ч)	[patri'ɔt]
hero	герой (ч)	[ɦɛ'rɔj]
heroine	героїня (ж)	[ɦɛro'jinʲa]

traitor	зрадник (ч)	['zradnɪk]
deserter	дезертир (ч)	[dɛzɛr'tir]
to desert (vi)	дезертирувати	[dɛzɛr'tiruwati]

mercenary	найманець (ч)	['najmanɛts]
recruit	новобранець (ч)	[nowo'branɛts]
volunteer	доброволець (ч)	[dobro'wɔlɛts]

dead (n)	убитий (ч)	[u'bitij]
wounded (n)	поранений (ч)	[po'ranɛnij]
prisoner of war	полонений (ч)	[polo'nɛnij]

155. War. Military actions. Part 1

war	війна (ж)	[wij'na]
to be at war	воювати	[woʲu'wati]
civil war	громадянська війна (ж)	[ɦroma'dʲansʲka wij'na]
treacherously (adv)	віроломно	[wiro'lɔmno]
declaration of war	оголошення (с)	[oɦo'lɔʃɛnʲa]

to declare (~ war)	оголосити	[oɦolo'siti]
aggression	агресія (ж)	[aɦ'rɛsiʲa]
to attack (invade)	нападати	[napa'dati]
to invade (vt)	захоплювати	[za'ɦoplʲuwati]
invader	загарбник (ч)	[za'ɦarbnik]
conqueror	завойовник (ч)	[zawo'jɔwnik]
defence	оборона (ж)	[obo'rɔna]
to defend (a country, etc.)	обороняти	[oboro'nʲati]
to defend (against ...)	оборонятися	[oboro'nʲatisʲa]
enemy	ворог (ч)	['wɔroɦ]
foe, adversary	супротивник (ч)	[supro'tiwnik]
enemy (as adj)	ворожий	[wo'rɔʒij]
strategy	стратегія (ж)	[stra'tɛɦiʲa]
tactics	тактика (ж)	['taktika]
order	наказ (ч)	[na'kaz]
command (order)	команда (ж)	[ko'manda]
to order (vt)	наказувати	[na'kazuwati]
mission	завдання (с)	[zaw'danʲa]
secret (adj)	таємний	[ta'ɛmnij]
battle	битва (ж)	['bitwa]
combat	бій (ч)	[bij]
attack	атака (ж)	[a'taka]
charge (assault)	штурм (ч)	[ʃturm]
to storm (vt)	штурмувати	[ʃturmu'wati]
siege (to be under ~)	облога (ж)	[ob'lɔɦa]
offensive (n)	наступ (ч)	['nastup]
to go on the offensive	наступати	[nastu'pati]
retreat	відступ (ч)	['widstup]
to retreat (vi)	відступати	[widstu'pati]
encirclement	оточення (с)	[o'tɔtʃɛnʲa]
to encircle (vt)	оточувати	[o'tɔtʃuwati]
bombing (by aircraft)	бомбардування (с)	[bombardu'wanʲa]
to drop a bomb	скинути бомбу	['skinuti 'bombu]
to bomb (vt)	бомбардувати	[bombardu'wati]
explosion	вибух (ч)	['wibuɦ]
shot	постріл (ч)	['pɔstril]
to fire (~ a shot)	вистрілити	['wistriliti]
firing (burst of ~)	стрілянина (ж)	[strilʲa'nina]
to aim (to point a weapon)	цілитися	['tsilitisʲa]
to point (a gun)	навести	[na'wɛsti]
to hit (the target)	влучити	['wlutʃiti]
to sink (~ a ship)	потопити	[poto'piti]
hole (in a ship)	пробоїна (ж)	[pro'bɔjina]

to founder, to sink (vi)	йти на дно	[jti na dno]
front (war ~)	фронт (ч)	[front]
evacuation	евакуація (ж)	[ɛwaku'atsi'a]
to evacuate (vt)	евакуювати	[ɛwaku'u'wati]

barbed wire	колючий дріт (ч)	[ko'l'utʃij drit]
barrier (anti tank ~)	загородження (с)	[zaɦo'rɔdʒɛn'a]
watchtower	вишка (ж)	['wiʃka]

military hospital	госпіталь (ч)	['ɦɔspital']
to wound (vt)	поранити	[po'raniti]
wound	рана (ж)	['rana]
wounded (n)	поранений (ч)	[po'ranɛnij]
to be wounded	одержати поранення	[o'dɛrʒati po'ranɛn'a]
serious (wound)	важкий	[waʒ'kij]

156. Weapons

weapons	зброя (ж)	['zbrɔ'a]
firearms	вогнепальна зброя	[woɦnɛ'pal'na 'zbrɔ'a]
cold weapons (knives, etc.)	холодна зброя (ж)	[ho'lɔdna 'zbrɔ'a]

chemical weapons	хімічна зброя (ж)	[hi'mitʃna 'zbrɔ'a]
nuclear (adj)	ядерний	[''adɛrnij]
nuclear weapons	ядерна зброя (ж)	[''adɛrna 'zbrɔ'a]

| bomb | бомба (ж) | ['bɔmba] |
| atomic bomb | атомна бомба (ж) | ['atomna 'bɔmba] |

pistol (gun)	пістолет (ч)	[pisto'lɛt]
rifle	рушниця (ж)	[ruʃ'nits'a]
submachine gun	автомат (ч)	[awto'mat]
machine gun	кулемет (ч)	[kulɛ'mɛt]

muzzle	дуло (с)	['dulo]
barrel	ствол (ч)	[stwol]
calibre	калібр (ч)	[ka'libr]

trigger	курок (ч)	[ku'rɔk]
sight (aiming device)	приціл (ч)	[pri'tsil]
magazine	магазин (ч)	[maɦa'zin]
butt (shoulder stock)	приклад (ч)	[prik'lad]

| hand grenade | граната (ж) | [ɦra'nata] |
| explosive | вибухівка (ж) | [wibu'hiwka] |

bullet	куля (ж)	['kul'a]
cartridge	патрон (ч)	[pat'rɔn]
charge	заряд (ч)	[za'r'ad]
ammunition	боєприпаси (мн)	[boɛpri'pasi]

bomber (aircraft)	бомбардувальник (ч)	[bombardu'wal'nik]
fighter	винищувач (ч)	[wi'niɕuwatʃ]
helicopter	вертоліт (ч)	[wɛrto'lit]

anti-aircraft gun	зенітка (ж)	[zɛ'nitka]
tank	танк (ч)	[tank]
tank gun	гармата (ж)	[ɦar'mata]

artillery	артилерія (ж)	[arti'lɛriʲa]
gun (cannon, howitzer)	гармата (ж)	[ɦar'mata]
to lay (a gun)	навести	[na'wɛsti]

shell (projectile)	снаряд (ч)	[sna'rʲad]
mortar bomb	міна (ж)	['mina]
mortar	мінломет (ч)	[mino'mɛt]
splinter (shell fragment)	осколок (ч)	[os'kɔlok]

submarine	підводний човен (ч)	[pid'wɔdnij 'ʧɔwɛn]
torpedo	торпеда (ж)	[tor'pɛda]
missile	ракета (ж)	[ra'kɛta]

to load (gun)	заряджати	[zarʲa'dʒati]
to shoot (vi)	стріляти	[stri'lʲati]
to point at (the cannon)	цілитися	['ʦilitisʲa]
bayonet	багнет (ч)	[baɦ'nɛt]

rapier	шпага (ж)	['ʃpaɦa]
sabre (e.g. cavalry ~)	шабля (ж)	['ʃablʲa]
spear (weapon)	спис (ч)	[spis]
bow	лук (ч)	[luk]
arrow	стріла (ж)	[stri'la]
musket	мушкет (ч)	[muʃ'kɛt]
crossbow	арбалет (ч)	[arba'lɛt]

157. Ancient people

primitive (prehistoric)	первісний	[pɛr'wisnij]
prehistoric (adj)	доісторичний	[doisto'riʧnij]
ancient (~ civilization)	стародавній	[staro'dawnij]

Stone Age	Кам'яний вік (ч)	[kamʲʲa'nij wik]
Bronze Age	Бронзовий вік (ч)	['brɔnzowij wik]
Ice Age	льодовиковий період (ч)	[lʲodowi'kɔwij pɛ'riod]

tribe	плем'я (с)	['plɛmʲʲa]
cannibal	людоїд (ч)	[lʲudo'jid]
hunter	мисливець (ч)	[mis'liwɛʦ]
to hunt (vi, vt)	полювати	[polʲu'wati]
mammoth	мамонт (ч)	['mamont]

cave	печера (ж)	[pɛ'ʧɛra]
fire	вогонь (ч)	[wo'ɦonʲ]
campfire	багаття (с)	[ba'ɦattʲa]
cave painting	наскальний малюнок (ч)	[na'skalʲnij ma'lʲunok]

tool (e.g. stone axe)	знаряддя (с) праці	[zna'rʲaddʲa 'praʦi]
spear	спис (ч)	[spis]
stone axe	кам'яна сокира (ж)	[kamʲʲa'na so'kira]

| to be at war | воювати | [woˈuˈwatⁱ] |
| to domesticate (vt) | приручати | [priruˈtʃatⁱ] |

idol	ідол (ч)	[ˈidol]
to worship (vt)	поклонятися	[pokloˈnⁱatisⁱa]
superstition	забобони (мн)	[zaboˈbɔnⁱ]

evolution	еволюція (ж)	[ɛwoˈlⁱutsⁱⁱa]
development	розвиток (ч)	[ˈrɔzwitok]
disappearance (extinction)	зникнення (с)	[ˈznⁱknɛnⁱa]
to adapt oneself	пристосовуватися	[pristosowuˈwatisⁱa]

archaeology	археологія (ж)	[arhɛoˈlɔhⁱⁱa]
archaeologist	археолог (ч)	[arhɛˈɔlofɦ]
archaeological (adj)	археологічний	[arhɛoloˈhitʃnⁱj]

excavation site	розкопки (мн)	[rozˈkɔpkⁱ]
excavations	розкопки (мн)	[rozˈkɔpkⁱ]
find (object)	знахідка (ж)	[znaˈhidka]
fragment	фрагмент (ч)	[frahˈmɛnt]

158. Middle Ages

people (ethnic group)	народ (ч)	[naˈrɔd]
peoples	народи (мн)	[naˈrɔdⁱ]
tribe	плем'я (с)	[ˈplɛmʲⁱa]
tribes	племена (мн)	[plɛmɛˈna]

barbarians	варвари (мн)	[ˈwarwarⁱ]
Gauls	гали (ч)	[ˈhalⁱ]
Goths	готи (мн)	[ˈfɦɔtⁱ]
Slavs	слов'яни (мн)	[sloˈwʲⁱanⁱ]
Vikings	вікінги (мн)	[ˈwikinfɦⁱ]

| Romans | римляни (мн) | [rimˈlⁱⁱanⁱ] |
| Roman (adj) | Римський Папа | [ˈrimsⁱkⁱj ˈpapa] |

Byzantines	візантійці (мн)	[wizanˈtijtsi]
Byzantium	Візантія (ж)	[wizanˈtiⁱa]
Byzantine (adj)	візантійський	[wizanˈtijsⁱkⁱj]

emperor	імператор (ч)	[impɛˈrator]
leader, chief (tribal ~)	вождь (ч)	[woʒdʲ]
powerful (~ king)	могутній	[moˈfɦutnij]
king	король (ч)	[koˈrɔlⁱ]
ruler (sovereign)	правитель (ч)	[praˈwitɛlⁱ]

knight	лицар (ч)	[ˈlⁱⁱtsar]
feudal lord	феодал (ч)	[fɛoˈdal]
feudal (adj)	феодальний	[fɛoˈdalⁱnij]
vassal	васал (ч)	[waˈsal]

| duke | герцог (ч) | [ˈfɦɛrtsofɦ] |
| earl | граф (ч) | [fɦraf] |

| baron | барон (ч) | [ba'rɔn] |
| bishop | єпископ (ч) | [ɛ'pɪskɔp] |

armour	лати (мн)	['latɪ]
shield	щит (ч)	[ɕit]
sword	меч (ч)	[mɛtʃ]
visor	забрало (с)	[za'bralo]
chainmail	кольчуга (ж)	[kolʲ'tʃuɦa]

| Crusade | хрестовий похід (ч) | [hrɛs'tɔwij po'hid] |
| crusader | хрестоносець (ч) | [hrɛsto'nɔsɛts] |

territory	територія (ж)	[tɛri'tɔriʲa]
to attack (invade)	нападати	[napa'dati]
to conquer (vt)	завоювати	[zawoʲu'wati]
to occupy (invade)	захватити	[zahwa'titi]

siege (to be under ~)	облога (ж)	[ob'lɔɦa]
besieged (adj)	обложений	[ob'lɔʒɛnij]
to besiege (vt)	облягати	[oblʲa'ɦati]

inquisition	інквізиція (ж)	[inkwi'zitsiʲa]
inquisitor	інквізитор (ч)	[inkwi'zitor]
torture	катування (с)	[katu'wanʲa]
cruel (adj)	жорстокий	[ʒor'stɔkij]
heretic	єретик (ч)	[ɛ'rɛtik]
heresy	єресь (ж)	['ɛrɛsʲ]

seafaring	мореплавання (с)	[morɛ'plawanʲa]
pirate	пірат (ч)	[pi'rat]
piracy	піратство (с)	[pi'ratstwo]
boarding (attack)	абордаж (ч)	[abor'daʒ]
loot, booty	здобич (ж)	['zdɔbitʃ]
treasure	скарби (мн)	[skar'bɪ]

discovery	відкриття (с)	[widkrit'tʲa]
to discover (new land, etc.)	відкрити	[wid'kriti]
expedition	експедиція (ж)	[ɛkspɛ'ditsiʲa]

musketeer	мушкетер (ч)	[muʃkɛ'tɛr]
cardinal	кардинал (ч)	[kardi'nal]
heraldry	геральдика (ж)	[ɦɛ'ralʲdika]
heraldic (adj)	геральдичний	[ɦɛralʲ'ditʃnij]

159. Leader. Chief. Authorities

king	король (ч)	[ko'rɔlʲ]
queen	королева (ж)	[koro'lɛwa]
royal (adj)	королівський	[koro'liwsʲkij]
kingdom	королівство (с)	[koro'liwstwo]

prince	принц (ч)	[prints]
princess	принцеса (ж)	[prin'tsɛsa]
president	президент (ч)	[prɛzi'dɛnt]

| vice-president | віце-президент (ч) | ['wɪtsɛ prɛzi'dɛnt] |
| senator | сенатор (ч) | [sɛ'nator] |

monarch	монарх (ч)	[mo'narh]
ruler (sovereign)	правитель (ч)	[pra'wɪtɛlʲ]
dictator	диктатор (ч)	[dɪk'tator]
tyrant	тиран (ч)	[ti'ran]
magnate	магнат (ч)	[mah'nat]

director	директор (ч)	[di'rɛktor]
chief	шеф (ч)	[ʃɛf]
manager (director)	управляючий (ч)	[upraw'lʲaʲutʃij]
boss	бос (ч)	[bos]
owner	господар (ч)	[hos'pɔdar]

head (~ of delegation)	голова (ж)	[holo'wa]
authorities	влада (ж)	['wlada]
superiors	керівництво (с)	[kɛriw'nitstwo]

governor	губернатор (ч)	[hubɛr'nator]
consul	консул (ч)	['kɔnsul]
diplomat	дипломат (ч)	[diplo'mat]
mayor	мер (ч)	[mɛr]
sheriff	шериф (ч)	[ʃɛ'rif]

emperor	імператор (ч)	[impɛ'rator]
tsar, czar	цар (ч)	[tsar]
pharaoh	фараон (ч)	[fara'ɔn]
khan	хан (ч)	[han]

160. Breaking the law. Criminals. Part 1

bandit	бандит (ч)	[ban'dɪt]
crime	злочин (ч)	['zlɔtʃin]
criminal (person)	злочинець (ч)	[zlo'tʃinɛts]

thief	злодій (ч)	['zlɔdij]
to steal (vi, vt)	красти	['krasti]
stealing (larceny)	крадеж (ч)	['kradɛʃ]
theft	крадіжка (ж)	[kra'diʒka]

to kidnap (vt)	викрадення	['wikradɛnʲa]
kidnapping	викрадення (с)	['wikradɛnʲa]
kidnapper	викрадач (ч)	[wikra'datʃ]

| ransom | викуп (ч) | ['wikup] |
| to demand ransom | вимагати викуп | [wima'hati 'wikup] |

| to rob (vt) | грабувати | [hrabu'wati] |
| robber | грабіжник (ч) | [hra'biʒnik] |

to extort (vt)	вимагати	[wima'hati]
extortionist	вимагач (ч)	[wima'hatʃ]
extortion	вимагання (с)	[wima'hanʲa]

to murder, to kill	вбити	['wbɨti]
murder	вбивство (с)	['wbɨwstwo]
murderer	вбивця (ч)	['wbɨwtsʲa]

gunshot	постріл (ч)	['pɔstril]
to fire (~ a shot)	вистрілити	['wistriliti]
to shoot to death	застрелити	[za'streliti]
to shoot (vi)	стріляти	[stri'lʲati]
shooting	стрілянина (ж)	[strilʲa'nina]

incident (fight, etc.)	подія (ж)	[po'diʲa]
fight, brawl	бійка (ж)	['bijka]
victim	жертва (ж)	['ʒɛrtwa]

to damage (vt)	пошкодити	[poʃ'kɔditi]
damage	шкода (ж)	['ʃkɔda]
dead body, corpse	труп (ч)	[trup]
grave (~ crime)	важкий	[waʒ'kij]

to attack (vt)	напасти	[na'pasti]
to beat (to hit)	бити	['biti]
to beat up	побити	[po'biti]
to take (rob of sth)	забрати	[za'brati]
to stab to death	зарізати	[za'rizati]
to maim (vt)	покалічити	[poka'litʃiti]
to wound (vt)	поранити	[po'raniti]

blackmail	шантаж (ч)	[ʃan'taʒ]
to blackmail (vt)	шантажувати	[ʃantaʒu'wati]
blackmailer	шантажист (ч)	[ʃanta'ʒist]

protection racket	рекет (ч)	['rɛkɛt]
racketeer	рекетир (ч)	[rɛkɛ'tir]
gangster	гангстер (ч)	['ɦanɦstɛr]
mafia	мафія (ж)	['mafiʲa]

pickpocket	кишеньковий злодій (ч)	[kiʃɛnʲ'kɔwij 'zlɔdij]
burglar	зломщик (ч)	['zlɔmɕik]
smuggling	контрабанда (ж)	[kontra'banda]
smuggler	контрабандист (ч)	[kontraban'dist]

forgery	підробка (ж)	[pid'rɔbka]
to forge (counterfeit)	підробляти	[pidrob'lʲati]
fake (forged)	фальшивий	[falʲ'ʃiwɨj]

161. Breaking the law. Criminals. Part 2

rape	зґвалтування (с)	[zgwaltu'wanʲa]
to rape (vt)	зґвалтувати	[zgwaltu'wati]
rapist	ґвалтівник (ч)	[gwaltiw'nik]
maniac	маніяк (ч)	[mani'ʲak]

| prostitute (fem.) | проститутка (ж) | [prosti'tutka] |
| prostitution | проституція (ж) | [prosti'tutsiʲa] |

pimp	сутенер (ч)	[sutɛ'nɛr]
drug addict	наркоман (ч)	[narko'man]
drug dealer	наркоторгівець (ч)	[narkotor'ɦiwɛts]

to blow up (bomb)	підірвати	[pidir'watɨ]
explosion	вибух (ч)	['wɨbuɦ]
to set fire	підпалити	[pidpa'lɨtɨ]
arsonist	підпалювач (ч)	[pid'palʲuwatʃ]

terrorism	тероризм (ч)	[tɛro'rɨzm]
terrorist	терорист (ч)	[tɛro'rɨst]
hostage	заручник (ч)	[za'rutʃnɨk]

to swindle (deceive)	обманути	[obma'nutɨ]
swindle, deception	обман (ч)	[ob'man]
swindler	шахрай (ч)	[ʃah'raj]

to bribe (vt)	підкупити	[pidku'pɨtɨ]
bribery	підкуп (ч)	['pidkup]
bribe	хабар (ч)	[ha'bar]

poison	отрута (ж)	[ot'ruta]
to poison (vt)	отруїти	[otru'jitɨ]
to poison oneself	отруїтись	[otru'jitisʲ]
suicide (act)	самогубство (с)	[samo'ɦubstwo]
suicide (person)	самовбивця (ч)	[samow'bɨwtsʲa]

to threaten (vt)	погрожувати	[poɦ'rɔʒuwatɨ]
threat	погроза (ж)	[poɦ'rɔza]
to make an attempt	вчинити замах	[wtʃɨ'nɨtɨ 'zamah]
attempt (attack)	замах (ч)	['zamah]

| to steal (a car) | украсти | [uk'rastɨ] |
| to hijack (a plane) | викрасти | ['wɨkrastɨ] |

| revenge | помста (ж) | ['pɔmsta] |
| to avenge (get revenge) | мстити | ['mstɨtɨ] |

to torture (vt)	катувати	[katu'watɨ]
torture	катування (с)	[katu'wanʲa]
to torment (vt)	мучити	['mutʃɨtɨ]

pirate	пірат (ч)	[pi'rat]
hooligan	хуліган (ч)	[huli'ɦan]
armed (adj)	озброєний	[oz'brɔɛnɨj]
violence	насильство (с)	[na'sɨlʲstwo]

| spying (espionage) | шпигунство (с) | [ʃpɨ'ɦunstwo] |
| to spy (vi) | шпигувати | [ʃpɨɦu'watɨ] |

162. Police. Law. Part 1

| justice | правосуддя (с) | [prawo'suddʲa] |
| court (see you in ~) | суд (ч) | [sud] |

judge	суддя (ч)	[sud'dʲa]
jurors	присяжні (мн)	[priˈsʲaʒni]
jury trial	суд (ч) присяжних	[sud priˈsʲaʒnih]
to judge, to try (vt)	судити	[suˈditi]
lawyer, barrister	адвокат (ч)	[adwoˈkat]
defendant	підсудний (ч)	[pidˈsudnij]
dock	лава (ж) підсудних	[ˈlawa pidˈsudnih]
charge	обвинувачення (с)	[obwinuˈwatʃɛnʲa]
accused	обвинувачений (ч)	[obwinuˈwatʃɛnij]
sentence	вирок (ч)	[ˈwirok]
to sentence (vt)	присудити	[prisuˈditi]
guilty (culprit)	винуватець (ч)	[winuˈwatɛts]
to punish (vt)	покарати	[pokaˈrati]
punishment	покарання (с)	[pokaˈranʲa]
fine (penalty)	штраф (ч)	[ʃtraf]
life imprisonment	довічне ув'язнення (с)	[doˈwitʃnɛ uˈwʲaznɛnʲa]
death penalty	смертна кара (ж)	[ˈsmɛrtna ˈkara]
electric chair	електричний стілець (ч)	[ɛlɛktˈritʃnij stiˈlɛts]
gallows	шибениця (ж)	[ˈʃibɛnitsʲa]
to execute (vt)	стратити	[ˈstratiti]
execution	страта (ж)	[ˈstrata]
prison	в'язниця (ж)	[wʲazˈnitsʲa]
cell	камера (ж)	[ˈkamɛra]
escort (convoy)	конвой (ч)	[konˈwoj]
prison officer	наглядач (ч)	[nahlʲaˈdatʃ]
prisoner	в'язень (ч)	[ˈwʲazɛnʲ]
handcuffs	наручники (мн)	[naˈrutʃniki]
to handcuff (vt)	надіти наручники	[naˈditi naˈrutʃniki]
prison break	втеча (ч)	[ˈwtɛtʃa]
to break out (vi)	утекти	[utɛkˈti]
to disappear (vi)	зникнути	[ˈzniknuti]
to release (from prison)	звільнити	[zwilʲˈniti]
amnesty	амністія (ж)	[amˈnistiʲa]
police	поліція (ж)	[poˈlitsiʲa]
police officer	поліцейський (ч)	[poliˈtsɛjsʲkij]
police station	поліцейський відділок (ч)	[poliˈtsɛjsʲkij ˈwiddilok]
truncheon	гумовий кийок (ч)	[ˈhumowij kiˈjok]
megaphone (loudhailer)	рупор (ч)	[ˈrupor]
patrol car	патрульна машина (ж)	[patˈrulʲna maˈʃina]
siren	сирена (ж)	[siˈrɛna]
to turn on the siren	увімкнути сирену	[uwimkˈnuti siˈrɛnu]
siren call	виття (с) сирени	[witˈtʲa siˈrɛni]
crime scene	місце (с) події	[ˈmistsɛ poˈdiji]
witness	свідок (ч)	[ˈswidok]

freedom	воля (ж)	['wolʲa]
accomplice	спільник (ч)	['spilʲnɨk]
to flee (vi)	зникнути	['znɨknutɨ]
trace (to leave a ~)	слід (ч)	[slid]

163. Police. Law. Part 2

search (investigation)	розшук (ч)	['rɔzʃuk]
to look for ...	розшукувати	[roz'ʃukuwatɨ]
suspicion	підозра (ж)	[pi'dɔzra]
suspicious (e.g., ~ vehicle)	підозрілий	[pido'zrilɨj]
to stop (cause to halt)	зупинити	[zupɨ'nitɨ]
to detain (keep in custody)	затримати	[za'trɨmatɨ]

case (lawsuit)	справа (ж)	['sprawa]
investigation	слідство (с)	['slidstwo]
detective	детектив (ч)	[dɛtɛk'tɨw]
investigator	слідчий (ч)	['slidtʃɨj]
hypothesis	версія (ж)	['wɛrsiʲa]

motive	мотив (ч)	[mo'tiw]
interrogation	допит (ч)	['dɔpɨt]
to interrogate (vt)	допитувати	[do'pɨtuwatɨ]
to question (~ neighbors, etc.)	опитувати	[o'pɨtuwatɨ]
check (identity ~)	перевірка (ж)	[pɛrɛ'wirka]

round-up (raid)	облава (ж)	[ob'lawa]
search (~ warrant)	обшук (ч)	['ɔbʃuk]
chase (pursuit)	погоня (ж)	[po'ɦonʲa]
to pursue, to chase	переслідувати	[pɛrɛs'liduwatɨ]
to track (a criminal)	слідкувати	[slidku'watɨ]

arrest	арешт (ч)	[a'rɛʃt]
to arrest (sb)	заарештувати	[zaarɛʃtu'watɨ]
to catch (thief, etc.)	зловити	[zlo'wɨtɨ]
capture	затримання (с)	[za'trɨmanʲa]

document	документ (ч)	[doku'mɛnt]
proof (evidence)	доказ (ч)	['dɔkaz]
to prove (vt)	доводити	[do'wɔdɨtɨ]
footprint	слід (ч)	[slid]
fingerprints	відбитки (мн) пальців	[wid'bɨtkɨ 'palʲtsiw]
piece of evidence	доказ (ч)	['dɔkaz]

alibi	алібі (с)	['alibi]
innocent (not guilty)	невинний	[nɛ'wɨnɨj]
injustice	несправедливість (ж)	[nɛsprawɛd'lɨwistʲ]
unjust, unfair (adj)	несправедливий	[nɛsprawɛd'lɨwɨj]

criminal (adj)	кримінальний	[krɨmi'nalʲnɨj]
to confiscate (vt)	конфіскувати	[konfisku'watɨ]
drug (illegal substance)	наркотик (ч)	[nar'kɔtɨk]
weapon, gun	зброя (ж)	['zbrɔʲa]

to disarm (vt)	обеззброїти	[obɛz'zbrɔjiti]
to order (command)	наказувати	[na'kazuwati]
to disappear (vi)	зникнути	['zniknuti]

law	закон (ч)	[za'kɔn]
legal, lawful (adj)	законний	[za'kɔnij]
illegal, illicit (adj)	незаконний	[nɛza'kɔnij]

| responsibility (blame) | відповідальність (ж) | [widpowi'dal'nist'] |
| responsible (adj) | відповідальний | [widpowi'dal'nij] |

NATURE

The Earth. Part 1

space	космос (ч)	['kɔsmos]
space (as adj)	космічний	[kos'mitʃnij]
outer space	космічний простір (ч)	[kos'mitʃnij 'prɔstir]
world, universe	всесвіт (ч)	['wsɛswit]
galaxy	галактика (ж)	[ɦa'laktika]
star	зірка (ж)	['zirka]
constellation	сузір'я (с)	[su'zirʲʲa]
planet	планета (ж)	[pla'nɛta]
satellite	супутник (ч)	[su'putnik]
meteorite	метеорит (ч)	[mɛtɛo'rit]
comet	комета (ж)	[ko'mɛta]
asteroid	астероїд (ч)	[astɛ'rɔjid]
orbit	орбіта (ж)	[or'bita]
to revolve (~ around the Earth)	обертатися	[obɛr'tatisʲa]
atmosphere	атмосфера (ж)	[atmos'fɛra]
the Sun	Сонце (с)	['sɔntsɛ]
solar system	Сонячна система (ж)	['sɔnʲatʃna sis'tɛma]
solar eclipse	сонячне затемнення (с)	['sɔnʲatʃnɛ za'tɛmnɛnʲa]
the Earth	Земля (ж)	[zɛm'lʲa]
the Moon	Місяць (ж)	['misʲats]
Mars	Марс (ч)	[mars]
Venus	Венера (ж)	[wɛ'nɛra]
Jupiter	Юпітер (ч)	[ʲu'pitɛr]
Saturn	Сатурн (ч)	[sa'turn]
Mercury	Меркурій (ч)	[mɛr'kurij]
Uranus	Уран (ч)	[u'ran]
Neptune	Нептун (ч)	[nɛp'tun]
Pluto	Плутон (ч)	[plu'tɔn]
Milky Way	Чумацький Шлях (ч)	[tʃu'matskij ʃlʲah]
Great Bear (Ursa Major)	Велика Ведмедиця (ж)	[wɛ'lika wɛd'mɛditsʲa]
North Star	Полярна Зірка (ж)	[po'lʲarna 'zirka]
Martian	марсіанин (ч)	[marsi'anin]
extraterrestrial (n)	інопланетянин (ч)	[inoplanɛ'tʲanin]

| alien | прибулець (ч) | [priˈbulɛts] |
| flying saucer | літальна тарілка (ж) | [liˈtalʲna taˈrilka] |

spaceship	космічний корабель (ч)	[kosˈmitʃnij koraˈbɛlʲ]
space station	орбітальна станція (ж)	[orbiˈtalʲna ˈstantsiʲa]
blast-off	старт (ч)	[start]

engine	двигун (ч)	[dwiˈɦun]
nozzle	сопло (с)	[ˈsɔplo]
fuel	паливо (с)	[ˈpaliwo]

cockpit, flight deck	кабіна (ж)	[kaˈbina]
aerial	антена (ж)	[anˈtɛna]
porthole	ілюмінатор (ч)	[ilʲumiˈnator]
solar panel	сонячна батарея (ж)	[ˈsɔnʲatʃna bataˈrɛʲa]
spacesuit	скафандр (ч)	[skaˈfandr]

| weightlessness | невагомість (ж) | [nɛwaˈɦɔmistʲ] |
| oxygen | кисень (ч) | [ˈkisɛnʲ] |

| docking (in space) | стикування (с) | [stɨkuˈwanʲa] |
| to dock (vi, vt) | здійснювати стикування | [ˈzdijsnʲuwatɨ stɨkuˈwanʲa] |

observatory	обсерваторія (ж)	[obsɛrwaˈtoriʲa]
telescope	телескоп (ч)	[tɛlɛˈskɔp]
to observe (vt)	спостерігати	[spostɛriˈɦatɨ]
to explore (vt)	досліджувати	[doˈslidʒuwatɨ]

165. The Earth

the Earth	Земля (ж)	[zɛmˈlʲa]
the globe (the Earth)	земна куля (ж)	[zɛmˈna ˈkulʲa]
planet	планета (ж)	[plaˈnɛta]

atmosphere	атмосфера (ж)	[atmosˈfɛra]
geography	географія (ж)	[ɦɛoˈɦrafiʲa]
nature	природа (ж)	[priˈrɔda]

globe (table ~)	глобус (ч)	[ˈɦlɔbus]
map	карта (ж)	[ˈkarta]
atlas	атлас (ч)	[ˈatlas]

| Europe | Європа (ж) | [ɛwˈrɔpa] |
| Asia | Азія (ж) | [ˈaziʲa] |

| Africa | Африка (ж) | [ˈafrika] |
| Australia | Австралія (ж) | [awˈstraliʲa] |

America	Америка (ж)	[aˈmɛrika]
North America	Північна Америка (ж)	[piwˈnitʃna aˈmɛrika]
South America	Південна Америка (ж)	[piwˈdɛna aˈmɛrika]

| Antarctica | Антарктида (ж) | [antarkˈtida] |
| the Arctic | Арктика (ж) | [ˈarktika] |

166. Cardinal directions

north	північ (ж)	['piwnitʃ]
to the north	на північ	[na 'piwnitʃ]
in the north	на півночі	[na 'piwnotʃi]
northern (adj)	північний	[piw'nitʃnij]
south	південь (ч)	['piwdɛnʲ]
to the south	на південь	[na 'piwdɛnʲ]
in the south	на півдні	[na 'piwdni]
southern (adj)	південний	[piw'dɛnij]
west	захід (ч)	['zahid]
to the west	на захід	[na 'zahid]
in the west	на заході	[na 'zahodi]
western (adj)	західний	['zahidnij]
east	схід (ч)	[shid]
to the east	на схід	[na 'shid]
in the east	на сході	[na 'shodi]
eastern (adj)	східний	['shidnij]

167. Sea. Ocean

sea	море (с)	['mɔrɛ]
ocean	океан (ч)	[okɛ'an]
gulf (bay)	затока (ж)	[za'tɔka]
straits	протока (ж)	[pro'tɔka]
continent (mainland)	материк (ч)	[matɛ'rik]
island	острів (ч)	['ɔstriw]
peninsula	півострів (ч)	[pi'wɔstriw]
archipelago	архіпелаг (ч)	[arhipɛ'laĥ]
bay, cove	бухта (ж)	['buhta]
harbour	гавань (ж)	['ĥawanʲ]
lagoon	лагуна (ж)	[la'ĥuna]
cape	мис (ч)	[mis]
atoll	атол (ч)	[a'tɔl]
reef	риф (ч)	[rif]
coral	корал (ч)	[ko'ral]
coral reef	кораловий риф (ч)	[ko'ralowij rif]
deep (adj)	глибокий	[ĥli'bɔkij]
depth (deep water)	глибина (ж)	[ĥlibi'na]
abyss	бездна (ж)	['bɛzdna]
trench (e.g. Mariana ~)	западина (ж)	[za'padina]
current (Ocean ~)	течія (ж)	['tɛtʃiʲa]
to surround (bathe)	омивати	[omiʲwati]
shore	берег (ч)	['bɛrɛĥ]
coast	узбережжя (с)	[uzbɛ'rɛzʲa]

flow (flood tide)	приплив (ч)	[prip'liw]
ebb (ebb tide)	відплив (ч)	[wid'pliw]
shoal	обмілина (ж)	[ob'milina]
bottom (~ of the sea)	дно (с)	[dno]

wave	хвиля (ж)	['hwilʲa]
crest (~ of a wave)	гребінь (ч) хвилі	['ɦrɛbinʲ 'hwili]
spume (sea foam)	піна (ж)	[pi'na]

storm (sea storm)	буря (ж)	['burʲa]
hurricane	ураган (ч)	[uraɦan]
tsunami	цунамі (с)	[ʦu'nami]
calm (dead ~)	штиль (ч)	[ʃtilʲ]
quiet, calm (adj)	спокійний	[spo'kijnij]

| pole | полюс (ч) | ['polʲus] |
| polar (adj) | полярний | [po'lʲarnij] |

latitude	широта (ж)	[ʃiro'ta]
longitude	довгота (ж)	[dowɦo'ta]
parallel	паралель (ж)	[para'lɛlʲ]
equator	екватор (ч)	[ɛk'wator]

sky	небо (с)	['nɛbo]
horizon	горизонт (ч)	[ɦori'zont]
air	повітря (с)	[po'witrʲa]

lighthouse	маяк (ч)	[ma'ʲak]
to dive (vi)	пірнати	[pir'nati]
to sink (ab. boat)	затонути	[zato'nuti]
treasure	скарби (мн)	[skar'bi]

168. Mountains

mountain	гора (ж)	[ɦo'ra]
mountain range	гірське пасмо (с)	[ɦirsʲ'kɛ 'pasmo]
mountain ridge	гірський хребет (ч)	[ɦirsʲ'kij ɦrɛ'bɛt]

summit, top	вершина (ж)	[wɛr'ʃina]
peak	шпиль (ч)	[ʃpilʲ]
foot (~ of the mountain)	підніжжя (с)	[pid'nizʲa]
slope (mountainside)	схил (ч)	[shil]

volcano	вулкан (ч)	[wul'kan]
active volcano	діючий вулкан (ч)	['diʲuʧij wul'kan]
dormant volcano	згаслий вулкан (ч)	['zɦaslij wul'kan]

eruption	виверження (с)	['wiwɛrʒɛnʲa]
crater	кратер (ч)	['kratɛr]
magma	магма (ж)	['maɦma]
lava	лава (ж)	['lawa]
molten (~ lava)	розжарений	[roz'ʒarɛnij]
canyon	каньйон (ч)	[kanʲ'jon]
gorge	ущелина (ж)	[u'ɕɛlina]

crevice	ущелина (c)	[uˈɕɛlina]
pass, col	перевал (ч)	[pɛrɛˈwal]
plateau	плато (c)	[ˈplato]
cliff	скеля (ж)	[ˈskɛlʲa]
hill	горб (ч)	[ɦorb]

glacier	льодовик (ч)	[lʲodoˈwik]
waterfall	водоспад (ч)	[wodosˈpad]
geyser	гейзер (ч)	[ˈɦɛjzɛr]
lake	озеро (c)	[ˈɔzɛro]

plain	рівнина (ж)	[riwˈnina]
landscape	краєвид (ч)	[kraɛˈwid]
echo	луна (ж)	[luˈna]

alpinist	альпініст (ч)	[alʲpiˈnist]
rock climber	скелелаз (ч)	[skɛlɛˈlaz]
to conquer (in climbing)	підкоряти	[pidkoˈrʲati]
climb (an easy ~)	піднімання (c)	[pidniˈmanʲa]

169. Rivers

river	ріка (ж)	[ˈrika]
spring (natural source)	джерело (c)	[dʒɛrɛˈlɔ]
riverbed (river channel)	річище (c)	[ˈritʃiɕɛ]
basin (river valley)	басейн (ч)	[baˈsɛjn]
to flow into …	упадати	[upaˈdati]

| tributary | притока (ж) | [priˈtɔka] |
| bank (river ~) | берег (ч) | [ˈbɛrɛɦ] |

current (stream)	течія (ж)	[ˈtɛtʃʲa]
downstream (adv)	вниз за течією (ж)	[wniz za ˈtɛtʃiɛʲu]
upstream (adv)	уверх по течії	[uˈwɛrh po ˈtɛtʃiji]

inundation	повінь (ж)	[ˈpowinʲ]
flooding	повінь (ж)	[ˈpowinʲ]
to overflow (vi)	розливатися	[rozliˈwatisʲa]
to flood (vt)	затоплювати	[zaˈtoplʲuwati]

| shallow (shoal) | мілина (ж) | [miliˈna] |
| rapids | поріг (ч) | [poˈriɦ] |

dam	гребля (ж)	[ˈɦrɛblʲa]
canal	канал (ч)	[kaˈnal]
reservoir (artificial lake)	водосховище (c)	[wodoˈshowiɕɛ]
sluice, lock	шлюз (ч)	[ʃlʲuz]

water body (pond, etc.)	водоймище (c)	[woˈdojmiɕɛ]
swamp (marshland)	болото (c)	[boˈlɔto]
bog, marsh	трясовина (ж)	[trʲasowiˈna]
whirlpool	вир (ч)	[wir]
stream (brook)	струмок (ч)	[struˈmɔk]
drinking (ab. water)	питний	[ˈpitnij]

fresh (~ water)	**прісний**	['prisnij]
ice	**крига** (ж)	['kriɦa]
to freeze over (ab. river, etc.)	**замерзнути**	[za'mɛrznuti]

170. Forest

| forest, wood | **ліс** (ч) | [lis] |
| forest (as adj) | **лісовий** | [liso'wij] |

thick forest	**хаща** (ж)	['haɕa]
grove	**гай** (ч)	[ɦaj]
forest clearing	**галявина** (ж)	[ɦa'lʲawina]

| thicket | **хащі** (мн) | ['haɕi] |
| scrubland | **чагарник** (ч) | [ʧa'ɦarnik] |

| footpath (troddenpath) | **стежина** (ж) | [stɛ'ʒina] |
| gully | **яр** (ч) | [jar] |

tree	**дерево** (с)	['dɛrɛwo]
leaf	**листок** (ч)	[lis'tɔk]
leaves (foliage)	**листя** (с)	['listʲa]

fall of leaves	**листопад** (ч)	[listo'pad]
to fall (ab. leaves)	**опадати**	[opa'dati]
top (of the tree)	**верхівка** (ж)	[wɛr'hiwka]

branch	**гілка** (ж)	['ɦilka]
bough	**сук** (ч)	[suk]
bud (on shrub, tree)	**брунька** (ж)	['brunʲka]
needle (of the pine tree)	**голка** (ж)	['ɦolka]
fir cone	**шишка** (ж)	['ʃiʃka]

tree hollow	**дупло** (с)	[dup'lɔ]
nest	**гніздо** (с)	[ɦniz'dɔ]
burrow (animal hole)	**нора** (ж)	[no'ra]

trunk	**стовбур** (ч)	['stɔwbur]
root	**корінь** (ч)	['korinʲ]
bark	**кора** (ж)	[ko'ra]
moss	**мох** (ч)	[moh]

to uproot (remove trees or tree stumps)	**корчувати**	[korʧu'wati]
to chop down	**рубати**	[ru'bati]
to deforest (vt)	**вирубувати**	[wi'rubuwati]
tree stump	**пень** (ч)	[pɛnʲ]

campfire	**багаття** (с)	[ba'hattʲa]
forest fire	**пожежа** (ж)	[po'ʒɛʒa]
to extinguish (vt)	**тушити**	[tu'ʃiti]

| forest ranger | **лісник** (ч) | [lis'nik] |
| protection | **охорона** (ж) | [oho'rɔna] |

to protect (~ nature)	охороняти	[ohoro'nʲatɨ]
poacher	браконьєр (ч)	[brako'nʲɛr]
steel trap	пастка (ж)	['pastka]

| to gather, to pick (vt) | збирати | [zbɨ'ratɨ] |
| to lose one's way | заблукати | [zablu'katɨ] |

171. Natural resources

natural resources	природні ресурси (мн)	[prɨ'rɔdni rɛ'sursɨ]
minerals	корисні копалини (мн)	['kɔrɨsni ko'palɨnɨ]
deposits	поклади (мн)	['pɔkladɨ]
field (e.g. oilfield)	родовище (с)	[ro'dɔwɨɕɛ]

to mine (extract)	добувати	[dobu'watɨ]
mining (extraction)	добування (с)	[dobu'wanʲa]
ore	руда (ж)	[ru'da]
mine (e.g. for coal)	копальня (ж)	[ko'palʲnʲa]
shaft (mine ~)	шахта (ж)	['ʃahta]
miner	шахтар (ч)	[ʃah'tar]

| gas (natural ~) | газ (ч) | [ɦaz] |
| gas pipeline | газопровід (ч) | [ɦazopro'wid] |

oil (petroleum)	нафта (ж)	['nafta]
oil pipeline	нафтопровід (ч)	[nafto'prɔwid]
oil well	нафтова вишка (ж)	['naftowa 'wɨʃka]
derrick (tower)	свердлова вежа (ж)	[swɛrd'lɔwa 'wɛʒa]
tanker	танкер (ч)	['tankɛr]

sand	пісок (ч)	[pi'sɔk]
limestone	вапняк (ч)	[wap'nʲak]
gravel	гравій (ч)	['ɦrawij]
peat	торф (ч)	[torf]
clay	глина (ж)	['ɦlɨna]
coal	вугілля (с)	[wu'ɦilʲa]

iron (ore)	залізо (с)	[za'lizo]
gold	золото (с)	['zɔloto]
silver	срібло (с)	['sriblo]
nickel	нікель (ч)	['nikɛlʲ]
copper	мідь (ж)	[midʲ]

zinc	цинк (ч)	['ʦɨnk]
manganese	марганець (ч)	['marɦanɛʦ]
mercury	ртуть (ж)	[rtutʲ]
lead	свинець (ч)	[swɨ'nɛʦ]

mineral	мінерал (ч)	[minɛ'ral]
crystal	кристал (ч)	[krɨs'tal]
marble	мармур (ч)	['marmur]
uranium	уран (ч)	[u'ran]

The Earth. Part 2

172. Weather

weather	погода (ж)	[poˈɦɔda]
weather forecast	прогноз (ч) погоди (ж)	[prɔɦˈnɔz pɔˈɦɔdɨ]
temperature	температура (ж)	[tɛmpɛraˈtura]
thermometer	термометр (ч)	[tɛrˈmɔmɛtr]
barometer	барометр (ч)	[baˈrɔmɛtr]
humidity	вологість (ж)	[wɔlɔɦistʲ]
heat (extreme ~)	спека (ж)	[ˈspɛka]
hot (torrid)	гарячий	[ɦaˈrʲatʃɨj]
it's hot	спекотно	[spɛˈkɔtno]
it's warm	тепло	[ˈtɛplo]
warm (moderately hot)	теплий	[ˈtɛplɨj]
it's cold	холодно	[ˈhɔlodno]
cold (adj)	холодний	[hoˈlɔdnɨj]
sun	сонце (с)	[ˈsɔntsɛ]
to shine (vi)	світити	[swiˈtiti]
sunny (day)	сонячний	[ˈsɔnʲatʃnɨj]
to come up (vi)	зійти	[zijˈtʲi]
to set (vi)	сісти	[ˈsistʲi]
cloud	хмара (ж)	[ˈhmara]
cloudy (adj)	хмарний	[ˈhmarnɨj]
rain cloud	хмара (ж)	[ˈhmara]
somber (gloomy)	похмурний	[pohˈmurnɨj]
rain	дощ (ч)	[dɔɕ]
it's raining	йде дощ	[jdɛ dɔɕ]
rainy (~ day, weather)	дощовий	[dɔɕoˈwɨj]
to drizzle (vi)	накрапати	[nakraˈpati]
pouring rain	проливний дощ (ч)	[prolɨwˈnɨj dɔɕ]
downpour	злива (ж)	[ˈzlɨwa]
heavy (e.g. ~ rain)	сильний	[ˈsilʲnɨj]
puddle	калюжа (ж)	[kaˈlʲuʒa]
to get wet (in rain)	мокнути	[ˈmɔknuti]
fog (mist)	туман (ч)	[tuˈman]
foggy	туманний	[tuˈmanɨj]
snow	сніг (ч)	[sniɦ]
it's snowing	йде сніг (ч)	[jdɛ sniɦ]

173. Severe weather. Natural disasters

thunderstorm	гроза (ж)	[ɦroˈza]
lightning (~ strike)	блискавка (ж)	[ˈblɪskawka]
to flash (vi)	блискати	[ˈblɪskatɪ]
thunder	грім (ч)	[ɦrim]
to thunder (vi)	гриміти	[ɦrɪˈmitɪ]
it's thundering	гримить грім	[ɦrɪˈmitʲ ɦrim]
hail	град (ч)	[ɦrad]
it's hailing	йде град	[jdɛ ɦrad]
to flood (vt)	затопити	[zatoˈpɪtɪ]
flood, inundation	повінь (ж)	[ˈpɔwinʲ]
earthquake	землетрус (ч)	[zɛmlɛtˈrus]
tremor, shoke	поштовх (ч)	[ˈpɔʃtowh]
epicentre	епіцентр (ч)	[ɛpiˈʦɛntr]
eruption	виверження (с)	[ˈwɪwɛrʒɛnʲa]
lava	лава (ж)	[ˈlawa]
twister	смерч (ч)	[smɛrʧ]
tornado	торнадо (ч)	[torˈnado]
typhoon	тайфун (ч)	[tajˈfun]
hurricane	ураган (ч)	[uraɦan]
storm	буря (ж)	[ˈburʲa]
tsunami	цунамі (с)	[ʦuˈnami]
cyclone	циклон (ч)	[ʦɪkˈlɔn]
bad weather	негода (ж)	[nɛˈɦɔda]
fire (accident)	пожежа (ж)	[poˈʒɛʒa]
disaster	катастрофа (ж)	[kataˈstrofa]
meteorite	метеорит (ч)	[mɛtɛoˈrit]
avalanche	лавина (ж)	[laˈwɪna]
snowslide	обвал (ч)	[obˈwal]
blizzard	заметіль (ж)	[zamɛˈtilʲ]
snowstorm	завірюха (ж)	[zawiˈrʲuha]

Fauna

174. Mammals. Predators

predator	**хижак** (ч)	[hi'ʒak]
tiger	**тигр** (ч)	[tiɦr]
lion	**лев** (ч)	[lɛw]
wolf	**вовк** (ч)	[wowk]
fox	**лисиця** (ж)	[lɨ'sɨts'a]
jaguar	**ягуар** (ч)	[jaɦu'ar]
leopard	**леопард** (ч)	[lɛo'pard]
cheetah	**гепард** (ч)	[ɦɛ'pard]
black panther	**пантера** (ж)	[pan'tɛra]
puma	**пума** (ж)	['puma]
snow leopard	**сніговий барс** (ч)	[sniɦo'wɨj bars]
lynx	**рись** (ж)	[ris']
coyote	**койот** (ч)	[ko'jot]
jackal	**шакал** (ч)	[ʃa'kal]
hyena	**гієна** (ж)	[ɦi'ɛna]

175. Wild animals

animal	**тварина** (ж)	[twa'rɨna]
beast (animal)	**звір** (ч)	[zwir]
squirrel	**білка** (ж)	['bilka]
hedgehog	**їжак** (ч)	[jɨ'ʒak]
hare	**заєць** (ч)	['zaɛts]
rabbit	**кріль** (ч)	[kril']
badger	**борсук** (ч)	[bor'suk]
raccoon	**єнот** (ч)	[ɛ'nɔt]
hamster	**хом'як** (ч)	[ho'm'ʲak]
marmot	**бабак** (ч)	[ba'bak]
mole	**кріт** (ч)	[krit]
mouse	**миша** (ж)	['mɨʃa]
rat	**щур** (ч)	[ɕur]
bat	**кажан** (ч)	[ka'ʒan]
ermine	**горностай** (ч)	[ɦorno'staj]
sable	**соболь** (ч)	['sɔbol']
marten	**куниця** (ж)	[ku'nɨts'a]
weasel	**ласка** (ж)	['laska]
mink	**норка** (ж)	['nɔrka]

| beaver | бобер (ч) | [bo'bɛr] |
| otter | видра (ж) | ['wɨdra] |

horse	кінь (ч)	[kinʲ]
moose	лось (ч)	[losʲ]
deer	олень (ч)	['ɔlɛnʲ]
camel	верблюд (ч)	[wɛr'blʲud]

bison	бізон (ч)	[bi'zɔn]
wisent	зубр (ч)	[zubr]
buffalo	буйвіл (ч)	['bujwil]

zebra	зебра (ж)	['zɛbra]
antelope	антилопа (ж)	[anti'lɔpa]
roe deer	косуля (ж)	[ko'sulʲa]
fallow deer	лань (ж)	[lanʲ]
chamois	сарна (ж)	['sarna]
wild boar	вепр (ч)	[wɛpr]

whale	кит (ч)	[kɨt]
seal	тюлень (ч)	[tʲu'lɛnʲ]
walrus	морж (ч)	[morʒ]
fur seal	котик (ч)	['kɔtɨk]
dolphin	дельфін (ч)	[dɛlʲ'fin]

bear	ведмідь (ч)	[wɛd'midʲ]
polar bear	білий ведмідь (ч)	['bilɨj wɛd'midʲ]
panda	панда (ж)	['panda]

monkey	мавпа (ж)	['mawpa]
chimpanzee	шимпанзе (ч)	[ʃimpan'zɛ]
orangutan	орангутанг (ч)	[oranɦu'tanɦ]
gorilla	горила (ж)	[ɦo'rɨla]
macaque	макака (ж)	[ma'kaka]
gibbon	гібон (ч)	[ɦi'bɔn]

elephant	слон (ч)	[slon]
rhinoceros	носоріг (ч)	[noso'riɦ]
giraffe	жирафа (ж)	[ʒɨrafa]
hippopotamus	бегемот (ч)	[bɛɦɛ'mɔt]

| kangaroo | кенгуру (ч) | [kɛnɦu'ru] |
| koala (bear) | коала (ч) | [ko'ala] |

mongoose	мангуст (ч)	[ma'nɦust]
chinchilla	шиншила (ж)	[ʃɨn'ʃɨla]
skunk	скунс (ч)	[skuns]
porcupine	дикобраз (ч)	[dɨko'braz]

176. Domestic animals

cat	кішка (ж)	['kiʃka]
tomcat	кіт (ч)	[kit]
horse	коняка (ж)	[ko'nʲaka]

| stallion (male horse) | жеребець (ч) | [ʒɛrɛ'bɛts] |
| mare | кобила (ж) | [ko'biɫa] |

cow	корова (ж)	[ko'rɔwa]
bull	бик (ч)	[bɨk]
ox	віл (ч)	[wil]

sheep (ewe)	вівця (ж)	[wiw'tsʲa]
ram	баран (ч)	[ba'ran]
goat	коза (ж)	[ko'za]
billy goat, he-goat	козел (ч)	[ko'zɛl]

| donkey | осел (ч) | [o'sɛl] |
| mule | мул (ч) | [mul] |

pig	свиня (ж)	[swɨ'nʲa]
piglet	порося (с)	[poro'sʲa]
rabbit	кріль (ч)	[krilʲ]

| hen (chicken) | курка (ж) | ['kurka] |
| cock | півень (ч) | ['piwɛnʲ] |

duck	качка (ж)	['katʃka]
drake	качур (ч)	['katʃur]
goose	гусак (ч)	[ɦu'sak]

| tom turkey, gobbler | індик (ч) | [in'dɨk] |
| turkey (hen) | індичка (ж) | [in'dɨtʃka] |

domestic animals	домашні тварини (мн)	[do'maʃni twa'rɨni]
tame (e.g. ~ hamster)	ручний	[rutʃ'nij]
to tame (vt)	приручати	[prɨru'tʃati]
to breed (vt)	вирощувати	[wɨ'rɔɕuwati]

farm	ферма (ж)	['fɛrma]
poultry	свійські птахи (мн)	['swijsʲki pta'hi]
cattle	худоба (ж)	[ɦu'dɔba]
herd (cattle)	стадо (с)	['stado]

stable	конюшня (ж)	[ko'nʲuʃnʲa]
pigsty	свинарник (ч)	[swɨ'narnɨk]
cowshed	корівник (ч)	[ko'riwnɨk]
rabbit hutch	крільчатник (ч)	[krilʲ'tʃatnɨk]
hen house	курник (ч)	[kur'nɨk]

177. Dogs. Dog breeds

dog	собака (ч)	[so'baka]
sheepdog	вівчарка (ж)	[wiw'tʃarka]
poodle	пудель (ч)	['pudɛlʲ]
dachshund	такса (ж)	['taksa]

| bulldog | бульдог (ч) | [bulʲ'dɔɦ] |
| boxer | боксер (ч) | [bok'sɛr] |

mastiff	мастиф (ч)	[mas'tif]
Rottweiler	ротвейлер (ч)	[rot'wɛjlɛr]
Doberman	доберман (ч)	[dobɛr'man]

basset	басет (ч)	[ba'sɛt]
bobtail	бобтейл (ч)	[bob'tɛjl]
Dalmatian	далматинець (ч)	[dalma'tinɛts]
cocker spaniel	кокер-спанієль (ч)	['kɔkɛr spani'ɛlʲ]

| Newfoundland | ньюфаундленд (ч) | [njufaund'lɛnd] |
| Saint Bernard | сенбернар (ч) | [sɛnbɛr'nar] |

husky	хаскі (ч)	[haski]
Chow Chow	чау-чау (ч)	[tʃau tʃau]
spitz	шпіц (ч)	[ʃpits]
pug	мопс (ч)	[mops]

178. Sounds made by animals

barking (n)	гавкіт (ч)	['hawkit]
to bark (vi)	гавкати	['hawkatɨ]
to miaow (vi)	нявкати	['nʲawkatɨ]
to purr (vi)	муркотіти	[murko'titɨ]

to moo (vi)	мукати	['mukatɨ]
to bellow (bull)	ревіти	[rɛ'witɨ]
to growl (vi)	ричати	[ri'tʃatɨ]

howl (n)	виття (c)	[wit'tʲa]
to howl (vi)	вити	['witɨ]
to whine (vi)	скиглити	['skihlitɨ]

to bleat (sheep)	бекати	['bɛkatɨ]
to oink, to grunt (pig)	рохкати	['rohkatɨ]
to squeal (vi)	вищати	[wɨ'ɕatɨ]

to croak (vi)	кумкати	['kumkatɨ]
to buzz (insect)	дзижчати	[dʑiʒ'tʃatɨ]
to chirp (crickets, grasshopper)	стрекотати	[strɛko'tati]

179. Birds

bird	птах (ч)	[ptah]
pigeon	голуб (ч)	['holub]
sparrow	горобець (ч)	[horo'bɛts]
tit (great tit)	синиця (ж)	[si'nɨtsʲa]
magpie	сорока (ж)	[so'rɔka]

raven	ворон (ч)	['wɔron]
crow	ворона (ж)	[wo'rɔna]
jackdaw	галка (ж)	['halka]

rook	грак (ч)	[ɦrak]
duck	качка (ж)	['katʃka]
goose	гусак (ч)	[ɦu'sak]
pheasant	фазан (ч)	[fa'zan]

eagle	орел (ч)	[o'rɛl]
hawk	яструб (ч)	['ʲastrub]
falcon	сокіл (ч)	['sɔkil]

| vulture | гриф (ч) | [ɦrif] |
| condor (Andean ~) | кондор (ч) | ['kɔndor] |

swan	лебідь (ч)	['lɛbidʲ]
crane	журавель (ч)	[ʒura'wɛlʲ]
stork	чорногуз (ч)	[tʃorno'ɦuz]

parrot	папуга (ч)	[pa'puɦa]
hummingbird	колібрі (ч)	[ko'libri]
peacock	пава (ж)	['pawa]

| ostrich | страус (ч) | ['straus] |
| heron | чапля (ж) | ['tʃaplʲa] |

| flamingo | фламінго (с) | [fla'minɦo] |
| pelican | пелікан (ч) | [pɛli'kan] |

| nightingale | соловей (ч) | [solo'wɛj] |
| swallow | ластівка (ж) | ['lastiwka] |

thrush	дрізд (ч)	[drizd]
song thrush	співучий дрізд (ч)	[spi'wutʃij 'drizd]
blackbird	чорний дрізд (ч)	['tʃornij 'drizd]

swift	стриж (ч)	['striʒ]
lark	жайворонок (ч)	['ʒajworonok]
quail	перепел (ч)	['pɛrɛpɛl]

woodpecker	дятел (ч)	['dʲatɛl]
cuckoo	зозуля (ж)	[zo'zulʲa]
owl	сова (ж)	[so'wa]
eagle owl	пугач (ч)	[pu'ɦatʃ]
wood grouse	глухар (ч)	[ɦlu'har]

| black grouse | тетерук (ч) | [tɛtɛ'ruk] |
| partridge | куріпка (ж) | [ku'ripka] |

starling	шпак (ч)	[ʃpak]
canary	канарка (ж)	[ka'narka]
hazel grouse	рябчик (ч)	['rʲabtʃik]

| chaffinch | зяблик (ч) | ['zʲablik] |
| bullfinch | снігур (ч) | [sni'ɦur] |

seagull	чайка (ж)	['tʃajka]
albatross	альбатрос (ч)	[alʲbat'rɔs]
penguin	пінгвін (ч)	[pinɦ'win]

180. Birds. Singing and sounds

to sing (vi)	співати	[spi'watɨ]
to call (animal, bird)	кричати	[kri'tʃatɨ]
to crow (cock)	кукурікати	[kuku'rikatɨ]
cock-a-doodle-doo	кукуріку	[kukuri'ku]

to cluck (hen)	кудкудакати	[kudku'dakatɨ]
to caw (crow call)	каркати	['karkatɨ]
to quack (duck call)	крякати	['krʲakatɨ]
to cheep (vi)	пищати	[pi'ɕatɨ]
to chirp, to twitter	цвірінькати	[tsʲwi'rinʲkatɨ]

181. Fish. Marine animals

bream	лящ (ч)	[lʲaɕ]
carp	короп (ч)	['kɔrop]
perch	окунь (ч)	['ɔkunʲ]
catfish	сом (ч)	[som]
pike	щука (ж)	['ɕuka]

| salmon | лосось (ч) | [lo'sɔsʲ] |
| sturgeon | осетер (ч) | [osɛ'tɛr] |

herring	оселедець (ч)	[osɛ'lɛdɛts]
Atlantic salmon	сьомга (ж)	['sʲomɦa]
mackerel	скумбрія (ж)	['skumbrʲia]
flatfish	камбала (ж)	[kamba'la]

zander, pike perch	судак (ч)	[su'dak]
cod	тріска (ж)	[tris'ka]
tuna	тунець (ч)	[tu'nɛts]
trout	форель (ж)	[fo'rɛlʲ]

eel	вугор (ч)	[wu'ɦor]
electric ray	електричний скат (ч)	[ɛlɛkt'ritʃnij skat]
moray eel	мурена (ж)	[mu'rɛna]
piranha	піранья (ж)	[pi'ranʲa]

shark	акула (ж)	[a'kula]
dolphin	дельфін (ч)	[dɛlʲ'fin]
whale	кит (ч)	[kɨt]

crab	краб (ч)	[krab]
jellyfish	медуза (ж)	[mɛ'duza]
octopus	восьминіг (ч)	[wosʲmi'niɦ]

starfish	морська зірка (ж)	[morsʲ'ka 'zirka]
sea urchin	морський їжак (ч)	[morsʲ'kij ji'ʒak]
seahorse	морський коник (ч)	[morsʲ'kij 'konɨk]

| oyster | устриця (ж) | ['ustrɨtsʲa] |
| prawn | креветка (ж) | [krɛ'wɛtka] |

| lobster | омар (ч) | [o'mar] |
| spiny lobster | лангуст (ч) | [lan'ɦust] |

182. Amphibians. Reptiles

| snake | змія (ж) | [zmi'ʲa] |
| venomous (snake) | отруйний | [ot'rujnɨj] |

viper	гадюка (ж)	[ɦa'dʲuka]
cobra	кобра (ж)	['kɔbra]
python	пітон (ч)	[pi'tɔn]
boa	удав (ч)	[u'daw]

grass snake	вуж (ч)	[wuʒ]
rattle snake	гримуча змія (ж)	[ɦri'mutʃa zmi'ʲa]
anaconda	анаконда (ж)	[ana'kɔnda]

lizard	ящірка (ж)	['ʲaɕirka]
iguana	ігуана (ж)	[iɦu'ana]
monitor lizard	варан (ч)	[wa'ran]
salamander	саламандра (ж)	[sala'mandra]
chameleon	хамелеон (ч)	[hamɛlɛ'ɔn]
scorpion	скорпіон (ч)	[skorpi'ɔn]

turtle	черепаха (ж)	[tʃɛrɛ'paha]
frog	жабка (ж)	['ʒabka]
toad	жаба (ж)	['ʒaba]
crocodile	крокодил (ч)	[kroko'dɨl]

183. Insects

insect	комаха (ж)	[ko'maha]
butterfly	метелик (ч)	[mɛ'tɛlik]
ant	мураха (ж)	[mu'raha]
fly	муха (ж)	['muha]
mosquito	комар (ч)	[ko'mar]
beetle	жук (ч)	[ʒuk]

wasp	оса (ж)	[o'sa]
bee	бджола (ж)	[bdʒo'la]
bumblebee	джміль (ч)	[dʒmilʲ]
gadfly (botfly)	овід (ч)	['ɔwid]

| spider | павук (ч) | [pa'wuk] |
| spider's web | павутиння (с) | [pawu'tɨnʲa] |

dragonfly	бабка (ж)	['babka]
grasshopper	коник (ч)	['kɔnik]
moth (night butterfly)	метелик (ч)	[mɛ'tɛlik]

| cockroach | тарган (ч) | [tar'ɦan] |
| tick | кліщ (ч) | [kliɕ] |

| flea | блоха (ж) | ['blɔha] |
| midge | мошка (ж) | ['mɔʃka] |

locust	сарана (ж)	[sara'na]
snail	равлик (ч)	['rawlɨk]
cricket	цвіркун (ч)	[ʦwir'kun]
firefly	світлячок (ч)	[switlʲa'ʧɔk]
ladybird	сонечко (с)	['sɔnɛʧko]
cockchafer	хрущ (ч)	[hruɕ]

leech	п'явка (ж)	['pʲʲawka]
caterpillar	гусениця (ж)	['husɛnɨʦʲa]
earthworm	черв'як (ч)	[ʧɛr'wʲʲak]
larva	личинка (ж)	[lɨ'ʧɨnka]

184. Animals. Body parts

beak	дзьоб (ч)	[dzʲob]
wings	крила (мн)	['krɨla]
foot (of the bird)	лапа (ж)	['lapa]
feathers (plumage)	пір'я (с)	['pirʲʲa]
feather	перо (с)	[pɛ'rɔ]
crest	чубчик (ч)	['ʧubʧɨk]

gills	зябра (мн)	['zʲabra]
spawn	ікра (ж)	[ik'ra]
larva	личинка (ж)	[lɨ'ʧɨnka]
fin	плавець (ч)	[pla'wɛʦ]
scales (of fish, reptile)	луска (ж)	[lus'ka]

fang (canine)	ікло (с)	['iklo]
paw (e.g. cat's ~)	лапа (ж)	['lapa]
muzzle (snout)	морда (ж)	['mɔrda]
mouth (cat's ~)	паща (ж)	['paɕa]
tail	хвіст (ч)	[hwist]
whiskers	вуса (мн)	['wusa]

| hoof | копито (с) | [ko'pɨto] |
| horn | ріг (ч) | [rih] |

carapace	панцир (ч)	['panʦɨr]
shell (mollusk ~)	мушля (ж)	['muʃlʲa]
eggshell	шкаралупа (ж)	[ʃkara'lupa]

| animal's hair (pelage) | шерсть (ж) | [ʃɛrstʲ] |
| pelt (hide) | шкура (ж) | ['ʃkura] |

185. Animals. Habitats

| habitat | середовище (с) проживання | [sɛrɛ'dɔwɨɕɛ proʒɨ'wanʲa] |
| migration | міграція (ж) | [mih'raʦiʲa] |

mountain	гора (ж)	[ɦoˈra]
reef	риф (ч)	[rif]
cliff	скеля (ж)	[ˈskɛlʲa]

forest	ліс (ч)	[lis]
jungle	джунглі (мн)	[ˈdʒunɦli]
savanna	савана (ж)	[saˈwana]
tundra	тундра (ж)	[ˈtundra]

steppe	степ (ч)	[ˈstɛp]
desert	пустеля (ж)	[pusˈtɛlʲa]
oasis	оаза (ж)	[oˈaza]

sea	море (с)	[ˈmɔrɛ]
lake	озеро (с)	[ˈɔzɛro]
ocean	океан (ч)	[okɛˈan]

swamp (marshland)	болото (с)	[boˈlɔto]
freshwater (adj)	прісноводний	[prisnoˈwɔdnij]
pond	став (ч)	[ˈstaw]
river	ріка (ж)	[ˈrika]

den (bear's ~)	барліг (ч)	[barˈliɦ]
nest	гніздо (с)	[ɦnizˈdɔ]
tree hollow	дупло (с)	[dupˈlɔ]
burrow (animal hole)	нора (ж)	[noˈra]
anthill	мурашник (ч)	[muraʃˈnɨk]

Flora

tree	дерево (с)	['dɛrɛwo]
deciduous (adj)	модринове	[mod'rinowɛ]
coniferous (adj)	хвойне	['hwɔjnɛ]
evergreen (adj)	вічнозелене	[wiʧnozɛ'lɛnɛ]

apple tree	яблуня (ж)	['ʲablunʲa]
pear tree	груша (ж)	['hruʃa]
sweet cherry tree	черешня (ж)	[ʧɛ'rɛʃnʲa]
sour cherry tree	вишня (ж)	['wiʃnʲa]
plum tree	слива (ж)	['sɫiwa]

birch	береза (ж)	[bɛ'rɛza]
oak	дуб (ч)	[dub]
linden tree	липа (ж)	['ɫipa]
aspen	осика (ж)	[o'sɨka]
maple	клен (ч)	[klɛn]
spruce	ялина (ж)	[ja'ɫina]
pine	сосна (ж)	[sos'na]
larch	модрина (ж)	[mod'rina]
fir tree	ялиця (ж)	[ja'ɫɨʦʲa]
cedar	кедр (ч)	[kɛdr]

poplar	тополя (ж)	[to'pɔlʲa]
rowan	горобина (ж)	[horo'bɨna]
willow	верба (ж)	[wɛr'ba]
alder	вільха (ж)	['wilʲha]
beech	бук (ч)	[buk]
elm	в'яз (ч)	[wʲʲaz]
ash (tree)	ясен (ч)	['ʲasɛn]
chestnut	каштан (ч)	[kaʃ'tan]

magnolia	магнолія (ж)	[mah'nɔlʲia]
palm tree	пальма (ж)	['palʲma]
cypress	кипарис (ч)	[kɨpa'rɨs]

mangrove	мангрове дерево (с)	['manhrowɛ 'dɛrɛwo]
baobab	баобаб (ч)	[bao'bab]
eucalyptus	евкаліпт (ч)	[ɛwka'lipt]
sequoia	секвоя (ж)	[sɛk'wɔʲa]

bush	кущ (ч)	[kuɕ]
shrub	кущі (мн)	[ku'ɕi]

| grapevine | виноград (ч) | [wino'hrad] |
| vineyard | виноградник (ч) | [wino'hradnik] |

raspberry bush	малина (ж)	[ma'lina]
redcurrant bush	порічки (мн)	[po'ritʃki]
gooseberry bush	аґрус (ч)	['agrus]

acacia	акація (ж)	[a'katsiˈa]
barberry	барбарис (ч)	[barba'ris]
jasmine	жасмин (ч)	[ʒas'min]

juniper	ялівець (ч)	[jali'wɛts]
rosebush	трояндовий кущ (ч)	[troˈandowij kuɕ]
dog rose	шипшина (ж)	[ʃip'ʃina]

188. Mushrooms

mushroom	гриб (ч)	[hrib]
edible mushroom	їстівний гриб (ч)	[jis'tiwnij hrib]
poisonous mushroom	отруйний гриб (ч)	[ot'rujnij hrib]
cap	шапка (ж)	['ʃapka]
stipe	ніжка (ж)	['niʒka]

cep, penny bun	білий гриб (ч)	['bilij 'hrib]
orange-cap boletus	підосичник (ч)	[pido'sitʃnik]
birch bolete	підберезник (ч)	[pidbɛ'rɛznik]
chanterelle	лисичка (ж)	[li'sitʃka]
russula	сироїжка (ж)	[siro'jiʒka]

morel	зморшок (ч)	['zmorʃok]
fly agaric	мухомор (ч)	[muho'mɔr]
death cap	поганка (ж)	[po'hanka]

189. Fruits. Berries

apple	яблуко (с)	['ˈabluko]
pear	груша (ж)	['hruʃa]
plum	слива (ж)	['sliwa]

strawberry (garden ~)	полуниця (ж)	[polu'nitsˈa]
sour cherry	вишня (ж)	['wiʃnˈa]
sweet cherry	черешня (ж)	[tʃɛ'rɛʃnˈa]
grape	виноград (ч)	[wino'hrad]

raspberry	малина (ж)	[ma'lina]
blackcurrant	чорна смородина (ж)	['tʃorna smo'rodina]
redcurrant	порічки (мн)	[po'ritʃki]
gooseberry	аґрус (ч)	['agrus]
cranberry	журавлина (ж)	[ʒuraw'lina]

| orange | апельсин (ч) | [apɛlˈ'sin] |
| tangerine | мандарин (ч) | [manda'rin] |

pineapple	ананас (ч)	[ana'nas]
banana	банан (ч)	[ba'nan]
date	фінік (ч)	['finik]

lemon	лимон (ч)	[lɪ'mɔn]
apricot	абрикос (ч)	[abri'kɔs]
peach	персик (ч)	['pɛrsɪk]
kiwi	ківі (ч)	['kiwi]
grapefruit	грейпфрут (ч)	[ɦrɛjp'frut]

berry	ягода (ж)	['ʲaɦoda]
berries	ягоди (мн)	['ʲaɦodɪ]
cowberry	брусниця (ж)	[brus'nitsʲa]
wild strawberry	суниця (ж)	[su'nitsʲa]
bilberry	чорниця (ж)	[t͡ʃor'nitsʲa]

190. Flowers. Plants

| flower | квітка (ж) | ['kwitka] |
| bouquet (of flowers) | букет (ч) | [bu'kɛt] |

rose (flower)	троянда (ж)	[tro'ʲanda]
tulip	тюльпан (ч)	[tʲulʲ'pan]
carnation	гвоздика (ж)	[ɦwoz'dɪka]
gladiolus	гладіолус (ч)	[ɦladi'ɔlus]

cornflower	волошка (ж)	[wo'lɔʃka]
harebell	дзвіночок (ч)	[d͡zwi'nɔt͡ʃok]
dandelion	кульбаба (ж)	[kulʲ'baba]
camomile	ромашка (ж)	[ro'maʃka]

aloe	алое (ч)	[a'lɔɛ]
cactus	кактус (ч)	['kaktus]
rubber plant, ficus	фікус (ч)	['fikus]

lily	лілея (ж)	[li'lɛʲa]
geranium	герань (ж)	[ɦɛ'ranʲ]
hyacinth	гіацинт (ч)	[ɦia'tsɪnt]

mimosa	мімоза (ж)	[mi'mɔza]
narcissus	нарцис (ч)	[nar'tsɪs]
nasturtium	настурція (ж)	[nas'turtsiʲa]

orchid	орхідея (ж)	[orhi'dɛʲa]
peony	півонія (ж)	[pi'wɔniʲa]
violet	фіалка (ж)	[fi'alka]

pansy	братки (мн)	[brat'kɪ]
forget-me-not	незабудка (ж)	[nɛza'budka]
daisy	стокротки (мн)	[stok'rɔtkɪ]

poppy	мак (ч)	[mak]
hemp	коноплі (мн)	[ko'nɔpli]
mint	м'ята (ж)	['mʲʲata]

lily of the valley	конвалія (ж)	[kon'waliʲa]
snowdrop	пролісок (ч)	['prɔlisok]
nettle	кропива (ж)	[kropɨ'wa]
sorrel	щавель (ч)	[ɕa'wɛlʲ]
water lily	латаття (с)	[la'tattʲa]
fern	папороть (ж)	['paporotʲ]
lichen	лишайник (ч)	[lɨ'ʃajnɨk]
conservatory (greenhouse)	оранжерея (ж)	[oranʒɛ'rɛʲa]
lawn	газон (ч)	[ɦa'zɔn]
flowerbed	клумба (ж)	['klumba]
plant	рослина (ж)	[ros'lɨna]
grass	трава (ж)	[tra'wa]
blade of grass	травинка (ж)	[tra'wɨnka]
leaf	листок (ч)	[lɨs'tɔk]
petal	пелюстка (ж)	[pɛ'lʲustka]
stem	стебло (с)	[stɛb'lɔ]
tuber	бульба (ж)	['bulʲba]
young plant (shoot)	паросток (ч)	['parostok]
thorn	колючка (ч)	[ko'lʲutʃka]
to blossom (vi)	цвісти	[tsvis'tɨ]
to fade, to wither	в'янути	['wʲʲanutɨ]
smell (odour)	запах (ч)	['zapah]
to cut (flowers)	зрізати	['zrizatɨ]
to pick (a flower)	зірвати	[zir'watɨ]

191. Cereals, grains

grain	зерно (с)	[zɛr'nɔ]
cereal crops	зернові рослини (мн)	[zɛrno'wi ros'lɨnɨ]
ear (of barley, etc.)	колос (ч)	['kɔlos]
wheat	пшениця (ж)	[pʃɛ'nɨtsʲa]
rye	жито (с)	['ʒɨto]
oats	овес (ч)	[o'wɛs]
millet	просо (с)	['prɔso]
barley	ячмінь (ч)	[jatʃ'minʲ]
maize	кукурудза (ж)	[kuku'rudza]
rice	рис (ч)	[ris]
buckwheat	гречка (ж)	['ɦrɛtʃka]
pea plant	горох (ч)	[ɦo'rɔh]
kidney bean	квасоля (ж)	[kwa'sɔlʲa]
soya	соя (ж)	['sɔʲa]
lentil	сочевиця (ж)	[sotʃɛ'wɨtsʲa]
beans (pulse crops)	боби (мн)	[bo'bɨ]

REGIONAL GEOGRAPHY

192. Politics. Government. Part 1

politics	політика (ж)	[po'litɪka]
political (adj)	політичний	[poli'tiʧnij]
politician	політик (ч)	[po'litɪk]
state (country)	держава (ж)	[dɛr'ʒawa]
citizen	громадянин (ч)	[ɦromadʲa'nin]
citizenship	громадянство (с)	[ɦroma'dʲanstwo]
national emblem	національний герб (ч)	[natsio'nalʲnij 'ɦɛrb]
national anthem	державний гімн (ч)	[dɛr'ʒawnij ɦimn]
government	уряд (ч)	['urʲad]
head of state	керівник (ч) країни	[kɛriw'nɪk kra'jini]
parliament	парламент (ч)	[par'lamɛnt]
party	партія (ж)	['partiʲa]
capitalism	капіталізм (ч)	[kapita'lizm]
capitalist (adj)	капіталістичний	[kapitalis'tiʧnij]
socialism	соціалізм (ч)	[sotsia'lizm]
socialist (adj)	соціалістичний	[sotsialis'tiʧnij]
communism	комунізм (ч)	[komu'nizm]
communist (adj)	комуністичний	[komunis'tiʧnij]
communist (n)	комуніст (ч)	[komu'nist]
democracy	демократія (ж)	[dɛmok'ratiʲa]
democrat	демократ (ч)	[dɛmok'rat]
democratic (adj)	демократичний	[dɛmokra'tiʧnij]
Democratic party	демократична партія (ж)	[dɛmokra'tiʧna 'partiʲa]
liberal (n)	ліберал (ч)	[libɛ'ral]
Liberal (adj)	ліберальний	[libɛ'ralʲnij]
conservative (n)	консерватор (ч)	[konsɛr'wator]
conservative (adj)	консервативний	[konsɛrwa'tiwnij]
republic (n)	республіка (ж)	[rɛs'publika]
republican (n)	республіканець (ч)	[rɛspubli'kanɛʦ]
Republican party	республіканська партія (ж)	[rɛspubli'kansʲka 'partiʲa]
elections	вибори (мн)	['wɪbori]
to elect (vt)	обирати	[obɪ'rati]
elector, voter	виборець (ч)	['wɪborɛʦ]
election campaign	виборча компанія (ж)	['wɪborʧa kom'paniʲa]
voting (n)	голосування (с)	[ɦolosu'wanʲa]

| to vote (vi) | голосувати | [ɦolosu'wati] |
| suffrage, right to vote | право (c) голосу (ч) | ['prawo 'ɦɔlosu] |

candidate	кандидат (ч)	[kandi'dat]
to run for (~ President)	балотуватися	[balotu'watisʲa]
campaign	кампанія (ж)	[kam'paniʲa]

| opposition (as adj) | опозиційний | [opozi'tsijnij] |
| opposition (n) | опозиція (ж) | [opo'zitsiʲa] |

visit	візит (ч)	[wi'zit]
official visit	офіційний візит (ч)	[ofi'tsijnij wi'zit]
international (adj)	міжнародний	[miʒna'rɔdnij]

| negotiations | переговори (мн) | [pɛrɛɦo'wɔri] |
| to negotiate (vi) | вести переговори | ['wɛsti pɛrɛɦo'wɔri] |

193. Politics. Government. Part 2

society	суспільство (c)	[sus'pilʲstwo]
constitution	конституція (ж)	[konsti'tutsiʲa]
power (political control)	влада (ж)	['wlada]
corruption	корупція (ж)	[ko'ruptsiʲa]

| law (justice) | закон (ч) | [za'kɔn] |
| legal (legitimate) | законний | [za'kɔnij] |

| justice (fairness) | справедливість (ж) | [sprawɛd'liwistʲ] |
| just (fair) | справедливий | [sprawɛd'liwij] |

committee	комітет (ч)	[komi'tɛt]
bill (draft law)	законопроект (ч)	[zakonopro'ɛkt]
budget	бюджет (ч)	[bʲu'dʒɛt]
policy	політика (ж)	[po'litika]
reform	реформа (ж)	[rɛ'fɔrma]
radical (adj)	радикальний	[radi'kalʲnij]

power (strength, force)	сила (ж)	['siɫa]
powerful (adj)	сильний	['silʲnij]
supporter	прибічник (ч)	[pri'bitʃnik]
influence	вплив (ч)	[wpliw]

regime (e.g. military ~)	режим (ч)	[rɛ'ʒim]
conflict	конфлікт (ч)	[kon'flikt]
conspiracy (plot)	змова (ж)	['zmɔwa]
provocation	провокація (ж)	[prowo'katsiʲa]

to overthrow (regime, etc.)	скинути	['skinuti]
overthrow (of a government)	скинення (c)	['skinɛnʲa]
revolution	революція (ж)	[rɛwo'lʲutsiʲa]

coup d'état	переворот (ч)	[pɛrɛwo'rɔt]
military coup	військовий переворот (ч)	[wijsʲ'kɔwij pɛrɛwo'rɔt]
crisis	криза (ж)	['kriza]

economic recession	економічний спад (ч)	[εkono'mitʃnij spad]
demonstrator (protester)	демонстрант (ч)	[dεmon'strant]
demonstration	демонстрація (ж)	[dεmon'stratsiʲa]
martial law	воєнний стан (ч)	[wo'εnij stan]
military base	військова база (ж)	[wijsⁱ'kɔwa 'baza]

| stability | стабільність (ж) | [sta'bilʲnistʲ] |
| stable (adj) | стабільний | [sta'bilʲnij] |

| exploitation | експлуатація (ж) | [εksplua'tatsiʲa] |
| to exploit (workers) | експлуатувати | [εkspluatu'wati] |

racism	расизм (ч)	[ra'sɨzm]
racist	расист (ч)	[ra'sɨst]
fascism	фашизм (ч)	[fa'ʃizm]
fascist	фашист (ч)	[fa'ʃist]

194. Countries. Miscellaneous

foreigner	іноземець (ч)	[ino'zεmεts]
foreign (adj)	іноземний	[ino'zεmnij]
abroad (in a foreign country)	за кордоном	[za kor'dɔnom]

emigrant	емігрант (ч)	[εmiĥ'rant]
emigration	еміграція (ж)	[εmiĥ'ratsiʲa]
to emigrate (vi)	емігрувати	[εmiĥru'wati]

the West	Захід (ч)	['zahid]
the East	Схід (ч)	[shid]
the Far East	Далекий Схід (ч)	[da'lɛkij shid]

civilization	цивілізація (ж)	[tsɨwili'zatsiʲa]
humanity (mankind)	людство (с)	['lʲudstwo]
the world (earth)	світ (ч)	[swit]
peace	мир (ч)	[mir]
worldwide (adj)	світовий	[swito'wij]

homeland	батьківщина (ж)	[batⁱkiw'ɕina]
people (population)	народ (ч)	[na'rɔd]
population	населення (с)	[na'sɛlɛnⁱa]
people (a lot of ~)	люди (мн)	['lʲudɨ]
nation (people)	нація (ж)	['natsiʲa]
generation	покоління (с)	[poko'linⁱa]

territory (area)	територія (ж)	[tɛri'toriʲa]
region	регіон (ч)	[rɛhi'ɔn]
state (part of a country)	штат (ч)	[ʃtat]

tradition	традиція (ч)	[tra'ditsiʲa]
custom (tradition)	звичай (ч)	['zwitʃaj]
ecology	екологія (ж)	[εko'lɔĥiʲa]

| Indian (Native American) | індіанець (ч) | [indi'anɛts] |
| Gypsy (masc.) | циган (ч) | [tsi'ĥan] |

| Gypsy (fem.) | циганка (ж) | [tsɨ'ɦanka] |
| Gypsy (adj) | циганський | [tsɨ'ɦansʲkij] |

empire	імперія (ж)	[im'pɛriʲa]
colony	колонія (ж)	[ko'loniʲa]
slavery	рабство (с)	['rabstwo]
invasion	навала (ж)	[na'wala]
famine	голодомор (ч)	[ɦolodo'mɔr]

195. Major religious groups. Confessions

| religion | релігія (ж) | [rɛ'liɦiʲa] |
| religious (adj) | релігійний | [rɛli'ɦijnɨj] |

faith, belief	віра (ж)	['wira]
to believe (in God)	вірити	['wiritɨ]
believer	віруючий	['wiruʲutʃij]

| atheism | атеїзм (ч) | [atɛ'jizm] |
| atheist | атеїст (ч) | [atɛ'jist] |

Christianity	християнство (с)	[hristɨ'ʲanstwo]
Christian (n)	християнин (ч)	[hristɨ'ʲanɨn]
Christian (adj)	християнський	[hristɨ'ʲansʲkij]

Catholicism	Католицизм (ч)	[katoli'tsɨzm]
Catholic (n)	католик (ч)	[ka'tolɨk]
Catholic (adj)	католицький	[kato'liɨskij]

Protestantism	Протестантство (с)	[protɛs'tantstwo]
Protestant Church	Протестантська церква (ж)	[protɛs'tantsʲka 'tsɛrkwa]
Protestant (n)	протестант (ч)	[protɛs'tant]

Orthodoxy	Православ'я (с)	[prawo'slaw⁷ʲa]
Orthodox Church	Православна церква (ж)	[prawos'lawna 'tsɛrkwa]
Orthodox (n)	православний	[prawos'lawnɨj]

Presbyterianism	Пресвітеріанство (с)	[prɛswitɛri'anstwo]
Presbyterian Church	Пресвітеріанська церква (ж)	[prɛswitɛri'ansʲka 'tsɛrkwa]
Presbyterian (n)	пресвітеріанин (ч)	[prɛswitɛri'anɨn]

| Lutheranism | Лютеранська церква (ж) | [lʲutɛ'ransʲka 'tsɛrkwa] |
| Lutheran (n) | лютеранин (ч) | [lʲutɛ'ranɨn] |

| Baptist Church | Баптизм (ч) | [bap'tɨzm] |
| Baptist (n) | баптист (ч) | [bap'tist] |

| Anglican Church | Англіканська церква (ж) | [anɦli'kansʲka 'tsɛrkwa] |
| Anglican (n) | англіканин (ч) | [anɦli'kanɨn] |

Mormonism	Мормонство (с)	[mor'mɔnstwo]
Mormon (n)	мормон (ч)	[mor'mɔn]
Judaism	Іудаїзм (ч)	[iuda'jizm]

Jew (n)	іудей (ч)	[iu'dɛj]
Buddhism	Буддизм (ч)	[bud'dɨzm]
Buddhist (n)	буддист (ч)	[bud'dɨst]
Hinduism	Індуїзм (ч)	[indu'jizm]
Hindu (n)	індуїст (ч)	[indu'jist]
Islam	Іслам (ч)	[is'lam]
Muslim (n)	мусульманин (ч)	[musulʲ'manɨn]
Muslim (adj)	мусульманський	[musulʲ'mansʲkij]
Shiah Islam	Шиїзм (ч)	[ʃi'jizm]
Shiite (n)	шиїт (ч)	[ʃi'jit]
Sunni Islam	Сунізм (ч)	[su'nizm]
Sunnite (n)	суніт (ч)	[su'nit]

196. Religions. Priests

priest	священик (ч)	[swʲa'ɕɛnɨk]
the Pope	Папа Римський	['papa 'rimsʲkij]
monk, friar	чернець (ч)	[tʃɛr'nɛts]
nun	черниця (ж)	[tʃɛr'nɨtsʲa]
pastor	пастор (ч)	['pastor]
abbot	абат (ч)	[a'bat]
vicar (parish priest)	вікарій (ч)	[wi'karij]
bishop	єпископ (ч)	[ɛ'pɨskop]
cardinal	кардинал (ч)	[kardɨ'nal]
preacher	проповідник (ч)	[propo'widnɨk]
preaching	проповідь (ч)	['prɔpowidʲ]
parishioners	парафіяни (мн)	[parafiʲ'ani]
believer	віруючий (ч)	['wiruʲutʃij]
atheist	атеїст (ч)	[atɛ'jist]

197. Faith. Christianity. Islam

Adam	Адам (ч)	[a'dam]
Eve	Єва (ж)	['ɛwa]
God	Бог (ч)	[boɦ]
the Lord	Господь (ч)	[ɦos'podʲ]
the Almighty	Всесильний (ч)	[wsɛ'sɨlʲnij]
sin	гріх (ч)	[ɦrih]
to sin (vi)	грішити	[ɦri'ʃɨtɨ]
sinner (masc.)	грішник (ч)	['ɦriʃnɨk]
sinner (fem.)	грішниця (ж)	['ɦriʃnɨtsʲa]
hell	пекло (с)	['pɛklo]

paradise	рай (ч)	[raj]
Jesus	Ісус (ч)	[i'sus]
Jesus Christ	Ісус Христос (ч)	[i'sus hris'tɔs]

the Holy Spirit	Святий Дух (ч)	[swʲa'tij duh]
the Saviour	Спаситель (ч)	[spa'sitɛlʲ]
the Virgin Mary	Богородиця (ж)	[boɦo'rɔdɨtsʲa]

the Devil	диявол (ч)	[diʲʲawol]
devil's (adj)	диявольський	[diʲʲawolʲsʲkij]
Satan	Сатана (ч)	[sata'na]
satanic (adj)	сатанинський	[sata'nɨnsʲkij]

angel	ангел (ч)	['anɦɛl]
guardian angel	ангел-охоронець (ч)	['anɦɛl oɦo'rɔnɛts]
angelic (adj)	ангельський	['anɦɛlʲsʲkij]

apostle	апостол (ч)	[a'pɔstol]
archangel	архангел (ч)	[ar'hanɦɛl]
the Antichrist	антихрист (ч)	[an'tɨhrist]

Church	церква (ж)	['tsɛrkwa]
Bible	Біблія (ж)	['bibliʲa]
biblical (adj)	біблійний	[bib'lijnɨj]

Old Testament	Старий Завіт (ч)	[sta'rij za'wit]
New Testament	Новий Завіт (ч)	[no'wɨj za'wit]
Gospel	Євангеліє (с)	[ɛ'wanɦɛliɛ]
Holy Scripture	Священне Писання (с)	[swʲa'ɕɛnɛ pɨ'sanʲa]
Heaven	Небо (с)	['nɛbo]

Commandment	заповідь (ж)	['zapowidʲ]
prophet	пророк (ч)	[pro'rɔk]
prophecy	пророцтво (с)	[pro'rɔtstwo]

Allah	Аллах (ч)	[a'lah]
Mohammed	Магомет (ч)	[maɦo'mɛt]
the Koran	Коран (ч)	[ko'ran]

mosque	мечеть (ж)	[mɛ'ʧɛtʲ]
mullah	мула (ч)	[mu'la]
prayer	молитва (ж)	[mo'lɨtwa]
to pray (vi, vt)	молитися	[mo'lɨtɨsʲa]

pilgrimage	паломництво (с)	[pa'lɔmnɨtstwo]
pilgrim	паломник (ч)	[pa'lɔmnik]
Mecca	Мекка (ж)	['mɛkka]

church	церква (ж)	['tsɛrkwa]
temple	храм (ч)	[hram]
cathedral	собор (ч)	[so'bɔr]
Gothic (adj)	готичний	[ɦo'tɨʧnij]
synagogue	синагога (ж)	[sɨna'ɦɔɦa]
mosque	мечеть (ж)	[mɛ'ʧɛtʲ]
chapel	каплиця (ж)	[kap'lɨtsʲa]
abbey	абатство (с)	[a'batstwo]

| convent | монастир (ч) | [monas'tɨr] |
| monastery | монастир (ч) | [monas'tɨr] |

bell (church ~s)	дзвін (ч)	[dzwin]
bell tower	дзвіниця (ж)	[dzwi'nɨtsʲa]
to ring (ab. bells)	дзвонити	[dzwo'nitɨ]

cross	хрест (ч)	[hrɛst]
cupola (roof)	купол (ч)	['kupol]
icon	ікона (ж)	[i'kɔna]

soul	душа (ж)	[du'ʃa]
fate (destiny)	доля (ж)	['dɔlʲa]
evil (n)	зло (с)	[zlo]
good (n)	добро (с)	[dob'rɔ]

vampire	вампір (ч)	[wam'pir]
witch (evil ~)	відьма (ж)	['widʲma]
demon	демон (ч)	['dɛmon]
spirit	дух (ч)	[duh]

| redemption (giving us ~) | спокута (ж) | [spo'kuta] |
| to redeem (vt) | спокутувати | [spo'kutuwatɨ] |

church service	меса (ж)	['mɛsa]
to say mass	служити	[slu'ʒɨtɨ]
confession	сповідь (ж)	['spowidʲ]
to confess (vi)	сповідатися	[spowi'datɨsʲa]

saint (n)	святий (ч)	[swʲa'tɨj]
sacred (holy)	священний	[swʲa'ɕɛnɨj]
holy water	свята вода (ж)	[swʲa'ta wo'da]

ritual (n)	ритуал (ч)	[ritu'al]
ritual (adj)	ритуальний	[ritu'alʲnɨj]
sacrifice	жертвування (с)	['ʒɛrtwuwanʲa]

superstition	забобони (мн)	[zabo'bonɨ]
superstitious (adj)	забобонний	[zabo'bonɨj]
afterlife	загробне життя (с)	[zaɦ'rɔbnɛ ʒɨt'tʲa]
eternal life	вічне життя (с)	['witʃnɛ ʒɨt'tʲa]

MISCELLANEOUS

background (green ~)	**фон** (ч)	[fon]
balance (of the situation)	**баланс** (ч)	[ba'lans]
barrier (obstacle)	**перешкода** (ж)	[pɛrɛʃ'kɔda]
base (basis)	**база** (ж)	['baza]
beginning	**початок** (ч)	[po'tʃatok]
category	**категорія** (ж)	[katɛ'hɔriʲa]
cause (reason)	**причина** (ж)	[pri'tʃina]
choice	**вибір** (ч)	['wibir]
coincidence	**збіг** (ч)	[zbih]
comfortable (~ chair)	**зручний**	[zrutʃ'nij]
comparison	**порівняння** (с)	[poriw'nʲanʲa]
compensation	**компенсація** (ж)	[kompɛn'satsiʲa]
degree (extent, amount)	**ступінь** (ч)	['stupinʲ]
development	**розвиток** (ч)	['rɔzwitok]
difference	**різниця** (ж)	[riz'nitsʲa]
effect (e.g. of drugs)	**ефект** (ч)	[ɛ'fɛkt]
effort (exertion)	**зусилля** (с)	[zu'silʲa]
element	**елемент** (ч)	[ɛlɛ'mɛnt]
end (finish)	**закінчення** (с)	[za'kintʃɛnʲa]
example (illustration)	**приклад** (ч)	['priklad]
fact	**факт** (ч)	[fakt]
frequent (adj)	**приватний**	[pri'watnij]
growth (development)	**зростання** (с)	[zros'tanʲa]
help	**допомога** (ж)	[dopo'mɔha]
ideal	**ідеал** (ч)	[idɛ'al]
kind (sort, type)	**вид** (ч)	[wid]
labyrinth	**лабіринт** (ч)	[labi'rint]
mistake, error	**помилка** (ж)	[po'milka]
moment	**момент** (ч)	[mo'mɛnt]
object (thing)	**об'єкт** (ч)	[o'bʲɛkt]
obstacle	**перешкода** (ж)	[pɛrɛʃ'kɔda]
original (original copy)	**оригінал** (ч)	[orihi'nal]
part (~ of sth)	**частина** (ж)	[tʃas'tina]
particle, small part	**частка** (ж)	['tʃastka]
pause (break)	**пауза** (ж)	['pauza]
position	**позиція** (ж)	[po'zitsiʲa]
principle	**принцип** (ч)	['printsip]
problem	**проблема** (ж)	[prob'lɛma]
process	**процес** (ч)	[pro'tsɛs]

progress	прогрес (ч)	[proɦ'rɛs]
property (quality)	властивість (ж)	[wlas'tiwistʲ]
reaction	реакція (ж)	[rɛ'aktsіʲa]
risk	ризик (ч)	['rizik]

secret	таємниця (ж)	[taɛm'nіtsʲa]
series	серія (ж)	['sɛrіʲa]
shape (outer form)	форма (ж)	['forma]
situation	ситуація (ж)	[sіtu'atsіʲa]
solution	рішення (с)	['rіʃɛnʲa]

standard (adj)	стандартний	[stan'dartnіj]
standard (level of quality)	стандарт (ч)	[stan'dart]
stop (pause)	перерва (ж)	[pɛ'rɛrwa]
style	стиль (ч)	[stіlʲ]

system	система (ж)	[sіs'tɛma]
table (chart)	таблиця (ж)	[tab'lіtsʲa]
tempo, rate	темп (ч)	[tɛmp]
term (word, expression)	термін (ч)	['tɛrmin]
thing (object, item)	річ (ж)	[rіtʃ]

truth (e.g. moment of ~)	істина (ж)	['istіna]
turn (please wait your ~)	черга (ж)	['tʃɛrɦa]
type (sort, kind)	тип (ч)	[tіp]
urgent (adj)	терміновий	[tɛrmi'nowіj]
urgently	терміново	[tɛrmi'nowo]

utility (usefulness)	користь (ж)	['korіstʲ]
variant (alternative)	варіант (ч)	[wari'ant]
way (means, method)	спосіб (ч)	['sposib]
zone	зона (ж)	['zona]

Printed in Great Britain
by Amazon

79678470R00106